THE SHORT, STRANGE LIFE
OF HERSCHEL GRYNSZPAN

THE SHORT, STRANGE LIFE OF HERSCHEL GRYNSZPAN

A BOY AVENGER, A NAZI DIPLOMAT, AND A MURDER IN PARIS

Jonathan Kirsch

LIVERIGHT PUBLISHING CORPORATION

A DIVISION OF W. W. NORTON & COMPANY

NEW YORK   LONDON

Photograph credits: Frontispiece: © Scherl / Sueddeutsche Zeitung / The Image Works. Part I: Mémorial de la Shoah, CDJC. Part II: Mémorial de la Shoah, CDJC. Part III: Yad Vashem.

For information about permission to reproduce selections from this book, write to Permissions, Liveright Publishing Corporation, a division of W. W. Norton & Company, Inc., 500 Fifth Avenue, New York, NY 10110

For information about special discounts for bulk purchases, please contact W. W. Norton Special Sales at specialsales@wwnorton.com or 800-233-4830

Manufacturing by RR Donnelley, Harrisonburg
Book design by Lovedog Studio
Production manager: Devon Zahn

Library of Congress Cataloging-in-Publication Data

Kirsch, Jonathan, 1949–
The short, strange life of Herschel Grynszpan : a boy avenger, a Nazi diplomat, and a murder in Paris / Jonathan Kirsch. — First Edition.
    pages cm
Includes bibliographical references and index.
ISBN 978-0-87140-452-7 (hardcover)
1. Grynszpan, Herschel Feibel, 1921–approximately 1943.
2. Vom Rath, Ernst, 1909–1938—Assassination. 3. Jewish refugees—France—Paris—Biography. 4. Jews—Germany—Hannover—Biography. 5. Jews—Germany—History—1933–1945.
6. Kristallnacht, 1938. I. Title.
DS134.42.G79K57 2013
940.53'1842—dc23

                                                                2012048899

Liveright Publishing Corporation
500 Fifth Avenue, New York, N.Y. 10110
www.wwnorton.com

W. W. Norton & Company Ltd.
Castle House, 75/76 Wells Street, London W1T 3QT

1 2 3 4 5 6 7 8 9 0

For my father, Robert

and my brother, Paul

and my father-in-law, Ezra Benjamin

and the *mishpocheh* for whom their memory is a blessing:

Ann, Adam, Jennifer, Remy, and Charles Ezra Kirsch

Marya and Ron Shiflett

Caroline Kirsch

Heather Kirsch

Joshua, Jennifer, Hazel, and Menashe Kirsch

CONTENTS

Part III
PARIS TO BERLIN

Prologue

THE BOY AVENGER

L IKE STILLS FROM A FILM NOIR, THE BLACK-AND-WHITE photographs of a seventeen-year-old boy named Herschel Grynszpan that have come down to us—police mug shots, newspaper photos, a souvenir snapshot taken at a Paris street fair—capture the various faces that he presented to the public during the fall of 1938.

With his hair brushed back off a high forehead, he seems to possess a certain swagger and style in some of the photographs. He is a diminutive but also darkly handsome fellow who was described in one official document as a "fashion designer," and, in a few of the snapshots, he resembles a matinee idol.[1] In others, he looks almost thuggish, like a little gangster dressed up in an expertly tailored suit. One candid photo, snapped through the window of a police car shortly after his arrest, portrays him as a lonely and frightened child. Yet all of these photos invariably depict the same human being, a troubled adolescent who boiled up out of a noisy Jewish neighborhood in a backwater of Paris and demanded the attention of the astonished world.

L'affaire Grynszpan, as his case came to be known, starts with a single act of violence behind the locked gates of the German embassy in Paris on November 7, 1938. But it is also a story replete with shock and scandal, mystery and perplexity. As in other and more recent episodes, the abundance of evidence does not rule out speculation. Was Herschel Grynszpan the cat's-paw of an international Jewish conspiracy that sought to provoke a war between France and Germany, as Nazi propaganda minister Joseph Goebbels imagined? Was he an agent provocateur who was charged by his Gestapo handler with the task of ridding Germany of an anti-Nazi diplomat and, at the same time, providing the Nazi regime with a pretext for a major escalation in the persecution of the Jews, as philosopher Hannah Arendt suggested? Does he deserve to be regarded as a proto-hero of the sexual liberation movement even though he lived in an era when gay men were sent to the camps along with Jews and Gypsies?

Precisely what transpired inside the ornate German embassy in Paris on that day remains a puzzlement, but even more baffling is the black hole of history into which Grynszpan has fallen since the end of World War II. Herschel Grynszpan was briefly famous, and it was his fame—or, as the Nazis saw it, his infamy—that accounts for the trove of historical detail that is available to us today. We know how much he weighed, how tall he was, and how much money his family received in welfare payments because he was investigated by both French and German police officers, and he was examined by physicians, psychiatrists, and social workers in the service of the French criminal courts and later by their counterparts in Nazi Germany, all in the greatest and most intimate detail. Grynszpan, still only an adolescent, was questioned by the famously efficient interrogators of the Gestapo and even by Adolf Eichmann, a self-styled expert on Jewish affairs in the Nazi bureaucracy and one of the masterminds of the Final Solution.

Today, however, Grynszpan remains a mystery, an irony if only because Grynszpan was among the most famous inmates of the Nazi concentration camp system. The names and deportation dates for

Jews who were sent from Paris to Auschwitz by the tens of thousands were meticulously recorded and preserved by the Nazis, but no such data is available for Herschel Grynzpan. Did he receive a quick death by *Genickschuss* in an interrogation cell at Gestapo headquarters in Berlin? Was he beheaded in the courtyard of a Nazi prison? Did he die in a German infirmary despite the frantic efforts of the SS doctors to keep him alive in case Hitler set a date for the long-delayed show trial in which Grynszpan was to play a starring role? Or did Grynszpan, as some have suggested, somehow survive the Second World War and show up in 1960 as a spectral figure in the public gallery of a German courtroom, where his unlikely life story was reprised?

Perhaps the most vexing aspect of the Grynszpan case is the fact that he has never been embraced as the heroic figure he earnestly sought to be. His fellow Jews, suffering through the catastrophic aftermath of his act of protest at the German embassy in Paris, "generally disapproved of it as useless, dangerous, and a great disservice to Jews everywhere," according to Gerald Schwab, one of the principal investigators of the Grynszpan case.[2] One of Grynszpan's own attorneys, richly paid to defend him in the French courts, dismissed him privately as "that absurd little Jew."[3] Hannah Arendt pronounced him to be "a psychopath" and, even more shockingly, accused him of serving as an agent of the Gestapo.[4] Jewish armed resistance against Nazi Germany is much studied and celebrated, but Grynszpan remains without honor even among the people whose avenger he imagined himself to be.

Grynzspan has indeed all but disappeared from the historical record. The first scholarly work on the Grynszpan affair, "Der Fall Grünspan," an article by historian Helmut Heiber, was published in 1957 in the German language only. The one monograph on the Grynszpan case published in English—a 1990 account by Gerald Schwab, an interpreter for the U.S. War Department at Nuremberg and a career employee of the U.S. State Department, who wrote a dissertation about the case for his master's degree at George Washington University—is long out of print. A book-length biography of Grynszpan written in the early 1960s by a French physician, Dr. Alain Cuénot, has never been published.*

Herschel Grynszpan himself is mostly a missing person when it comes to the vast literature of the Second World War and the Holocaust. When Grynszpan is mentioned at all, it is only to note that his act of violent protest in Paris was seized upon by Joseph Goebbels, propaganda minister of the Third Reich, as a pretext for Kristallnacht, the pogrom that marked an escalation in Hitler's war against the Jews. At Yad Vashem, for example, a single grainy snapshot of Grynszpan appears for a couple of seconds in a slide show about Kristallnacht, and he is mentioned not all in the accounts of Jewish resistance to Nazi Germany.

The effacement of Herschel Grynszpan, who wrote and spoke so ardently about his deed to lawyers, judges, politicians, and reporters in the months and years following his arrest, would have broken the boy's heart. His prison journals, which were carefully preserved and studied by both French and German authorities, reveal that the lonely and frightened adolescent yearned not merely for attention

---

*A monograph by Friedrich Karl Kaul, *Der Fall des Herschel Grynszpan*, was published in German in 1965. Ron Roizen, an independent researcher, conducted an original study of the Grynszpan case for an article published in *Holocaust and Genocide Studies* in 1986. Early in his career, the distinguished Holocaust historian Michael R. Marrus surveyed the case for a 1988 article in the *American Scholar*. An abridged English translation of Cuénot's unpublished manuscript was commissioned by an American businessman named David Rome, who donated copies of the typescript to various libraries and institutions. Such is the scholarly literature of the Grynzpan case in its entirety. Heiber, Kaul, and Cuénot are deceased, but Roizen and Marrus generously agreed to be interviewed by the author of this book.

THE BOY AVENGER   XV

but for a place of consequence in the saga of the Jewish people. "He thought the only end to isolation was to reach the point where he was no longer separated from the true struggles that went on around him," writes Don DeLillo of Lee Harvey Oswald in the novel *Libra*, but the same words surely apply to Grynszpan. "The name we give to this point is history."[5]

Grynszpan can be seen as another Oswald, a lone gunman whose private obsession finally drove him to a public act of violence. Sometimes he seems like a character in a mystery so deeply layered with conspiracy and intrigue, erotic scandal and rough justice, that it resembles a hardboiled detective novel. He can even be regarded as the hero he fancied himself to be—a righteous avenger who engaged in armed resistance against Nazi Germany. Long after the official date of his death, which is only a legal fiction established by the decree of a German court, he was rumored to be alive, a ghost who haunted the bombed-out cities where he spent the last years of his short, strange life. I do not argue that he is one or another of these figures, although the reader may reach his or her own conclusion. What I seek to do now is restore Herschel Grynszpan to his rightful place in history.

PART I

FROM HANOVER TO PARIS

1

THE DAY HITLER
DINED ALONE

O N AN OTHERWISE UNREMARKABLE DAY IN THE FALL OF
1932, a man entered a Munich restaurant called the Osteria
Bavaria, took a seat at an empty table, and ordered a vegetarian meal.

With his brush mustache and an unruly apostrophe of black hair
across his forehead, the solitary diner was already famous around
the world as the "leader"—the familiar German word is *Führer*—of
the Nazi Party. Only a few months later, on January 30, 1933, he
would be raised to the formal rank of chancellor of Germany.
Remarkably, his customary entourage of bodyguards and cronies
was absent from the crowded restaurant.

Adolf Hitler was dining alone.

"There he sat, a raw-vegetable Genghis Khan," recalled the patron
who happened to be sitting at the next table, "a teetotaling Alexander, a womanless Napoleon, an effigy of Bismarck who would certainly have had to go to bed for four weeks if he had ever tried to eat
just one of Bismarck's breakfasts. . . ."[1]

The gentleman who observed Hitler eat his meal was Friedrich
Percyval Reck-Malleczewen, an erstwhile doctor and now a journalist. Born into the Prussian Junker class, he moved in privileged circles and had encountered Hitler, Joseph Goebbels ("our Minister of

Lies"), and Hermann Göring ("obviously mentally deranged") in the salons of their rich and powerful benefactors. Reck-Malleczewen, however, was one aristocrat who held the Nazis in contempt, and he imagined that Hitler grew uncomfortable under his critical gaze on that day in the Osteria Bavaria.[2]

"Since at that time, September, 1932, the streets were already quite unsafe, I had a loaded revolver with me," Reck-Malleczewen later recorded in his journal. "In the almost deserted restaurant, I could easily have shot him. If I had had an inkling of the role this piece of filth was to play, and of the years of suffering he was to make us endure, I would have done it without a second thought. But I took him for a character out of a comic strip, and did not shoot."[3]

Fate never afforded Reck-Malleczewen another opportunity to take a shot at Hitler. Still, the same thought occurred to other and bolder men. The most memorable attempt took place on July 20, 1944, when a German officer named Klaus von Stauffenberg—a titled member of the German nobility—planted a bomb in the Wolf's Lair, the field headquarters where Hitler was meeting with his military high command, but the explosion failed to kill the Führer, and the co-conspirators were quickly identified and arrested, tried and convicted. The failed assassins were tortured and then hung from meat hooks on lengths of piano wire. "Ah, now really, gentlemen, this is a little late," Reck-Malleczewen confided to his journal. "You made this monster, and as long as things were going well you gave him whatever he wanted. You turned Germany over to this arch-criminal."[4]

The entries in his secret journal ended abruptly in October 1944, when Reck-Malleczewen was arrested and confined in the concentration camp at Dachau. He had attracted the attention of the Gestapo because he insisted on using the traditional German greeting—*Grüss Gott!* (God be praised!)—rather than the obligatory *Heil Hitler!* Such verbal eccentricity was enough to constitute an act of resistance in Nazi Germany, and he came to be wrongly suspected of participation in Count von Stauffenberg's failed assassination plot. The formal penalty for Reck-Malleczewen's crime was beheading, but he was actually murdered—like countless other victims of the industrial-scale abbatoir that was the Third Reich—with a *Genickschuss*, a single gunshot to the nape of the neck.*

✦   ✦   ✦

THE IDEA THAT ONE can divert the currents of history by committing a single homicide is ancient, powerful, and enduring. The Bible offers an early example in the account of an ingenious and successful assassin named Ehud ben Gera, who contrives to carry a concealed weapon into the court of the king of Moab and then plunges his two-edged sword into the royal belly. Shakespeare, writing in the Elizabethan age but conjuring up the ancients, celebrates the killing of Julius Caesar as a righteous act of tyrannicide: "Did not great Julius bleed for justice' sake?" muses Brutus in *Julius Caesar*.⁵ And, four centuries later, the world went to war when Archduke Franz Ferdinand, the heir-apparent to the Austro-Hungarian throne, was shot to death by a nineteen-year-old Slav nationalist on the streets of Sarajevo in June 1914.

Precisely because the murder of the archduke had such world-changing consequences, assassination was even more popular in certain political circles in the unsettled decade that followed the end of the First World War. For example, Rosa Luxemburg and Karl Liebknecht, founders of the German revolutionary party known as the Spartacists, were assassinated by right-wing freebooters in Berlin in

---

* Reck-Malleczewen's journal was sufficiently well concealed to escape the attention of the officers who arrested him, and it was discovered and published in a German edition in 1947. Hannah Arendt called attention to the journal in *Eichmann in Jerusalem* (1963), but not until 1970 was an English translation published, under the title *Diary of a Man in Despair*.

1919—Luxemburg was beaten to death with rifle butts, and Lieb-knecht died of a *Genickschuss*, a single shot to the nape of the neck. In 1921, a former Turkish grand vizier known as Talaat Bey was felled in Berlin by a foreign student whose family had been among the victims of the mass murder of Armenians during World War I. Two years later, an aggrieved Russian émigré opened fire on a party of Soviet diplomats at a restaurant table in Lausanne to avenge him-self for the death of his father and uncle in Bolshevik Russia.

So the lone gunman with a score to settle was a familiar figure during the early years of the twentieth century. One noteworthy assassination took place in Paris in 1926 at a time when the "City of Lights" became a place of refuge for thousands of men and women who sought to escape the revolutionary tumult in Russia and eastern Europe and a stalking ground for agents of the Bolshe-vik secret police who were tracking down their class enemies. The overheated politics of postwar Paris is suggested in a lighthearted way in *Ninotchka*, a 1939 movie whose plot turns on the exploits of four clownish Bolshevik commissars who are dispatched to Paris to sell off the jewelry that has been expropriated from fleeing aristocrats.

"I was wounded before Warsaw," says Ninotchka, memorably played by Greta Garbo, to the Russian count who seeks to seduce her in his swanky Paris apartment. "A Polish lancer. I was sixteen."

"Poor Ninotchka."

"Don't pity me. Pity the poor Polish lancer. After all, I'm still alive."

Among the real expatriates who were living in Paris in the 1920s was Simon Petliura, the former ataman (commander) of an army that fought for Ukrainian independence against the Bolsheviks between 1919 and 1921—the same nasty little war in which the fic-tional Ninotchka sustained her wound. Amid the general carnage, the soldiers of Petliura's army carried out a series of pogroms against the Jewish communities of Ukraine that led to a death toll numbering in the tens of thousands, although Petliura himself later insisted that such excesses were against his will and beyond his control. After his army was finally defeated and Ukraine was absorbed into the Soviet Union, Petliura managed to make his way to Paris and set himself up in 1924 as the head of a government-in-exile and the publisher of the *Trident*, a weekly newspaper for his fellow Ukrainian exiles in Paris. Significantly, the newspaper was named after the symbol that adorned the flag of Petliura's army as they rounded up Jewish families and subjected them to horrific acts of torture and murder.

Petliura's fellow refugees in Paris included a Jewish poet and activist from Ukraine named Sholom Schwartzbard, who read about the arrival of Petliura in a Russian-language émigré newspaper. Schwartzbard counted fifteen members of his family among the victims of the pogroms in Ukraine, and he resolved to avenge himself on Petliura in the name of the Jewish people. He studied the only picture of Petliura that he was able to find—a sketch in the pages of the *Encyclopédie Larousse*—and he armed himself with a 9-millimeter Browning semiautomatic pistol. Schwartzbard once targeted a Ukrainian-speaking man in a crowd of sightseers outside the Musée de Cluny, but he did not pull the trigger because he was not entirely sure that he had found the right man.

Not until two years later did Schwartzbard finally come across a photograph of Petliura in another newspaper, *Les Nouvelles Ukrainiennes*, which also disclosed that Petliura took his lunch every day at the Chartier Restaurant near the corner of rue Racine and boulevard St. Michel in the Latin Quarter. Schwartzbard was waiting outside the restaurant on May 25, 1926, when Petliura finished his solitary meal.

"Are you Simon Petliura?" asked Schwartzbard, apparently still unsure of his target, first in Ukrainian and a second time in French.

The man did not answer, but when he raised his walking stick in self-defense, Schwartzbard fired five shots from his Browning.[6]

"Assassin!" cried Schwartzbard in a moment of profound but unintended irony. "This is for the pogroms!"[7]

Petliura fell at Schartzbard's feet. "*Assez!*" he cried out—Enough!—or so said one of the eyewitnesses. Or perhaps the victim merely whimpered in pain—"*Aiee!*"—as Schwartzbard later insisted.[8] All we know with certainty is that Schwartzbard fired two more shots as a coup de grâce, and Petliura was dead.

Schwartzbard was promptly placed under arrest by a couple of passing gendarmes, whose timely arrival may have spared him from lynching at the hands of the crowd that witnessed the assassination. Once on trial in a Paris courtroom in 1927 on a single count of murder, however, Schwartzbard appealed to the public conscience in France and around the world by turning the proceedings into a trial of the dead man on charges of genocide. Significantly, Schwartzbard portrayed the tortured and murdered men, women, and children of Ukraine as the latest victims in the long history of Jewish martyrdom, but he presented himself a kind of Jew that the world had not seen for some eighteen centuries—a Jew who fought back.

"Enough of slavery, enough outpouring of tears, an end to imploring, crying, bribing," he wrote in a letter from his prison cell to *Der Fraye Arbeiter Shtimme* (The Free Workers' Voice), a Yiddish newspaper in America to which he had contributed poetry under the pen name Baal Khaloymes (The Dreamer). "I was too kind to this murderer under whose command thousands, tens of thousands of Jews, infants at the breast, old white-haired men, women and men, were exterminated, and bands under his command raped, pillaged, extorted and burned. They spared the bullets; kikes aren't worth the price of the bullets. They had to be put to the saber, so went the order of the ataman-bandits. Well, I didn't spare any bullets for this murderer. I fired five shots into his ugly body!"[9]

To the surviving members of his own family—who lived on an Odessa street named after Rosa Luxemburg in what was now the Soviet republic of Ukraine—Schwartzbard addressed an open letter that called on the Jewish people to follow his own example of armed resistance. "Spread the inspiring message—an outraged Jew has had his revenge," he wrote. "The blood of the murderer Petliura, spilled in the eminent city of Paris, will awaken the world from its lethargy and remind it of the vicious crimes committed so recently upon the poor and abandoned Jewish people."[10]

Precisely the same appeal was made to the jury of Frenchmen who were charged with deciding Schwartzbard's fate. "A Jew who would lift a stick to defend himself was an unknown phenomenon," conceded his defense attorney, Henri Torres, who pointed out that Schwartzbard had joined the Foreign Legion and earned the Croix de Guerre after being wounded in battle during World War I. "Well! I say that when one becomes a French citizen as did Schwartzbard, when one experiences the freedom, full of life, among the Parisians, when a French soldier in a trench has held a hot steel in his hand, a new soul, ardent and trembling with excitement, then is awakened within him, that one strikes out for the sake of justice."[11]

The duty of the jury, argued Torres, was to acquit Schwartzbard for the assassination of Petliura, thereby symbolically condemning his army for the mass murder of Jewish men, women, and children in Ukraine. And Torres explicitly charged the jury with the duty to prevent future acts of violence against the Jewish people. On that very day in 1927, Adolf Hitler remained nothing more than a rabble-rouser on the radical fringe of German politics, and the horrors of the Holocaust were as yet unimagined and perhaps unimaginable. Torres intended his words to be prophetic, but he was tragically wrong: "Gentlemen of the jury," he concluded, "to condemn the pogroms of yesteryear is to prevent those of the future."[12]

Only three decades earlier, the conviction of a Jewish army officer named Alfred Dreyfus on false charges of treason—a public scandal known as *l'affaire Dreyfus*—showed the world that anti-Semitism still tainted French justice.* Now, however, the jury agreed with Schwartzbard's attorney, and the defendant was acquitted after less than half an hour of deliberation. He went on to write a couple of books, both in Yiddish, and he conducted a speaking tour in the United States, where a defense fund had been organized during his trial and where he was now hailed as a hero. Schwartzbard, a celebrity in some circles and all the more credible after the steady escalation of Nazi persecution of the Jews of Germany, traveled to Cape Town, South Africa, to raise funds for a publishing project in 1938. There, as it happened, he fell ill and died in bed, and the man known admiringly in Hebrew as *Ha Nokem* (The Avenger) was given a funeral befitting a hero by the swelling Jewish population of South Africa.

✦   ✦   ✦

ON THE SAME OCTOBER day in 1927 when Sholom Schwartzbard was surprisingly set free by a French jury, a six-year-old boy was at play in the school yard of Public School No. 1 in the northern German city of Hanover. His given name was Herschel—a common Yiddish name derived from the German word for "stag"—but his parents called him Hermann. As Polish Jews struggling to make a living in Germany in the 1920s, Zindel and Rivka Grynszpan had decided that a German name was preferable to a Yiddish one.† Their

---

* One of the journalists who covered *l'affaire Dreyfus* was a highly assimilated Jew named Theodor Herzl, the Paris correspondent for an Austrian newspaper. The spectacle of French anti-Semitism was among the experiences that persuaded Herzl that the Jewish people needed a country of their own, and he went on to play a leading role in the Zionist movement.
† The transliteration of Yiddish words and names from Hebrew characters into Roman characters is not standardized. "Grynszpan," a German word that literally means "verdigris," can also be spelled Grünspan (which

hope was that Hermann would assimilate into the culture of their new homeland and escape the anti-Semitism that had afflicted them in Poland. Surely the Grynszpans followed the coverage of the Schwartzbard trial in the Yiddish newspapers, but they could not have imagined that their son, too, was destined to write himself into the headlines.

As a boy, Herschel was always short and thin. Even in adolescence, although he possessed exotic good looks and a taste for well-cut clothing, he still weighed only a hundred pounds and stood only an inch over five feet. He may have suffered from rickets in infancy and was a habitual nail-biter. No doubt ridiculed by his classmates for his slight lisp, he was subject to bouts of "stomach trouble" that required a special diet.[13] Even so, when Herschel started going to school, he quickly acquired the reputation of a "quarreler" and proved to be quite capable of defending himself in the school yard. His classmates nicknamed him Maccabee, a Hebrew word that literally means "hammer" and refers to Judah Maccabee, the heroic leader of a successful war of national liberation fought by the Jewish people in antiquity.[14]

The Grynszpan family belonged to the *Ostjuden* (Eastern Jews), which set them apart from the native-born Jews of Germany who had been recognized as full-fledged citizens in the nineteenth century. The Jews who wandered westward from the shtetls of Poland, Russia, and other countries of eastern Europe were seen as odd, alien, and threatening, not only by Germans but even by the highly assimilated Jewish community in Germany, "who found them prim-

---

is how the family name appears in some German public records), Gruenspann, Grinszpan, Grinspun, or Grünspahn, among other variant spellings. "Zindel" is sometimes spelled Sindel. "Rivka" is sometimes spelled Rifka. I have adopted the most common English spellings of the family names, but the sources sometimes use variant spellings. Grynszpan is the spelling used by Herschel Grynszpan himself.

itive and felt they held up a grubby mirror to their more refined selves."[15] The newcomers were suspected of carrying with them the contagion of Bolshevism; Rosa Luxemburg and Sholom Schwartz-bard, for example, were both *Ostjuden* whose radical words and deeds seemed to confirm a Jewish stereotype that was later viciously and relentlessly caricatured in Nazi propaganda.

"We know him, the Jew," Reichsführer-SS Heinrich Himmler later declared in a classic, if also cracked, expression of Nazi iconography, "this people composed of the waste products of all the people and nations of this planet on which it has imprinted the features of its Jewish blood, the people whose goal is the domination of the world, whose breath is destruction, whose will is extermination, whose religion is atheism, whose idea is Bolshevism."[16]

Zindel Grynszpan, however, hardly conformed to the caricature of Judaism that was so prominently featured in Nazi propaganda. He was neither a radical nor a revolutionary. Like most other Jews who had reached Germany from eastern Europe, he sought only to escape the Jew-hatred that persisted like an ineradicable pestilence in his native land. Indeed, the recent experience of Jews suggested that Germany was far more civilized than the Russian empire and, for that reason, a safe refuge for the Jewish people. After all, the pogroms that provoked Schwartzbard to kill Petliura had taken place in Ukraine, where acts of crude and ubiquitous anti-Semitic violence contrasted with the peace and prosperity that were available to the Jews who lived in Bavaria, Saxony, or Prussia.

So it was that the Grynszpans fled Radomsk, a Polish backwater town, in 1911 and took up residence in the German city of Hanover. As if to symbolize the elevated status of German civilization, their apartment at 36 Burgstrasse was not far from the Church of the Holy Cross, where the philosopher and mathematician Gottfried Wilhelm Leibniz had been buried. Yet there was nothing very civilized about the neighborhood, which was located near the bustling railroad station and the bazaar-like stalls of the Scheiber Market. The most notorious of the malefactors who stalked the streets around the Grynszpan apartment was the so-called Butcher of Hanover, a predator who lured teenaged boys into his home in order to murder them and sell their flesh as comestibles. He went to the gallows in 1925, when Herschel was four years old.

"Swindlers, receivers of stolen goods, homosexuals and prostitutes," writes Dr. Alain Cuénot, Grynszpan's self-appointed biographer, "lived together in a sort of medieval 'court of miracles,' where everyone knew one another."[17]

Zindel worked as a milkman, a plumber, a junk dealer, and a tailor—all of these were common occupations for *Ostjuden* in Germany (and elsewhere around the Western world, including America) at a time when German Jews were able to aspire to careers in commerce and government, the arts and the professions. Indeed, the Grynszpans, unlike the affluent and assimilated Jews of Germany, remained poor and sometimes desperately so. Between July 10, 1933, and October 15, 1934, for example, the Grynszpan family survived on welfare payments totaling 2,042 reichsmarks, a gesture of public generosity that would soon be withdrawn from the Jewish residents of Germany by the Nazi regime.

The more existential threat, of course, was not the end of the dole but the crusade undertaken by Hitler and the Nazi Party to eliminate all Jews from Germany, starting with the *Ostjuden* but not stopping until the Third Reich was emptied of its Jewish population—*Judenrein*, as the Nazis put it. Once the Nazis achieved absolute power in Germany in 1933, the Grynszpans, like tens of thousands of their fellow Jews, struggled to find a way out but lacked the two essential resources—money and a destination.

Ultimately, they managed to spare only their youngest child, Herschel, by sending him out of Nazi Germany while the rest of the family remained behind in Hanover. The Grynszpans were observant Jews—"With God's help" appears repeatedly in their exchanges of correspondence—and they would have recognized the parallel between Herschel's flight from Nazi Germany in 1935 and the biblical life story of Moses, who is spared from slaughter by Pharaoh when he is set afloat on the Nile in a little boat fashioned out of reeds.[18]

So it was that Herschel, then only fifteen years old and even younger in appearance, reached what appeared to be a place of refuge in Paris. Two years later, on November 7, 1938, he walked into the German embassy on the rue de Lille, and what he did there abruptly put his name into the world headlines. Nothing in his upbringing predicted that he possessed the will, the courage, or the strength to carry out an act of armed resistance against Nazi Germany. Yet, precisely as he had intended, Herschel Grynszpan catapulted himself into celebrity and earned an uncertain but ineradicable place in history.

Dorothy Thompson, a famous newspaper columnist of the 1930s and a self-appointed advocate for the Jews of Germany, organized a defense fund in America and raised money to engage a similarly celebrated Corsican defense attorney to represent young Herschel in the French courts.* Leon Trotsky, an archenemy of Soviet dictator Joseph Stalin who had briefly sought refuge in France and was now living in exile in Mexico, was moved to declare his "open moral solidarity" with Grynszpan.[19] British composer Michael Tippett did the same in an oratorio titled *A Child of Our Time*: "Grynszpan," he

* Dorothy Thompson interviewed Adolf Hitler in 1931 and published a book about him, *I Saw Hitler*. Outraged by her depiction of Hitler and her coverage of Nazi Germany, the Nazi authorities expelled her in 1934. Although she worked tirelessly on behalf of Herschel Grynszpan as a victim of German anti-Semitism, she was also an early and ardent champion of Palestinian Arabs who were displaced after the founding of the State of Israel, a position that led to harsh criticism of her in Jewish circles during the 1950s.

explained, "seemed to me the protagonist of a modern passion story."[20]

Almost alone among the six million victims of the Final Solution, Zindel and Rivka Grynszpan's youngest child was known by name in the highest circles of the Nazi leadership, including Hitler, who personally presided over the fate of Herschel Grynszpan.

2

THE PRODIGAL
SON

MINIATURE VERSION OF THE HOLOCAUST WAS VISITED
upon thousands of innocents in Germany in the spring of
1942. The unfortunate victims of this little-known atrocity, however, were not human beings. Rather, they were cats, dogs, and other
household animals, and their only misdemeanor was that their owners happened to be Jews.

"On May 15, Jews were forbidden to keep pets," wrote Victor
Klemperer, a Jewish convert to Protestantism, in a journal entry
about the fate of his beloved cat. "[I]t is also forbidden to give the
animals away to be looked after. This is the death sentence for Mus-
chel. Tomorrow he is to be taken to the vet."[1]

The euthanizing of a cat, a triviality in the vast annals of suffering
and death that make up the history of the Second World War, allows
us to understand the ever-tightening noose that Hitler placed around
Jewish necks in Germany, starting in 1933 and continuing without
pause until the final defeat of the Third Reich in 1945. Long before
they were rounded up, packed into freight cars and cattle cars, and
sent to die in gas chambers, the Jews of Europe—men, women, children, and babies—were subjected to indignities and outrages that
had not been seen since the Middle Ages. Indeed, medieval anti-

Semitism seems almost quaint by comparison with the brutal German version.

The "war against the Jews," to use a phrase coined by Hitler and immortalized by historian Lucy Dawidowicz, began on January 30, 1933, when Hitler, as the leader of the largest party in the Reichstag, was appointed to the office of chancellor in the democratic government that had been established at Weimar at the end of the First World War.[2] Less than a month later, on February 27, a fire of suspicious origins—blamed on the Communists but almost certainly set by the Nazis—broke out in the Reichstag building. On the very next day, Hitler, relying on the Reichstag fire as a thin pretext, seized absolute power in Germany "for the protection of the People and the State."[3] The virulent Jew-hatred that Hitler had openly displayed in the pages of *Mein Kampf* ceased to be merely the ranting of a political crank and was now written into law and imposed on approximately half a million Jews who resided in Germany.

Beginning in 1933, and continuing over the next several years, German Jews were stripped of their citizenship and reduced to the status of "subjects" of the Third Reich. Their passports were recalled and reissued with a large red letter *J* to identify each one as a *Jude*,* and they were eventually required to wear a yellow Star of David marked with the same word on their outer clothing as an unmistakable badge of their Jewishness. They were excluded from schools and universities, the arts and the press, the military and the government, and the professions, including medicine, law, and banking. At the same time that they were denied the opportunity to work, they were also struck from the welfare rolls.

---

* The red *J* was applied to Jewish passports by Nazi Germany at the behest of the Swiss government, which specified that the ink used by German printers be indelible. "The Swiss made sure that it could not be effaced." Saul Friedländer, *The Years of Extermination: Nazi Germany and the Jews, 1939–1945* (New York: HarperPerennial, 2007), 91.

A certain German obsession with minutiae may explain the bizarre list of legal prohibitions that was compiled and enforced by Nazi bureaucrats. Jews were forbidden to own carrier pigeons or ice-skate on a public rink or display the German national flag. Their driver's licenses were canceled, and they were banned from trolleys and trains—or, more precisely, a Jew was not permitted to enter the dining or sleeping cars of a train: "We will kick him out," hooted Hermann Göring, Hitler's second-in-command, "and he will have to sit all alone in the toilet all the way!"[4]

Jews, moreover, were excluded from movies, concerts, cabarets, theaters, and circuses. They could not use the public baths or swimming pools. Their shops were boycotted, vandalized, and looted, and their apartments, businesses, artworks, and other possessions were "Aryanized," a euphemism for the seizure and sale of Jewish property at nominal prices to non-Jews. A live Jew could reside only in a building owned by another Jew, a dead Jew could not be buried in a municipal cemetery, and a Jewish cemetery could not decline to bury a Jew who had converted to Christianity.

Notably, the laws of Nazi Germany decreed Jewish identity to be a matter of blood rather than faith, and various anti-Semitic measures were imposed on anyone in whom the Nazis detected even the faintest trace of Jewishness. Converts to Christianity remained fully Jewish according to German law, and anyone with at least one Jewish grandparent was regarded as a fractional Jew known as a *Mischling*. Sex and marriage between Jewish and non-Jewish Germans were criminalized, and so were many of the ritual observances of Judaism. As a result, the Jews in Germany—and their children and grandchildren, too—could neither practice their faith nor abandon it, and they were all punished for the fact of their Jewishness.

The extermination order issued against pets owned by Jews, which may strike us as a wholly gratuitous act of cruelty, underscores the compulsiveness with which the Nazis pursued a solution to what they called the *Judenfrage*—a word that literally means "the Jewish Question" but is sometimes rendered as "the Jewish Problem."*5 From the outset, the ultimate goal of the Nazi program was to make Germany *Judenrein*, and the crucial first step, as they saw it, was to remove Jews from every aspect of ordinary life in Nazi Germany. Thus, Jews were deemed to be unworthy of the most trivial privileges, whether it was attending a music recital, or sitting on a park bench, or stroking a beloved family pet. The point of every little outrage was to inflict on the Jews of Germany a kind of "social death," as historian Peter Longerich puts it.[6]

Yet the official program of discrimination and degradation did not remain merely a matter of "social" death. Jews began to find themselves at risk of attracting the attention of the brawlers in brown shirts who belonged to the SA (Sturmabteiling, or storm troopers), an armed unit of the Nazi Party that was routinely used to terrorize and punish its adversaries and enemies. For example, a Jew might be dragged out of his home by night and left dead in a forest, or set upon and beaten with truncheons on the street in broad daylight, or forced to scrub a public urinal with a toothbrush, or made to drink from a spittoon from a saloon. Sometimes a gesture of contempt was expressed in a cruel joke, as when the town of Ludwigshaven posted an official sign on a perilous stretch of road: "Drive Carefully, Sharp Curve—Jews, 75 miles an hour!"[7]

The pervasive Nazi propaganda apparatus was deployed against the Jews under the personal direction of Joseph Goebbels, minister of propaganda, president of the Chamber of Culture, *Gauleiter* of

* Among historians the favored translation of *Judenfrage* is "Jewish Question." Some scholars, however, translate the term as "Jewish Problem," especially when referring to Nazi usage, because it more readily conveys the notion that the Jewish people were a problem for which mass murder was to provide the "Final Solution." For that reason, I have adopted "Jewish Problem," except when quoting a source that uses "Jewish Question."

Berlin, and a particularly slavish member of Hitler's inner circle. "I've dictated a sharp article against the Jews," boasted Goebbels in a journal entry in 1933. "At its mere announcement the whole *mischpoke* [*sic*] broke down."[8] The word used by Goebbels, a mangled version of the Yiddish word for "family" (*mishpocheh*), signals the special contempt in which the Nazis held the Yiddish-speaking *Ostjuden*. But his public pronouncements were far more vicious and played to the old and enduring traditions of German anti-Semitism that the Nazi Party always sought to exploit.

"Forget it never, comrades!" wrote Goebbels in his newspaper, *Der Angriff* (The Attack). "Tell it to yourself a hundred times a day, so that it may follow you in your deepest dreams: the Jews are guilty! And they will not escape the punishment they deserve."[9]

The logic at work in all of these early exertions, if the Nazis can be credited with any measure of rationality, was simple if also brutal. Germany had to be transformed into a land so hateful and dangerous for Jews that they would leave on their own initiative. Where the Jews would go and how they would get there were, at first, matters of utter indifference to Hitler and his comrades. America, Palestine, and even Madagascar were mentioned as possible dumping grounds in the Nazi master plan to make Germany *Judenrein*. The Nazis soon discovered, however, that not a single country was willing to welcome the Jews of Germany in any significant numbers, and appealing destinations like New York, Tel Aviv, or Capetown were replaced with more apparitional names like Auschwitz and Babi Yar, Bergen-Belsen and Treblinka.

✦   ✦   ✦

SOME JEWS WERE FORTUNATE enough to put themselves out of reach of the Nazis soon after Hitler came to power. Albert Einstein, for example, was already abroad on the day when Hitler took the oath of office as chancellor, and the famous scientist never again set foot on German soil. Following Einstein's example, composers Kurt Weill and Arnold Schönberg, conductors Otto Klemperer and Bruno Walter, and directors Fritz Lang (whose mother was a Jewish convert to Catholicism) and Billy Wilder (who co-wrote the screenplay for *Ninotchka* after he arrived in Hollywood) were able to reach America. A pair of German-Jewish intellectuals, Hannah Arendt and Walter Benjamin, managed to find a place of temporary refuge in Paris, but Benjamin ultimately took his own life when he was turned back at the Spanish border. Suicide, as it turned out, was the only escape route for some Jews trapped in the Third Reich.

Other Jews in Germany, however, were not eager to leave their homeland, and especially not at first. After all, the Jewish experience in the Diaspora had always been blighted by occasional periods of oppression and outbreaks of violence, but the Jews endured and even prospered in the countries of Europe, and nowhere more splendidly than in Germany, the birthplace of the paterfamilias of the Rothschilds, among other wealthy and powerful Jewish families with German origins. The survival strategy that had proven largely successful over the previous two millennia was to simply wait it out, and the same strategy was embraced by the leadership of the Jewish community in Germany.

"Fear? We have shown by a thousand martyrs that we have no fear of the deeds of human beings," announced Bruno Weill, vice president of the Central Association of German Citizens of the Jewish Faith, to his embattled community. "Hope? Yes. The hope that coexistence through centuries with the German people will prove itself stronger than all prejudices."[10]

More than one Jew in Germany comforted himself with the notion that this, too, shall pass. "Through the intensive study of history I have reached the, if I may say so, scientific conclusion that, in the end, reason must triumph over madness and that we cannot consider an eruption of madness such as the one in Germany as something that can last more than a generation," wrote the novelist Lion Feuchtwanger to a fellow Jewish writer, Arnold Zweig, in 1935. "And we are already at the end of the third year."[11]

Even those Jews who recognized the new and deadly threat that Nazism represented and who sought to leave the Third Reich, however, were confronted with serious and sometimes insurmountable obstacles. Many Jews in Germany, for example, could not afford to bear the expense of emigration to another country even if they were able to find a place of refuge—and a visa was the rarest of commodities. Even the most affluent Jews were hindered by German currency laws, which imposed confiscatory taxes on emigrants, compelled them to purchase foreign currency at reduced exchange rates, and limited the amount of money they could lawfully take out of Germany. For the less affluent Jews, of course, such measures were beside the point, because they had no money and no place to go.

"The problem was not to make the rich Jews leave," observed Reinhard Heydrich, who served in the highest ranks of the SS until his death by assassination in 1942, "but to get rid of the Jewish mob."[12]

When SS officer Adolf Eichmann—a "Jewish specialist" under Heydrich's command—set up the so-called Central Office for Jewish Emigration, in the Rothschild Palais in Vienna in 1938, for example, the formal title of his office accurately described its function. "You put in at the one end a Jew who still has capital and has, let us say, a factory or a shop or an account in a bank," said one witness who testified at the Eichmann trial in 1961, "and he passes through the entire building from counter to counter, from office to office— [and when] he comes out at the other end, he has no money, he has no rights, only a passport in which is written: You must leave this country within two weeks: if you fail to do so, you will go to a concentration camp."[13]

Heydrich and Eichmann, of course, were among the key executors of the Final Solution of the Jewish Problem (*Endlösung der Juden-frage*). Historians have debated for decades whether the extermination of the Jews was already among Hitler's desiderata on the day he came to power in Germany in 1933, or whether it was embraced as an achievable goal only after the world went to war in 1939, but it is beyond argument that the infrastructure that would be required to kill Jews on an industrial scale did not yet exist in the 1930s. Emigration rather than extermination remained both the official and the actual policy of Nazi Germany until the outbreak of World War II.

"The life opportunities of the Jews have to be restricted," warned an internal memo prepared for Heydrich in 1934 by the Security Service (Sicherheitsdienst, or SD) of the SS. "To them Germany must become a country without a future, in which the old generation may die off with what still remains for it, but in which the young generation should find it impossible to live, so that the incentive to emigrate is constantly in force." The Nazis were intent on maintaining order in the Third Reich, and so it was decreed, "Violent mob anti-Semitism must be avoided." Yet the same memo reserved the right to decide when and how violence was to be used, and its author shared a startling vision of the things to come: "One does not fight rats with guns but with poison and gas."[14]

Indeed, the Nazi approach to solving the Jewish Problem—and the official vocabulary used to describe it—evolved as the inevitable march to war afforded new opportunities to the Third Reich. "In 1938 'emigration' was a euphemism for 'expulsion,'" explains Lucy Dawidowicz in *The War Against the Jews*. "Once war began, 'evacuation' became a euphemism for 'deportation,' which, in turn signified transportation to a place of death."[15]

At first, however, the Third Reich lacked the means to carry out the mass murder of the Jews, and so German bureaucrats came up with gentler approaches to the Jewish Problem than the one that Heydrich and Eichmann would administer in the years ahead. Perhaps the most remarkable of these was the so-called Ha'avara agreement, derived from the Hebrew word for "transfer," a mechanism that was set up by Nazis in Germany and Zionist leaders in Palestine, where the British had earlier agreed to establish a "Jewish national home."* Under the Ha'avara program, German Jews bound for Palestine were permitted to use a portion of their blocked bank accounts for the purchase of export goods, and they received credit for the value of the purchases on arrival in their new homeland. By such means, some 20,000 Jews were able to reach Palestine along with approximately $30 million worth of German merchandise.

"Not an earthshaking sum even then," comments Israeli historian Tom Segev in *The Seventh Million*. "The immigrants themselves were forced to wait a long time for their money, sometimes as much as two or three years. They lost up to 35 percent of their capital, but according to calculations by proponents of the haavara, they would have lost more had they tried to transfer their capital in any other legal way."[16]

Still, as Heydrich himself readily conceded, the Nazi program of compulsory Jewish emigration would always be hindered by two fundamental flaws—a Jew who sought to leave Germany needed both money and a visa, and both were scarce. To take advantage of the Ha'avara program, for example, a Jewish emigrant in Nazi Germany required both a bank account with a generous balance and permission from the British authorities to enter Palestine. Hundreds

---

* The Ha'avara program was opposed by the right-wing faction in the Zionist movement known as the Revisionists, who complained that Jewish honor "had been sold to Hitler for a whore's wages." Quoted in Tom Segev, *The Seventh Million*, trans. Haim Watzman (New York: Hill and Wang, 1993), 24. One Zionist leader who had participated in the negotiations with Nazi Germany, Haim Arlosoroff, was shot to death in Tel Aviv by a pair of attackers shortly after returning from Berlin. The assassins have never been identified, but the Labor Zionists have always assumed that they were Revisionists.

of thousands of Jews had no bank accounts with which to bargain for their lives. Even if they did, the British sharply limited the total number of Jewish entry permits for Palestine during the 1930s and, six months before the outbreak of the Second World War, "reneged on its commitments and for all practical purposes closed the doors of Palestine to Jewish immigration," as Saul Friedländer points out.[17]

Among the unfortunate Jews in Germany who found themselves in this predicament was a wholly obscure Jewish family living at 36 Burgstrasse in Hanover.

✦   ✦   ✦

BY 1933, ZINDEL AND Rivka Grynszpan had already lived in Germany for more than two decades, but they were still made to feel like aliens. Born in Polish towns under the rule of the Russian empire, they were married in Radomsk, Rivka's birthplace, shortly after Zindel completed his service in the Russian army. Like thousands of other *Ostjuden*, they sought to distance themselves from the unremitting poverty and discrimination, as well as the sporadic outbreaks of anti-Semitic violence, that afflicted the Jews of Poland, Byelorussia, and Ukraine. As speakers of Yiddish—a language that originated as a fusion of Hebrew and medieval German—they were also more comfortable in a German-speaking country. "The little Eastern Jew has a somewhat exaggerated fear of a *completely* foreign language," wrote the journalist and novelist Joseph Roth, an astute observer of his fellow Jews, in *The Wandering Jew*. "German is almost a mother tongue to him. He would far rather go to Germany than France."[18]

Arriving in Hanover in the twilight of Germany's Wilhelmine era, the Grynszpans never achieved wealth or comfort and struggled constantly merely to make a living. They even failed to earn the status of German citizens, although their legal citizenship was changed from Russian to Polish when Poland was restored to sovereignty at the end of World War I—a fact of life that allows us to see how ordinary people can be transformed by the great events of history. In the eyes of their resentful German neighbors, the Grynszpans were merely another cluster of *Ostjuden* who lived at the margins of a once powerful nation and reminded them of its defeat and despoliation.

All six of the Grynszpan children were born in Germany, but they, too, were considered Polish citizens under German law. Three of them did not survive their impoverished childhoods in Hanover: one died at birth in 1912, another died of scarlet fever in 1928, and a third child died in a traffic accident in 1931. Zindel and Rivka Grynszpan's remaining three offspring grew up in the fragile Weimar Republic, which always teetered on the brink of ruination from its creation in 1919 to its fall in 1933. Indeed, they were eyewitnesses to the end of the failed experiment in German democracy: Esther turned seventeen on the day after the Nazis came to power in Germany, Mordecai was thirteen, and the youngest child, Herschel Feibel Grynszpan, born on March 28, 1921, was eleven.

The Grynszpans lived in a crowded apartment at 36 Burgstrasse. Zindel worked variously as a tailor and a junk dealer, but his meager earnings were not enough to support the family. Esther found a job as a secretary, and Mordecai became a plumber's apprentice. Like the other Russian and Eastern Jews who came from Russia, the Grynszpans adopted German names in an effort to blend into their adopted country: Zindel was called Siegmund, Rivka was Regina, Esther was Berta, and Mordecai was Marcus. The baby of the family, still enrolled in Public School (*Volksschule*) No. 1, was called Hermann by his doting *mishpocheh*. Significantly, the Grynszpans used these German names not only outside the home but even in their most intimate encounters with each other—they may have been derogated as *Ostjuden* in the eyes of the Nazis, but the Grynszpans themselves clung to their aspirations to make a life in Germany.

After 1933, however, even the use of German names was forbidden to the Jews in Nazi Germany precisely because it served as a kind of protective coloration. If a Jew did not already possess a name that was readily identifiable as Jewish, the Nazis decreed, one would be imposed by law: Jewish men were to add "Israel" to their names, and Jewish women were to add "Sarah." Legal name changes previously granted by the German courts were canceled because, according to one German official, "national pride is deeply wounded by those cases in which Jews with Eastern Jewish names have adopted particularly nice German surnames."[19]

Zindel and Rivka Grynszpan therefore resolved to save whom they could. If the family lacked the resources to leave Germany together, they would somehow find a way to save the children—and they would start with their youngest son. Here, too, the Grynszpans were typical of the Jewish communal effort to spare the children from the spiraling peril of Nazi persecution: "The only thing to do," said Rabbi Leo Baeck, a prominent Jewish leader in Germany, to a Zionist emissary in 1934, "is to get them out."[20] Thus began the grim struggle of one disenfranchised family of *Ostjuden* to find a place of refuge outside of Germany for their last-born child.

Herschel possessed none of the qualities that might have assisted his parents in finding an opportunity for escape. He had entered the *Volksschule* when he was six and left the same school at fourteen, the age at which German law no longer compelled him to attend school. His teachers remarked that he was "a quick study and of above-average intelligence," and his best subject was "Drawing," but his grades in many categories—"German," "Behavior," and "Industry" —were mediocre, his homework was often "deficient," and he was required to repeat sixth grade.

Later, Herschel himself asserted that he did not do well in school because Jewish students were "treated as outcasts," but his report cards actually improved after 1933. And Herschel did not do any better in the Jewish day care center that he attended after school hours. According to the director, Klara Dessau, he was a "difficult child" who was repeatedly excluded from class and "the only child whom she ever had occasion to slap." By contrast, his older brother and sister were "model children," according to Dessau, and even Herschel's mother complained about her youngest son.[21]

Herschel also belonged to a Jewish sports club called Bar-Kochba Hannover, a name that referred to a heroic Jewish resistance fighter who was martyred in antiquity. An acquaintance from the sports club recalled that Herschel was nicknamed "the Hun King" because he was "dark complected and very hot tempered,"[22] and we have already seen that his classmates later called him "Maccabee," another name with martial associations in Jewish history.[23] Some who knew him in childhood remembered him as "mean-spirited, ill-tempered, sullen, and taciturn," a lonely child who associated only with his fellow Jews "but was without comrades," and "a fighter who made use of his fists."[24]

Herschel placed himself in even greater peril when he dropped out of school at the age of fourteen in 1935. He was handed an *Abgangszeugnis*—a certificate indicating his departure from school —but he had failed to complete even the eight-year program that comprised an elementary school education. Small in stature, frail and sometimes sickly, impoverished and lacking both a diploma and a trade, young Herschel was unemployable in Germany and hardly represented the kind of "human material" that was welcomed in the countries where Jews were seeking to find refuge.[25]

"Human material" is the harsh term used in Zionist circles to describe the human beings who competed for the limited number of entry certificates issued by the British authorities in Palestine. "We must save children first, because they are the best material for the *yishuv*," wrote one functionary of the Zionist movement, using the Hebrew term for the Jewish community in Palestine. "The pioneer youth must be saved but specifically those who have received training and are spiritually able to perform Zionist labor."[26] Since Herschel did not as yet belong to any of the Zionist youth movements that prepared their members for emigration—and since he did not appear to be suitable for the hard work of pioneering in the Jewish homeland—his mother and father were forced to find another way to send their youngest son out of Germany.

One option they did not consider was simply putting Herschel on a train to Poland. After all, the boy may have been born in Hanover but he remained a Polish citizen, and Poland was the only country in the world for which he did not need an entry visa. Various relatives of both Zindel and Rivka Grynszpan still lived in the Polish town of Radomsk, including Herschel's paternal and maternal grandmothers. Although Herschel did not speak Polish, his command of Yiddish would have been enough to enable him to take up an apprenticeship with one or another of his various uncles on both sides of the family; one was a coppersmith, another owned a bakery, and a third operated a photography shop.

Yet the Grynszpans knew that the Jews who lived in Poland—more than three million of them, a Jewish population six times greater than Germany's—endured their own version of anti-Semitic persecution under the military dictatorship of Marshal Rydz-Smigly. Pogroms had broken out in Polish towns and cities in 1936, and the Polish government pandered to these undercurrents of violence by issuing an official decree requiring Jewish shopkeepers to display their birth names on their store signs. The law was aimed at the Polish counterparts of men like Zindel's brother, Abraham Grynszpan, whose tailoring shop in Paris was called Maison Albert, and was intended to clearly identify which businesses in Poland were owned by Jews. DON'T BUY AT JEWISH SHOPS was one of the items of graffiti that soon appeared like a foul refrain on the storefronts, and another one mimicked the slogans that could be seen across the border in Nazi Germany: GET OUT TO PALESTINE![27]

Indeed, the Polish Jews were no less anxious than the German Jews to get out. Isaac Bashevis Singer—another *Ostjude* from a town in Poland whose literary genius later earned him a Nobel Prize—managed to reach New York in 1935, but his visa had expired and he lived in fear of arrest and deportation by the American authorities as an illegal alien. Even in the mid-1930s, he was mindful of the aggressive intentions of Nazi Germany toward Poland and understood that it was not a safe refuge from Nazism. "While shaving, I made a decision: I would not let them deport me to Poland," Singer writes in an autobiographical short story titled *A Day in Coney Island.* "I would not fall into Hitler's paws. I would stay illegally." [28] So it was for tens of thousands of Polish Jews, the Grynszpans among them. No Jewish family that had already managed to flee the asperities that characterized life in Poland yearned to return.

Among the limited options for emigration from Germany, all of them discouraging in one way or another, Palestine remained the first choice of the Grynszpan family. Zindel and Rivka registered their son with the Jewish office in Berlin that coordinated emigration to Palestine, thus putting Herschel's name at the bottom of the long list of contenders for the limited number of entry certificates, and they prevailed upon him to belatedly join the Mizrachi Youth Organization. Unlike the leading Zionist movements—the left-wing Labor Zionists and the right-wing Revisionists, both of which embraced a secular approach to Jewish nation building in Palestine—Mizrachi alloyed Zionism with strict religious observance. "The land of Israel for the people of Israel," was the slogan of Mizrachi, "according to the Torah of Israel."[29]

Significantly, the secular Zionist movements encouraged the young men and women in their ranks to reinvent themselves as a new kind of Jew. At meetings and outings in the countries of the Diaspora, the Jewish youths studied modern Hebrew rather than the biblical version that is used for prayer, study, and ritual. They were taught how to work the land, how to operate and repair machinery, and how to use weapons to defend themselves. They proudly wore the distinctive garb of the various Zionist organizations, and they went on hikes and camping trips that were intended to toughen them for the hard work ahead. They sang anthems and marching songs that were meant to stir a sense of destiny, solidarity, and self-empowerment in the young Zionists: "Our hope is not yet lost," according to the words of *Hatikvah* (The Hope), "to be a free people in our land, the land of Zion and Jerusalem."[30]

Mizrachi, too, trained the sons of tailors to become farmers and taught them to use Hebrew as a lingua franca as well as the *Loshen Kodesh* (Holy Tongue), but the religious Zionists also preserved the ancient beliefs and practices that the rest of the Zionist movement had abandoned. If Herschel seemed too young and too frail to perform physical labor, as the apparatchiki of the Labor Zionists saw him, Mizrachi offered another and more traditional role for a skinny Jewish boy—he could still study the Torah.

While waiting to find out whether he would receive one of the certificates for Palestine, Herschel was sent to a yeshiva in Frankfurt am Main to enroll in a five-year program whose students aspired to become rabbis and teachers. The Jewish communal organization in Hanover, already struggling to cope with the ever-increasing burdens that resulted from Nazi persecution, managed to scrape up fifteen reichsmarks as a monthly contribution in support of Herschel's studies. On May 9, 1935, fourteen-year-old Herschel Grynszpan started the studies that were intended to eventually deliver him to safety in Palestine, or so his mother and father hoped and prayed.

His stern and demanding instructors at the yeshivah later recalled Herschel as "a student of average aptitude and intelligence." Given his lack of interest in schoolwork, he was clearly out of his element in a rabbinical seminary and did not possess the discipline that was required for the study of the Talmud and the Torah. Rather, he was apparently attracted to the street life—and the nightlife—of a cosmopolitan city. Although Herschel remained at the Frankfurt yeshiva for nearly a full year, returning home only once for a six-week visit between semesters, he eventually dropped out, just as he had done at public school, and reappeared in Hanover on April 15, 1936, in the same predicament that he had faced a year earlier.

"I searched in vain to find work as an apprentice plumber or mechanic," he later told the French authorities. "In the streets I suffered many troublesome incidents with the Hitlerites. I was kicked more than twice a day, even by little boys, who called me 'dirty Jew.'"[31]

Herschel later spoke of a crucial conversation that put him on an entirely different path. He may have abandoned the yeshiva, but he continued to adhere to the religious practices of Judaism, keeping the Sabbath and praying at the local synagogue. There he found himself in conversation with a man he described as "old Katz, the watchmaker." Herschel insisted later, rather curiously, "I don't like to talk with men whom I don't know," but, on this occasion, "I accepted the old man's invitation."[32] Old Katz lectured the boy on the danger of tarrying in Nazi Germany while waiting for an opportunity to emigrate to Palestine: "A boy like you can't stay here under such conditions," he warned Herschel. "In Germany, a Jew is not a man, but is treated like a dog."[33]

The Grynszpan family, as it happened, was scattered across Europe, not only in Poland and Germany but also in Belgium and France, where various of Zindel Grynszpan's brothers lived and worked. For the *Ostjuden*, the countries of western Europe represented beacons of light and places of refuge that were much easier to reach than the Holy Land or America. But young Herschel, who was apparently an attentive newspaper reader even in early adolescence, understood that Jews were being denied entry visas all over the world.

"I told him that all the governments were closed to me," Herschel later recalled about his conversation with old Katz. "He advised me to go to France."[34]

✦ ✦ ✦

ONE NEWSPAPER STORY THAT is likely to have attracted the attention of the Grynszpan family carried a dateline from Davos, Switzerland. On February 4, 1936, a twenty-six-year-old Jewish medical student, David Frankfurter, assassinated Wilhelm Gustloff, a Nazi functionary who was operating in Switzerland, with the stated intention of taking vengeance against the Third Reich for the crimes that had been committed against the Jewish people. "If you ask me why I made the decision to kill Gustloff," Frankfurter later told the Swiss judge who heard his case, "I can tell you the following: A wave of hate against everything that was connected with Brown Shirts or Nazis overcame me."[35]

Frankfurter, like the Grynszpans, was an *Ostjude*. His father was a rabbi from Russia, and Frankfurter himself had been born in Yugoslavia. He studied medicine in Leipzig and Frankfurt but fled from Germany to Switzerland after the Nazi seizure of power in 1933. An indifferent student, Frankfurter was agitated and distressed by the atrocities taking place in Germany, and he resolved to strike back against the Nazis, if only symbolically. He purchased a revolver and ammunition in December 1935, and he fantasized about finding a way to reach and kill Hitler, Göring, or Goebbels. But when Frankfurter read about Gustloff's mission of recruitment and propaganda on behalf of Nazi Germany in the newspapers that were published for Jewish émigrés in Switzerland, he found his target.

Frankfurter packed his weapon, traveled to Davos, and took a hotel room. He ascertained the location of the Gustloff home and knocked on the front door. Precisely because Gustloff's appointment as the Nazi emissary to the German community in Switzerland obliged him to receive a daily stream of strangers, Frankfurter was granted entry by Gustloff's wife and invited to take a chair in Gustloff's study while he finished a call on the hall telephone. The young man waited politely until Gustloff entered the room and asked the purposes of his visit. Then Frankfurter rose from the armchair, coolly drew the loaded revolver from his coat pocket and fired the fatal shots at Gustloff from a distance of a few feet.

Frankfurter left Gustloff dead on the floor of the study and, amid the commotion that followed the sound of gunshots, pushed past Gustloff's wife and fled through the front door. But he soon decided that escape was futile; when he passed a police station, the medical student turned assassin surrendered himself. When asked by a police interrogator whether he regretted his deed, Frankfurter answered, "Not in the slightest." After he submitted to medical and psychiatric examinations while in custody, no one mistook the message that the assassin sought to send to Nazi Germany and the rest of the world. "Frankfurter aimed the revolver with premeditation," testified the medical expert, "with the intention of killing a representative of an enemy of his people, as a protest, and out of wounded Jewish pride."[36]

Nazi Germany saw in the slain Gustloff a martyr who offered rich opportunities for propaganda. His body was ceremoniously returned to Germany. A state funeral was organized, and Hitler himself delivered an oration in which he acknowledged that Frankfurter had fully intended to strike a blow against Germany and blamed the deed on "the hate-filled power of our Jewish foe."[37] Hitler issued an open and ominous threat to any other Jew who dared to follow David Frankfurter's example by resisting the iron will of the Third Reich through an act of armed resistance: "We understand the challenge," were Hitler's ominous words, "and we accept it."[38]

To maximize the propaganda value of the Frankfurter affair, an attorney named Friedrich Grimm was appointed to represent the interests of the victim's family—and the German government—in the Swiss legal proceedings, and an official of the Ministry of Propaganda named Wolfgang Diewerge was given the task of extracting useful material for books and pamphlets, newspaper dispatches and radio broadcasts. *A Jew Has Fired (Ein Jude hat geschossen)*, the booklet that Diewerge wrote about the Frankfurter case, took up the sinister theme that Hitler had unveiled at Gustloff's funeral—the young medical student could be nothing else than a cat's-paw of Hitler's favorite bogeyman, the international Jewish conspiracy.

"I had the impression that the young straying Jewish student could not have committed the crime on his own initiative, but that certain powers of International Jewry must be behind him," Grimm later insisted. "[A]t the end of December around Christmas, when Christendom celebrates the festival of love and peace, [Frankfurter] made the decision to kill and then let [the plan] slowly ripen to fruition."[39]

Frankfurter was put on trial and adjudged to be guilty in a Swiss courtroom in Coire. "The court cannot share the opinion of the defense about justifiable vengeance," the judge announced, "even though Switzerland does not accept the methods used by Germany to resolve the Jewish problem."[40] If the German emissaries hoped for the death sentence or life imprisonment, they were disappointed, for the young defendant was sentenced to a term of eighteen years at hard labor, which meant that he was locked away safely in a Swiss prison when Nazi Germany commenced the Final Solution of the Jewish Problem in its own brutal way. For that reason alone, and remarkably enough, the assassin of Wilhelm Gustloff survived the war.*

Significantly, the Third Reich did not use the Gustloff assassination as the pretext for official or "spontaneous" violence against the Jews at the time of the assassination. An accident of history provides the explanation: the winter games of the 1936 Olympics were sched-

---

*David Frankfurter was pardoned and released from prison in 1945. He emigrated to Palestine, later served as an officer in the Israel Defense Forces, and died in Tel Aviv in 1982.

uled to open in Garmisch-Partenkirchen, in the Bavarian Alps, on February 6, 1936, two days after the assassination, and the Nazi regime wanted to make sure that tourists and reporters would not witness any outrages while attending the Olympics.

"Within a few hours a strict order was issued," writes Saul Friedländer. "Because of the Olympic Games, all anti-Jewish actions were prohibited. And indeed no outbursts of 'popular anger' occurred." The ruse was successful, and the rest of the world was fooled: "One sees no Jewish heads being chopped off, or even roundly cudgeled," went one report on the summer games in the *Nation* in August 1936. "Everything is terrifyingly clean and the visitor likes it all."[41]

Still, the Nazi regime did not allow the Jewish population of the Third Reich to go wholly unpunished. Hitler called for the imposition of a collective fine that "would make the whole of Jewry responsible for all damage some individual members of this gang of criminals caused the German economy and thereby the German people."[42] As a symbolic gesture, Hitler wanted the fine to be announced by the end of the trial of David Frankfurter, but various intrigues and rivalries within the Nazi economic bureaucracy produced a delay. In fact, the fine was not actually imposed until another Jewish avenger struck another Nazi target only two years later.

In the meantime, the daily lives of the Jews who remained in the Third Reich, the Grynszpans among them, continued to deteriorate as the Nazis tightened the noose they had placed around Jewish necks with ever more restrictive rules and regulations. The point, as it had been from the first day of the Nazi regime, was to make life in Germany so unbearable for the Jews that even the most stubborn among them would flee. "This Jewish pestilence must be eradicated," wrote Joseph Goebbels in his diary in the aftermath of the Gustloff affair. "Totally. None of it should remain."[43]

Yet the Nazi leaders were not merely venting their rage on paper, nor were they incapable of imagining more decisive solutions to the Jewish Problem. By 1936, Reichsführer Heinrich Himmler, then only thirty-six years old, was raised to the command of "Germany's entire repression and terror system," including the SS and the Gestapo, and the thirty-two-year-old Obergruppenführer Reinhard Heydrich was installed as his second-in-command.[44] If the Jews did not leave voluntarily, the infrastructure required to carry out the threats that Goebbels confided to his diary would be ready.

Five months after the Gustloff assassination, the Grynszpan family finally heeded the advice of old Katz and put into effect a plan of their own to spare their youngest child.

✦   ✦   ✦

LACKING ANY OTHER MEANS, the parents of Herschel Grynszpan could rely only on the *mishpocheh*. One of Zindel's four younger brothers, Isaac, lived in Essen, a city on the Ruhr, not far from the border with Belgium. Two other brothers, both working as tailors, had already left Germany altogether; Abraham settled in Paris in 1923, and Wolf reached Brussels in 1933. The fourth brother, Salomon, also ended up in Paris, which meant that Herschel had two uncles and their families living in the French capital.

When old Katz urged Herschel to leave Germany, the boy demonstrated a certain willfulness by insisting on a single destination: "I myself wanted to go to Palestine," he later declared.[45] Katz, however, took the matter up with Herschel's father, who eventually agreed to send the boy to France, but only on the condition that Abraham agree to shelter him somewhere amid the sewing machines and bolts of fabrics in the apartment identified by a sign on the door as Maison Albert. Zindel wrote to his brother, who promptly agreed to take in Herschel and even offered to adopt him—a gesture that would surely make it easier for Herschel to remain in France as a legal immigrant and perhaps even to achieve French citizenship.

The escape plan required paperwork from the outset. On July 9, 1936, only three months after dropping out of the yeshiva in Frankfurt, Herschel presented himself at the police station in Hanover and filed a formal application for an exit visa. His stated destination was Belgium, and he declared his intention to live with his uncle Wolf in Brussels while waiting for permission to travel on to Palestine. He also explained that an entry visa would be granted by Belgium only if he already possessed a document that would permit him to return to Germany. The point, of course, was that Belgium was unwilling to accept a Jewish refugee from Nazi Germany unless he could be sent back whenever it was convenient to do so. The applicant who was forced to master the immigration law of three countries—a challenge faced by everyone who sought a way out of the Third Reich—was fifteen years old.

A week later, on July 16, the police in Hanover issued two crucial documents—an exit visa that would allow Herschel to leave Nazi Germany, and a reentry visa that would allow him to return. To remain in compliance with German law, Herschel would have to return to the Third Reich no later than April 1, 1937. As a citizen of Poland, he also carried a passport issued by the Polish consulate in Hamburg, Passport no. 1585/35, and a German residence permit, both of which would expire on June 3, 1937. After that date, he could neither stay abroad nor return to Germany. A countdown clock was set in motion on the day that Herschel left the police station with documents in hand, and the awareness that time was running out was yet another stress on an adolescent who was already a nail-biter with a nervous stomach.

Herschel must have experienced both relief and excitement as he packed a few belongings, bid farewell to his parents and siblings, and set out on the journey that would carry him out of Nazi Germany. His doting family was comforted to know that he would be beyond the reach of the thugs in uniforms who were legally empowered and officially mandated to treat Jews like curs, and everyone in the Grynszpan family hoped that the boy would not see the Third Reich again. Yet, at the same moment, all of the Grynszpans must have been heartsick, and no one was more distraught than young Herschel, who was being sent away from home at fifteen and charged with the task of saving his own life.

Herschel was high-strung and sometimes histrionic, but the emotional life of the entire Grynszpan family was no less troubled. Zindel and Rivka quarreled openly, or so said Rivka's brother: "I myself often heard Zindel heap insults upon his wife." Like the biblical Jacob and Esau, or Joseph and his brothers, the two Grynszpan brothers who lived in Paris, Abraham and Salomon, were "on bad terms." Various of their many cousins and in-laws had innumerable feuds of their own, creating a skein of rancor that extended across Europe. Remarkably, the single most aggrieved and embittered member of the tribe was its matriarch, Herschel's paternal grandmother, who still lived in Radomsk, wholly estranged from her four sons. "The Grynszpans talked a great deal about their family," observes biographer Dr. Alain Cuénot, "but in reality they did not like each other."[46]

The most remarkable evidence of the dysfunction in the Grynszpan family are the letters that Herschel's paternal grandmother, Gika (née Poper) Grynszpan, sent to her sons in Paris from Radomsk—a one-way correspondence that carries a certain grim irony in light of the events to come. As we parse these long and overwrought letters, we realize that her sons were simply ignoring their mother's urgent pleas "to send me a little money." The letters are so self-pitying and so plainly intended to make her sons feel guilty that they would read like a parody of the stereotypical Jewish mother who otherwise exists only in Jewish jokes if the letters were not also so earnest and so heartrending. Gika, as if plucked from *Fiddler on the Roof* or a story by Isaac Bashevis Singer, invokes her own poverty, the various illnesses of the family members in her care, the urgent need for two hundred zlotys to send their sister Lea to Cracow for an operation ("For you it is so little and for me it is an enormous sum"), and her bewilderment at the silence of her scattered sons.[47]

"Dear children, you may not wish to know anything about me, but I, your mother, wish to know how you are doing, what you are doing, how your health is, how your work is going, etc." wrote Gika Grynszpan. "Believe me, I am crying as I write this letter. My dear son, I don't know how I have offended you. I write you letters and you are silent and don't write to me. I am after all your mother. Why do you treat me this way? Every day I await an answer from you. But almost two years have already elapsed and you still do not answer. This time, do not behave the same way, for all our hopes are placed in you."[48]

Even if they ignored their mother's pleas and plaints, however, the brothers Grynszpan were willing to assist in the boy's escape from Nazi Germany during that fraught summer of 1936. When he finally trudged off to the station in Hanover, Herschel boarded a train to Essen, where he stayed for two weeks with his uncle Isaac. From Essen, he traveled alone in the direction of Brussels, and he was able to show all of the papers that were necessary to cross the international border from Germany to Belgium as a legal visitor, no simple task in 1936. By the end of July, he presented himself at the apartment of his uncle Wolf in Brussels.

Brussels, of course, was merely a stopping point on the way to Uncle Abraham's apartment-workshop in Paris. But France was reluctant to accept Jewish refugees from Nazi Germany. German law prohibited the "export of capital" and thus permitted Jews to take only ten reichsmarks out of Germany—a pittance that amounted to less than five U.S. dollars—and French law prohibited indigent refugees from entering at all. So Herschel was forced to tarry in Brussels until he could either acquire enough money to legally enter

France by showing "proof of economic independence" or find some other way across the French border.[49] Although his papers would have permitted him to linger in Brussels for almost a full year, it was never his intention to do so.

If the Grynszpan brothers could not or would not scrape up two hundred zlotys to pay for their sister's operation in Cracow, however, it was even less likely that they would give or lend their nephew enough money to qualify for an entry visa from the French consulate in Brussels. Indeed, as Herschel described his arrival at Wolf Grynszpan's apartment in Brussels, his aunt and uncle "welcomed me rather coldly because I arrived with no funds and my sojourn imposed additional expense upon them." They soon contrived to move him into the nearby apartment of a neighbor named Zaslawsky, "who is vaguely related to my family," but his new host also "[let] me know at the same time that I was not to outstay my welcome there."[50] As a result, Herschel was forced to shuttle between the two apartments, taking his meals with Uncle Wolf and sleeping at the Zaslawskys'.

Since he had no realistic expectation that he could stay in Brussels until he received a permit to enter Palestine, as he had told the police back in Hanover, or that he would accumulate enough money to qualify for a French entry visa, he urgently had to find another way out of Belgium. The Grynszpan family may have advised Herschel to smuggle himself into France from the very outset, or the alert young man may have discerned the necessity of doing so after his arrival in Brussels. In any event, Herschel succeeded in finding someone who possessed a set of skills quite different from the ones needed to obtain entry and exit visas, German residence permits, and certificates for Palestine. His unlikely benefactor was a rather mysterious woman whom we know only as Madame Rosenthal.

✦   ✦   ✦

MADAME ROSENTHAL, A RELATIVE of the Zaslawkys, showed up in Brussels in the late summer of 1936 on her way back to her home in Paris after a vacation at the beach resort in Ostend. She appears to have taken a kindly interest in the adolescent lodger whom she met in the Zaslawskys' apartment, a slightly built boy, intense and handsome, with brooding brown eyes and slicked-back hair. With the assent of Uncle Wolf, who was surely pleased to rid himself of his indigent nephew, and possibly with the contrivance of Uncle Abraham in Paris, Madame Rosenthal tutored young Herschel in the art of escape.

The key item of intelligence provided by Madame Rosenthal focused on the small town of Quiévrain on the Franco-Belgian border. Belgian workers who lived along the border crossed back and forth between the two countries by taking the tram that ran between Quiévrain and Valenciennes, a French industrial town, where they were employed in the steel and textile factories. Somehow Madame Rosenthal knew that the papers of passengers on the trams were rarely checked by the French border police, especially if the passenger carried no luggage. Here was a clandestine route into France that required no passports, no visas, and no proof of economic independence.

On September 15, 1936, Herschel traveled in the company of Madame Rosenthal as far as Quiévrain, where he followed her instructions to board the tram to Valenciennes. Despite his age and stature, he apparently managed to mingle with the workers en route to their jobs in France and avoided the attention of the police officers who sometimes boarded the trams and checked the identity papers of suspicious-looking passengers. At the other end of line, he may have been met at the tram station in Valenciennes by Uncle Abraham by prior arrangement with Madame Rosenthal or the Zaslawskys, although both Herschel and Abraham would later tell quite a different story about how the boy reached Paris.

What we know with certainty is that Herschel managed to make his way from Brussels to Quiévrain to Valenciennes to Paris, where he showed up at Maison Albert and dropped his meager baggage in a corner of the cramped apartment. At last, the boy was safely beyond the reach of the Third Reich, or so both Herschel and his family back in Hanover now assumed.

3

TOUT VA BIEN

O N THE DAY IN 1936 WHEN HERSCHEL GRYNSZPAN FIRST
saw Paris, it was a city under siege from within. Demonstrations washed through the grand avenues at unsettlingly frequent intervals, sometimes mounted by workers on strike and sometimes by the paramilitary corps of the French right. The shrill headlines in the daily newspapers reported on political confrontation, business scandal, economic crisis, and the mounting tension between a resurgent Nazi Germany and the rest of Europe. Yet, at the same time, Paris still glittered with its old joie de vivre even as the foundations of the Third Republic were rotting away.

"I feel driven to inform you *personally* that Paris is the capital of the world, and that you must come here," Joseph Roth had written to his editor back in Frankfurt when he first arrived in Paris to serve as a foreign correspondent.[1] And the French themselves shared the same high opinion of their premier city: "If I can't wake up in Paris," says one character in the 1937 French film *Pépé le Moko*, a French woman who suffers from homesickness while on a visit to the Casbah in colonial Algiers, "I want to go back to sleep."[2]

French cheer in the face of catastrophe was parodied in a hit song by bandleader Ray Ventura that Herschel surely heard on the radio soon after his arrival in Paris. "Tout va très bien, Madame la Marquise" tells the darkly comic story of a noblewoman who places a telephone call to her country estate to find out how things are going in her absence. One by one, the servants reluctantly reveal a concatenation of dire events: her husband accidently set the château on fire, the fire spread to the stables, her favorite horse was burned to death, and her husband then committed suicide out of remorse. But each servant reassures the Marquise with the same cheerful refrain: "Aside from that, all is very well, Marquise."[3]

The song was readily understood by the residents of Paris as a wry and ironic commentary on the ruinous state of affairs in France in 1936. Only two years earlier, the Place de la Concorde had been the scene of a bloody riot by right-wing demonstrators in the wake of a financial scandal involving a Jewish émigré from Ukraine named Serge-Alexandre Stavisky. The same fear and loathing now focused on Léon Blum, a former theater critic turned politician who served as the first Jewish prime minister of France in a coalition of leftist political parties that banded together to cope with the mounting threat of fascism, both in France and elsewhere in Europe.* All the while, mindful of the carnage of World War I, France comforted itself with the imagined impregnability of the Maginot Line, a series of fortifications that ran along the Franco–German border, and did nothing when Hitler sent the Wehrmacht into the demilitarized zone that had been established in the Rhineland under the Treaty of Versailles.

"They are resting on the soft pillow of the Maginot Line," despaired a French colonel named Charles de Gaulle in 1936, but his

---

* "Whenever Léon Blum, the elegantly mustached socialist prime minister, appeared in newsreels, there were loud jeers and boos interspersed with cries of 'sale Juif—dirty Jew,'" recalls Victor Brombert, who grew up in France in the 1930s. Brombert, *Trains of Thought: From Paris to Omaha Beach, Memories of a Wartime Youth* (New York: Anchor Books, 2004), 22.

senior officers assumed a more passive stance toward the once and future enemy: "*Pas des histoires, pas des provocations, pas de bruit*," that is, "no fuss, no provocations, no noise."[4]

Paris, despite all of the internal turbulence and foreign peril, was still regarded as the City of Light, a place of enchantment that had always attracted artists, writers, performers, and intellectuals from around the world—Ernest Hemingway and F. Scott Fitzgerald from America, James Joyce and Samuel Beckett from Ireland, Pablo Picasso and Salvador Dalí from Spain, among many others. "I have two loves, my country and Paris," exclaimed Josephine Baker, the celebrated African American chanteuse who was a fixture at the Folies Bergère.[5] Her signature song, "J'ai Deux Amours," spoke for tens of thousands of foreigners who had lived in Paris and its environs, some as cultural expatriates like Gertrude Stein, some as political exiles like Leon Trotsky, and others as obscure illegal aliens like Herschel Grynszpan.*

"I love France, second only to America," declared aviator Charles Lindbergh, who settled in the fashionable Sixteenth Arrondissement to escape the media frenzy that accompanied the kidnapping and murder of his baby, although his admiration for the Nazis prompted him to consider making his home in the Third Reich.[6]

Above all else, Paris was a mecca that excited the appetites of pleasure-seekers and thrill-seekers, bohemians and romantics, eccentrics and decadents. Josephine Baker, for example, performed the so-called *Danse sauvage* for the tourists at the Folies Bergère with exposed breasts and a skirt fashioned out of faux bananas, a spectacle that would have attracted the attention of the vice squad

* France granted asylum to Leon Trotsky in 1933, but his request to take up residence in Paris was refused. By 1935, his presence was considered a diplomatic liability, and he moved first to Norway and finally to Mexico, where an assassin in the service of Joseph Stalin finally caught up with Trotsky in 1940, delivering a fatal wound with the blow of an ice ax.

back in her hometown of St. Louis. James Joyce's *Ulysses* and Henry Miller's *Tropic of Cancer* were both condemned as obscene in their native countries, but copies of the French editions were on sale at Shakespeare and Company on rue de l'Odéon. As if to symbolize the sexual services that were available from the *filles de joie* in the brothels and the *poules* on the boulevards, posters featuring a skull and crossbones and a stern warning—DEFENDEZ-VOUS CONTRE LA SYPHILIS—were displayed on the public urinals that were such a distinctive feature of the Paris streetscape.[7]

"One memorable night at Bricktop's a wealthy American woman tipped the members of the band ten dollars each to play jazz in the nude," writes William Wiser in *The Twilight Years*, referring to the Paris nightclub operated by an African American woman whose nickname referred to the color of her hair. "[N]ighttime Paris allowed for equal time to women imitating the privilege of a male audience paying to see Josephine Baker naked at the Folies Bergère."[8]

So, even as ordinary French men and women suffered the privations of the Great Depression, Paris remained a watering spot for the rich and famous, who favored the Ritz, the Crillon, and the Meurice as the hotels of choice but ranged more adventurously through the neighborhoods of Paris in search of sensation. By night, an affluent visitor from abroad might show up at the salon of a French aristocrat or socialite and then catch a cabaret performance by chanteuse Édith Piaf at Au Lapin Agile or jazz guitarist Django Reinhardt at the Hot Club de France. Duke Ellington joined the house band at Bricktop's when he was performing elsewhere in Paris, and the Duke of Windsor, who had only recently abdicated the throne of England, might be spotted on the dance floor with the notorious American divorcée who was then still known as Mrs. Wallis Simpson.

By day, a proverbial American in Paris might shop at the ateliers of Gabrielle "Coco" Chanel or Elsa Schiaparelli or the bijouteries of Cartier or Van Cleef and Arpels around the Place Vendôme, or carry glasses of champagne through the galleries where the latest works of Marc Chagall, Max Ernst, or Joan Miró were on display, or take an aperitif on the terrace at Café le Dôme on boulevard de Montparnasse in the hope of glimpsing an authentic artist or writer at the tables where Pablo Picasso and Ernest Hemingway had once idled and where a young Henry Miller used to cadge drinks. The grinding austerities of the New Deal could be forgotten amid the opulence and exoticism that were still available in Paris in the 1930s.

Even Adolf Hitler noted the extravagances of the Parisian scene and saw in them a strategic advantage in the approaching confrontation between France and Germany. He fancied himself to be an artist, and he coveted the treasures of civilization in the Louvre, but he simultaneously held the Parisian joie de vivre in contempt. "Does the spiritual health of the French people matter to you?" Hitler asked Albert Speer, his favorite architect and confidant. "Let's let them degenerate. All the better for us."[9] Indeed, the skull and crossbones that could be seen on the pissoirs of Paris were a fitting symbol for more than sexually transmitted disease; French politics, too, were in perilous health.

Eighteen rioters died, for example, and hundreds were wounded under gunfire from the horse-mounted Garde Mobile when a right-wing demonstration in the Place de la Concorde in 1934 boiled over into an attack on the nearby Chamber of Deputies. Two years later, Léon Blum himself was pulled from his car and cruelly beaten by thugs from the right-wing Camelots du Roi who may have been inspired by the provocative words of their leader Charles Maurras: "He is a man who must be shot," Maurras said of Blum, "but in the back."[10] The same hateful sentiment was embraced by novelist Céline: "I don't want to go to war for Hitler, I insist, but I don't want to wage war against him for the Jews," he declared in an inflammatory pamphlet titled *Trifles for a Massacre*. "Rather a dozen Hitlers to an all-powerful Blum."[11]

Not since the trial of Alfred Dreyfus in 1894 had France been so dangerously riven by social, cultural, and political passions. The darkening horizon around the City of Light can be discerned in the dispatches of Joseph Roth, the longtime Paris correspondent of the *Frankfurter Zeitung*. Paris, he had enthused in a letter that he wrote to his editor back in Germany on his arrival in 1925, "is free, open, intellectual in the best sense, and ironic in its magnificent pathos. Every cab driver here is wittier than any one of our authors."[12]

Even the age-old burden of Jew-hatred, according to Roth, rested more lightly on Jewish refugees in France than elsewhere in Europe. "Admittedly there is anti-Semitism in France," he wrote. "But it is not one hundred proof. Eastern Jews, accustomed to a far stronger, cruder, more brutal anti-Semitism, are perfectly happy with the French version." When Roth asked the Jewish proprietor of his favorite restaurant why he had chosen to come to Paris, M. Weingrod answered, "*Excusez, Monsieur*, why not to Paris? In Russia they throw me out, in Poland they lock me up, in Germany they give me no visa. Why should I not come to Paris, *hein*? [Eh?]"[13]

By the late 1930s, however, Roth offered a much different perspective of France from the Paris bistro where he came every night to sit among actors and stagehands, cops and postmen, and sip a cup of black coffee that had been spiked with kirsch "because it isn't just a matter of staying awake but also of being in the mood to stay awake," as he explained to his readers.

"I tell you, it'll all come to a bad end, if the world carries on the way it's headed," said one of his fellow patrons. "Look at us, standing here over our drinks, who knows whether we'll still be around to do this in a year's time?"[14]

✦　✦　✦

THE ELFIN LAD FROM Hanover who slipped into Paris on a summery day in late September of 1936 surely glimpsed some of the iconic sights—the Eiffel Tower or the Arc de Triomphe, the grand boulevards and the ornate bridges over the Seine—but his destination was Maison Albert, the cramped two-room apartment at 23 boulevard Richard Lenoir where his uncle Abraham and his aunt Chava lived and worked.

Although he was no doubt relieved and perhaps slightly awestruck to find himself in France at last, Herschel Grynszpan quickly apprehended that he was back among his fellow *Ostjuden* in the modest but bustling streets on the edge of Belleville, a neighborhood that sheltered many of his fellow stateless refugees from eastern Europe. As Herschel followed his uncle into the building and up the stairs, he would have caught snatches of conversation in Yiddish from the other apartments and the familiar aroma of Jewish dishes prepared with onion and carrots, parsley and dill, chicken and flanken, and schmaltz rather than *beurre* or *huile d'olive*, all more redolent of the kitchens of Radomsk than the haute cuisine for which Paris was so celebrated.

Abraham was among the thousands of other Jewish refugees who had settled in and around the narrow and twisting streets of the Marais, the medieval Jewish quarter that remained the center of gravity of Jewish life in Paris. The place was especially baffling to greenhorns like Herschel, if only because the cobbled lanes tended to run at angles rather than in a neat grid, and a single thoroughfare might have a different street name on every block. Unlike the stately boulevards and elegant blocks of the more fashionable districts of Paris, the Marais was odorous, congested, and knotted, a backwater where the accents and dialects of points farther east were more common than French.

At the heart of the Marais was the neighborhood known light-heartedly as the Pletzel, a Yiddish word for a traditional kind of flat bread covered with onions and poppy seeds. Here was found the greatest concentration of synagogues, schools and bookstores, bakeries and restaurants, all of which catered to the growing but also impoverished Jewish community. On the edges of the Marais were the neighborhoods of the Tenth and Eleventh Arrondissements where newly arrived Jewish garment workers like the Grynszpan family set up their sewing machines and struggled to make a living at the highly portable trade of tailoring. Few, if any, American tourists ventured into the Marais in the 1930s, and the Jewish immigrants who lived there struggled to earn a living on the ragged edges of Paris.

Herschel's middle-aged aunt and uncle had no children of their own, and they extended a warmer welcome than the boy had received from Uncle Wolf in Brussels. Given the bolts of fabric, the cutting table and tools, the sewing machines and the stacks of finished goods that filled the apartment, Maison Albert was a hectic and noisy place. Still, they managed to find a spare bedstead and set it up in the room that already served as both a workshop and a dining room. From his own earnings—600 francs in a good week, about 15 American dollars—Uncle Abraham handed Herschel a weekly allowance of 30 or 40 francs so that his nephew would have some money in his pocket when he ventured out of the apartment.

Not long after Herschel's arrival, his father sent a legal document that formally imposed on Abraham both the authority and the responsibility to act as the boy's guardian. Abraham did not shirk his duty. Herschel lacked the French residence permit known as a *permis de séjour*, which put him at risk of arrest, imprisonment, and deportation if a gendarme stopped him on the streets of Paris and demanded to see his papers, but Abraham was fully credentialed as his surrogate father. Zindel may have settled upon Abraham a sum of money to provide for the support of his son, but all of the particulars—how much money was sent, how the Grynszpans came up with it, and how it was smuggled out of Germany—would soon figure crucially in the larger mystery of the *l'affaire Grynszpan*.

Herschel's slow-motion escape from Nazi Germany over the summer of 1936 had left him anxious, depressed, and exhausted. Still only flirting with one hundred pounds of weight, standing barely five feet, he suffered from occasional bouts of the stomach distress that afflicted him at moments of tension. Although he lived in close quarters with his aunt and uncle in the apartment-workshop on boulevard Richard Lenoir, and occasionally saw Aunt Chava's sister and brother-in-law, Herschel was bitterly homesick for his family back in Hanover, a state of mind that was exacerbated by his difficulty in learning to speak French. His uncle Salomon lived nearby, but the two Grynszpan brothers in Paris were estranged from each other. Uncle Abraham himself was described by those who knew him as "affable though taciturn, reserved, and rarely confiding in others."[15] So it was that Herschel remained isolated and fearful during those first days and weeks in Paris, and his own excitable nature only intensified the emotional spikes that could be observed in any adolescent.

"If there was one attribute which characterized Herschel, it was that of an emotional person who cared a great deal about the people close and dear to him," writes Gerald Schwab. "His eyes filled with tears when there was talk of his family or the misfortunes of the Jews." According to the other tenants of the apartment house who came to know the new arrival, Herschel was regarded as "a gentle, self-effacing, obliging, affectionate and sensitive young man with occasional sudden mood changes, that is, a temper."[16]

Soon after his arrival, Abraham moved the family—and Maison Albert—to 8 rue Martel, a sprawling apartment block with an interior courtyard just off the boulevard de Strasbourg in the Tenth Arrondissement and not far from the Gare de l'Est railroad station, in another busy working-class district where Jewish tailors like himself plied their trade among the greengrocers, shopkeepers, and other tradesmen. Mindful of his role as a surrogate father, Abraham sent his nephew to a doctor who prescribed a special diet that seemed to settle the boy's stomach.

Yet another attempt at schooling did not appeal to the unsettled teenager, and Herschel did not show any aptitude for or interest in joining his uncle at the sewing machines. As Herschel began to venture out of the apartment, however, he soon befriended a few of the other Jewish boys in the neighborhood, all of them more at ease in Yiddish than in French and all of them living in "a second city, a Paris apart," according to William Wiser, "where émigrés were associated by former nationality, a common language, and dependence on one another."[17]

As time passed, Herschel remained slight in stature and "gave the impression of being more a child than an adolescent," according to Gerald Schwab, the American war crimes investigator who documented Grynszpan's life and exploits. "In fact, his aunt and uncle still considered him a child at seventeen and always referred to him as such."[18] Yet the photographs of Herschel in mid-adolescence show that he was capable of cutting a compelling and even dashing figure despite his age and size. His complexion was swarthy, his lashes black and heavy, his hair and eyes dark brown, all of which contributed to his exotic good looks. Surely the fact that he lived in a tailor's workshop accounts for his attire, including bespoke suits that were both fashionable and flattering. Although his work at Maison Albert consisted mostly of doing chores for his uncle and running errands for his aunt, a curious item eventually entered the public record—Herschel was fancifully identified in one court document as a "fashion designer."[19]

Both the stresses and the seductions of life in Paris inevitably shaped young Herschel as he settled into the daily life of a refugee family. Uncle Abraham brought home copies of at least a couple of the many newspapers that circulated among the Jewish émigrés, including *La Journée Parisienne* and the Yiddish-language *Pariser Haint*, where the stories of Isaac Bashevis Singer, a landsman from Poland whose literary career was still confined to the Yiddish press, were sometimes reprinted. Herschel read the papers every day, but what attracted his eye were the news dispatches from Germany, Austria, and Czechoslovakia that chronicled the mounting belligerency of the Nazis and the ever-worsening persecution of the Jewish subjects of the Third Reich. Poring over a newspaper account of the Dreyfus affair, which linked the anti-Semitic persecution of the French army officer in the preceding century to the persecution of the Jews in contemporary Europe, Herschel apparently concluded that the plight of his parents and siblings back in Hanover was not merely a private tragedy.

"With God's help" was an expression heard often in the Grynszpan household, and it appears reflexively and perhaps even obsessively in the notes and letters that circulated among the family members. "I am, like my parents, a strict observer of religious precepts, as opposed to those who rarely practice or are free thinkers," Herschel would later declare at a time when it was especially convenient to do so. "I have always followed religious services regularly for, to me, religion is a serious matter."[20] As it turned out, however, Herschel was not always or especially pious, and he soon acquired a taste for the pleasures of life in Paris.

Abraham and Chava, for example, took Herschel to the movies every week. He preferred war movies and love stories, and his favorites included the escapist entertainment offered by the spectacular MGM production of *Ben Hur*; *Michel Strogoff*, a political thriller based on a novel by Jules Verne and set in nineteenth-century Russia; and *Dark Eyes*, a melodrama about a love affair between an Italian man and a Russian woman. On his own, Herschel was more adventurous, and he fell into the habit of taking long walks along the streets and boulevards of Paris and the occasional hike in the countryside outside of Paris. When he could scrape up the money out of his weekly allowance or his meager earnings, he attended a stage show or ventured onto the floor of the El Dorado dance hall on the boulevard de Strasbourg.

Herschel also began to attend social events at the *club sportif* Aurore on rue Vielle du Temple, where he met other Jewish refugees from eastern Europe who had managed to reach the safety of Paris. Unlike Herschel, who had joined the religious Zionist organization known as Mizrachi back in Hanover, most of the boys and girls he now met at the Aurore belonged to the progressive factions in the Zionist movement that embraced secularism and socialism in their mission to pioneer a Jewish homeland in Palestine. The little stage band covered, if a bit thinly, the hit tunes that could also be heard on the radio or the dance floor at Bricktop's, but now and then the crowd might have called for a familiar and beloved klezmer tune. And the conversation among his new friends at the Aurore surely turned Herschel's attention from movies and haberdashery to the grim prospects that faced his generation.

So Herschel's *chaverim* must have engaged the newcomer in urgent and weighty conversation about the assassination of Wilhelm Gustloff by a Jewish medical student in Switzerland, which had taken place only a few months before, and what portended for the Jews of Germany. Perhaps they likened David Frankfurter's lone act of armed resistance in Davos to the Jewish self-defense units that were organized when Petliura's army was ravaging the shtetls of Ukraine. Since the Soviet Union was already seen as a crucial counterweight to the Third Reich, they assiduously followed the breaking news out of Moscow regarding the show trials in which Old Bolsheviks were accused of the high crime of Trotskyism—the same trials that were joked about in *Ninotchka* were regarded with solemnity and even terror by young Jewish socialists.

Herschel would not have overheard quite the same table talk back in Hanover or at Maison Albert. The Grynszpans invoked God's help in the face of hardship and bent their heads over the piecework on the worktable. Quite another conversation, however, was conducted among Jewish activists—Communists and socialists, left-

wing Zionists and right-wing Zionists—who were convinced that
the old strategies for survival that had sustained the Jews of the
Diaspora for twenty centuries were useless against the rude beast of
fascism. Daily prayer struck them as less worthwhile than calisthen-
ics and day hikes, and the ability to fieldstrip a rifle was valued more
highly than the repair of a balky sewing machine. Here were Jews
who were preparing to fight back.

Herschel's best friends, however, were neither intellectuals nor
militants. Rather, they were a couple of boys from the neighborhood, both Jewish refugees like himself—Naftali Kaufmann,
whom he knew as Nathan, and Salomon Schenkier, who was called
Sam. Herschel himself was already known as Hermann. Nathan
and Sam soon became his constant companions, and they often
joined up with each other to attend the dances at the Aurore or the
El Dorado, or to take in a movie at the Saint Martin or the Globe
or the Scala Cinema, or to stroll through the prettified precincts
around the Place de l'Opéra, where they could window-shop at the
fashionable boutiques or glimpse the stylish crowd at the Café de
la Paix.

Like most boys of their age, then, Herschel and his friends occupied themselves with movies and dances, sports and excursions, anything that might divert them from the dreariness of daily life in the
Pletzel. They were necessarily mindful of world politics, if only
because it had already impinged on their lives and threatened to
impose even greater hardships on them, but they also sought the
diversions that would help them put Hitler out of mind. What is
entirely missing from the historical record, however, is any sign of
entanglement with girls. Aside from the connections that Herschel
might have made in idle conversation or on the dance floor, no diary
entries or love letters suggest that he had any romantic attachments,
and he would later confide to his attorneys that he remained a virgin
at seventeen.

Above all, Herschel and his chums frequented a noisy café near the corner of boulevard Saint-Denis and boulevard de Strasbourg, an urban crossroads filled with shoppers during the day and street-walkers late into the night. Across the boulevard from the café stood the Porte Saint-Denis, an elaborate arch of triumph that had been erected in 1672 to commemorate the victory of King Louis XIV over a German army in a battle at the Rhine. The monument had long been outscaled and overshadowed by the teeming apartment blocks that now filled the Faubourg Saint-Denis, and the landmark proba-bly signified nothing more to Herschel than the portal through which he passed on the way from rue Martel to his favorite meeting place.

Herschel had little him to keep him away from the café. The young man was "something of an idler," according to Gerald Schwab, "a kind of stroller of streets, a dreamer."[21] He liked to tinker with mechanical devices, and there was no dearth of sewing machines that required maintenance and repair in his uncle's apartment and the other workshops around the neighborhood, but he never managed to turn his interests into a trade. To be sure, Herschel talked about apprenticing as an electrician or a mechanic, but it was nothing but talk; instead, he preferred to show up at the café and drift endlessly and aimlessly into conversation with his friends about matters great and small—the next dance at the Aurore or the latest Nazi outrage to afflict their loved ones who were still trapped in Germany or Poland.

Sometimes, when his allowance ran out, Herschel could not afford to take a table and order a beverage or a meal at the café on the boul' Saint-Denis. Still, he would hang out on the crowded side-walk, smoking a cigarette, bantering with his friends, and perhaps keeping an eye out for a generous stranger with enough pocket money to treat him to a coffee or a bite to eat.

The café at 15 boulevard Saint-Denis was called Tout Va Bien— All Is Well.

✦   ✦   ✦

ONE OF THE WALKS that Herschel evidently came to know well would have taken him along the boulevard de Strasbourg in the direction of the Left Bank and delivered him to quite a different district of Paris. He left behind the congested streets of the Tenth Arrondissement—bars and cafés, groceries and bottle shops, little hotels and all-night movie houses, all of them a bit shabby and catering mostly to workers and travelers—and passed through the affluent precincts whose restaurants and grand hotels, galleries and salons, museums and public buildings, symbolized Paris to the rest of the world. Then he crossed over the Pont au Change, passing the high medieval walls of the Préfecture de Police on the Île de la Cité, and finally reached the Left Bank.

Along the embankment of the Seine called the Quai d'Orsay stood the stately building where the French Ministry of Foreign Affairs was headquartered, and clustered in the same elegant neighborhood were the embassies and consulates representing the nations of the world as it existed in the fall of 1938. At 78 rue de Lille, around the corner from the Gare d'Orsay railroad station, stood the embassy of Nazi Germany, the nation that would conquer so many others—and wipe some of them off the map entirely—in less than a year. Herschel Grynszpan knew the route to the German diplomatic mission precisely because passports and visas imprinted with the ominous figure of the eagle and the swastika of the Third Reich figured so powerfully in his life.

A guarded portal stood between the public street and the inner courtyard of the German embassy, but throngs of visitors sought entry to 78 rue de Lille every day, not only diplomats from allied or aggrieved nations but also the friends and relatives of those who were desperately seeking a way out of Germany, entrepreneurs and speculators and outright con men who saw Germany as a place where careers and fortunes might be made even in these troubled times, and, now and then, the agents and operatives whose dealings with the German diplomats required the greatest degree of discretion. As the listening post of the Third Reich in the capital city of its most likely enemy in the next war, the embassy, an entrepôt of intrigue behind a façade of diplomatic gentility, fairly hummed with energy and activity. "Spies were admitted to the rue de Lille Embassy," shrilled one Paris newspaper, "and one had only to be announced as an intelligence agent to be received without difficulty."[22]

Among the diplomats who attended to the work of the German embassy was a young man with the aristocratic name of Ernst Eduard Adolf Max vom Rath. Born into a wealthy and privileged family in Frankfurt am Main on June 3, 1909, Ernst vom Rath was the son of a distinguished attorney who had spent many years in public service as a *Regierungsrat*, or government counselor, before retiring to run the family business, a sugar factory.

The younger Rath followed his father into law and government: he attended law school in Königsberg, passed his law examinations in 1932, and briefly apprenticed in the Magistrate's Court, first in Zinter and later in Berlin. With his thin lips, high forehead, and even features, the handsome young man cut an elegant figure in the courtroom. But a career in the law was unappealing to the ambitious Rath, who had a taste for life in exotic places, and he resolved in 1934 to pursue an appointment to the German foreign service.

Here, too, Rath was able to call on influential family connections. In fact, an uncle, Roland Koester, held the appointment of German ambassador to France and presided over the embassy at 78 rue de Lille. Uncle Roland generously invited his nephew to spend the summer of 1934 in Paris so that he could prepare for the language test that was included among the examinations administered to all applicants. His private tutor, a certain Mlle Taulin, later attested to the young man's "great intelligence and perfect manners," his "extreme reserve and calm disposition," all of which would become points of interest and consequence only a few years latter.[23] When Rath returned to Berlin, he passed the exams on his first sitting and then served a six-week training and evaluation program at the German embassy in Budapest. On April 13, 1935, he was sworn into the German foreign service with the rank of attaché.

Rath was mindful of the fact that Germany was in the midst of the Nazi revolution, and he did not rely only on his aristocratic bloodline. Rather, he was careful to position himself for a future in the foreign service of what was now the Third Reich by joining the Nazi Party while he was still a student at the University of Königsberg in the summer of 1932. His timing turned out to be ideal. Because his date of enrollment was six months before Hitler was named chancellor of Germany and party membership became de rigueur, if not strictly obligatory, Rath was eligible for the elevated status of *Alter Kämpfer* (Old Fighter).

Later, Rath even joined the paramilitary unit of the party known as the Sturmabteilung—storm troops or, more colloquially, the Brownshirts—in April of 1933. As a cultivated member of the German gentry, he may have felt out of place among the thuggish Brownshirts, but he understood that it only added luster to his Nazi credentials at a time when Nazi Party membership alone was no longer as much of a distinction in Germany. Clearly, he understood what an enterprising young diplomat needed to do in order to advance his career in the Third Reich.

The other aspiring diplomats who were trained and tested in the company of young Rath could not have been surprised when his first post as a newly minted attaché turned out to be Paris—perhaps the most coveted of all German diplomatic missions—and his first assignment was to serve as personal secretary to his uncle, who promptly put the elegant young man in charge of matters of protocol. Tellingly, Rath's posting in the Paris embassy came to an abrupt end when his uncle died in 1936, and he was promptly recalled to Berlin and then shipped out to the German consulate in Calcutta, a far less desirable place, where he came down with an ailment that might have been dysentery or perhaps something more exotic. Struggling to recover his health in the punishing heat and humidity of India, Rath was eventually granted a medical evacuation to Germany for treatment at the Berlin Institute of Radiology. There he was diagnosed with pulmonary tuberculosis—again, the diagnosis would come to be the subject of speculation—and spent another four months in a sanatorium in the Black Forest.

All the while, Rath longed for the comforts and pleasures that he had first experienced in Paris. To improve his command of the French language, he corresponded with Mlle Taulin and asked her to mark any errors in his letters and return them for his further instruction. The letters they exchanged were all perfectly proper, or so Mlle Taulin later affirmed: "I never observed the slightest indication in his thought or expression," she declared, "that he was either violent or vulgar."[24] Later, the Nazi propaganda minister, Joseph Goebbels, and even the Führer himself, would come to regard it as a matter of urgent interest and historic importance to determine whether Ernst vom Rath was capable of flirting with a woman. For the time being, however, the letters that Rath composed in a convalescent's bed in the Black Forest and mailed to Mlle Taulin in Paris remained a private affair.

So it was that Ernst vom Rath was momentarily absent from Paris on the day in 1936 when Herschel Grynszpan arrived there. Not until the summer of 1938 was Rath deemed fit enough to resume his diplomatic service, and only then was he sent back to the German embassy in Paris to assume the new rank of *Legationssekretär* (legation secretary) in charge of cultural affairs. After the privations of Calcutta and the frustrations of a long convalescence in Germany, the young man was glad to be back at his desk in Paris and accruing the years in service that would be necessary to attain a diplomatic rank worthy of the family name.

✦ ✦ ✦

HERSCHEL TURNED SEVENTEEN ON March 28, 1938. Adolf Hitler had confidently predicted that the Third Reich would last a thousand years, and the events that marked 1938—"*the* crucial year in the history of Nazi Germany before Europe tumbled into war," according to historian and journalist Giles MacDonogh—only seemed to prove him right. "Every month," writes MacDonogh, "resounded with shocks or sensations."[25] Each of these acts of aggression was described in the Yiddish newspapers that were read so attentively in the Grynszpan apartment. Each one was the cause for yet more aggravated conversation among Herschel's circle of friends, and each only exacerbated the anxiety that afflicted Herschel in that tumultuous year in Paris.

"Even for a teenager very taken with himself, it was hard to be unaware of events," recalls critic and scholar Victor Brombert, whose family also emigrated from Russia to Germany to France, about his own anxious adolescence in Paris in the 1930s. "Newsreels, radio programs, ubiquitous arguments and discussions—all kept us sensitized."[26]

On March 11, 1938, for example, the government of Austria was persuaded to name a Nazi collaborator as chancellor under the threat of German invasion. Exactly how much persuasion was required remains a matter of historical debate. In any case, the chancellor promptly "invited" the Wehrmacht to cross the international border, and Austria was formally absorbed into the Third Reich two days later. The *Anschluss*, as it was called, reduced another 185,000 Jews to the status of subjects of the Third Reich, literally overnight, and the Austrian Nazis all too eagerly aped their brethren in Germany by taking to the streets to terrorize the Jewish citizenry of Vienna, whose Jewish population was the largest of any city in German-speaking Europe.

"Fluffy Viennese blondes [fought] to get closer to the elevating spectacle of an ashen-faced Jewish surgeon on his hands and knees before half a dozen young hooligans with Swastika armlets and dog-whips," wrote a correspondent for the London *Morning Chronicle*. "His delicate fingers, which must have made the swift and confident incisions that had saved the lives of many Viennese, held a scrubbing brush."[27]

The Jews of Austria now faced the same dilemma that had confronted the Jews of Germany for the last five years, and they had no better or more numerous escape routes. Czechoslovakia promptly sealed its borders against a new wave of refugees and granted entry only to those whose passports had been stamped with an entry visa. Twenty-five thousand passport applications were received by the government of Poland from Jews in Vienna, many of them *Ostjuden* who had ended up in Austria after the dismemberment of the Austro-Hungarian Empire after World War I. A few prominent Jewish figures—psychoanalyst Sigmund Freud, composer Arnold Schönberg, and director Otto Preminger among them—found a place of refuge in England or America. Less illustrious Austrian Jews, however, remained in deadly peril.

"The Jewish question," observed Joseph Goebbels, "has become a global problem once again."[28]

Goebbels may have been cackling with self-congratulation, but he was not wrong. Concern over the fate of Jewish refugees from the Third Reich finally prompted President Franklin D. Roosevelt to convene an international conference in the French resort town of Evian on July 6, 1938. "We cannot stand aside in view of the suffering of human beings and fail to respond to their cry for help," commented the French Catholic newspaper *La Croix* in a prescient editorial. "We cannot be partners to a solution of the Jewish question by means of their extinction, by means of the complete extermination of a whole people."[29] The Evian conference, however, demonstrated only that the world was unwilling to stand up to Nazi Germany or to afford a sanctuary to its Jewish refugees. "No country, America not excepted," explains historian Saul Friedländer, "declared itself ready to accept unconditionally any number of Jews."[30]

A headline in the Nazi Party newspaper *Völkischer Beobachter* accurately summed up the attitude of the participants in the Evian conference toward the Jews of Germany and Austria—"Nobody wants them"—and Hitler himself later described the impotence and indifference of the Western democracies with a characteristic taunt. "Now, as the nation is not willing any more to be sucked dry by these parasites, cries of pain arise all over," he declared in a 1938 speech to the Nuremberg party rally. "But it does not mean that these democratic countries have now become ready to replace their hypocritical remarks with acts of help; on the contrary, they affirm with complete coolness that over there, evidently, there is no room! In short, no help, but preaching, certainly!"[31]

Hitler counted on such complacency and hypocrisy in his next act of aggression. On the pretext that the German-speaking population of the Sudetenland, a region of Czechoslovakia, was the victim of persecution by the Czech government, Hitler ordered the Wehrmacht to prepare for yet another invasion. The French and British responded to the military threat by calling up their reserves, but they did not share Germany's willingness to go to war. The British prime minister, Neville Chamberlain, resolved to bargain away a chunk of Czechoslovakia in exchange for what he infamously called "peace with honor."[32]

Chamberlain flew to Germany on September 15, 1938, and abjectly offered the Sudetenland to Germany in the Führer's alpine retreat at Berchtesgaden. Chamberlain and Hitler agreed to redraw the boundaries of a sovereign nation and thus presented the Czech democracy with a cynical fait accompli. At ceremonies held in Munich on September 29, Chamberlain was joined by the enervated French prime minister, Edouard Daladier, as the leaders of these two Western democracies added their signatures to those of the Führer of the Third Reich and *Il Duce* of Fascist Italy, Benito Mussolini, on the treaty that formally dismembered Czechoslovakia.

The shameful peace that the Western democracies purchased from the Third Reich in 1938 at the expense of Czechoslovakia proved to be ephemeral. Moreover, it sent an unmistakable message to the rest of the world, including heads of state and Jewish refugees huddled in the Pletzel. Germany might want to rid itself of its Jewish population, but its appetite for the territory of its neighbors meant that its Jewish population only increased with each new acquisition. What remained of Czechoslovakia was still at risk, and Poland would surely be next.

✦　✦　✦

THE BALEFUL STORIES IN the Yiddish newspapers merely added to the stress that consumed Herschel Grynszpan. Although he did not join his friends in a glass of *vin ordinaire* at the Tout Va Bien, instead ordering a black coffee or a glass of orange juice, Herschel was smoking three packs of harsh French cigarettes each week. Now seventeen, he remained short and skinny, and he was still afflicted with occasional bouts of stomach distress.

Now and then, Herschel made despairing comments that led his friends and relatives to suspect that he was entertaining thoughts of suicide, a prospect that was all the more plausible because so many Jews took their own lives when they could find no other way to escape Nazi persecution. On other occasions, he was given to gestures of adolescent grandiosity, as when he wrote a letter to the president of the United States, audaciously pleading for an entry visa, or when he announced his intention to leave his uncle's apartment once and for all and join the French Foreign Legion.

"He refused to eat and wanted to enlist," Abraham Grynszpan later attested. "I even gave him 200 francs to take the necessary steps."[33]

What the Foreign Legion could have offered a stateless refugee living illegally in France was a path to French citizenship. Like the hundreds of thousands of Jews whose fate was debated at the Evian conference, Herschel was caught in a tragically familiar dilemma: he could neither stay in France nor return to Germany, and no other sanctuary presented itself. Although Herschel seemed unlikely to meet the recruiting standards of France's elite military unit, any adolescent who believed that the president of the United States would read, much less answer, his plaintive letter was also capable of imagining himself in the snappy uniform of the *Légion étrangère*, if one could be found in his boyish size.

Indeed, the Grynszpan family had been struggling with Herschel's precarious legal status ever since his arrival in France in the summer of 1936. Abraham dutifully registered his houseguest at the local police station, as required by law, but the fact that Herschel's passport was not stamped with a French entry visa led to a fine of 1,000 francs. Then Abraham petitioned the Central Committee for Aid to Immigrant Jews for assistance in filing the necessary papers to secure an identity card and a *permis de séjour* for his nephew, but no help was forthcoming until January 25, 1937. The application was eventually lodged with the Ministry of the Interior and forwarded to the prefect of police, and the receipt that was issued to Herschel served in lieu of an identity card while the paperwork was being processed.

Meanwhile, both his German reentry visa and his Polish passport were about to expire. Back in Hanover, Zindel Grynszpan was able to secure a brief extension of the visa on behalf of his absent son, and

Herschel himself reported to the Polish consulate in Paris that his original passport had been lost, which was almost certainly a fiction but resulted in the issuance of a new passport that would remain in effect through January 7, 1938. When his German reentry visa finally expired, Herschel addressed a letter to the German consulate in Paris with a request for a new visa on the grounds that "his studies in Paris were taking longer than anticipated," which was merely another ploy since he had not undertaken any schoolwork since arriving in France and had never claimed that he intended to do so.[34]

Abraham presented himself at the German consulate in September 1937 to plead the case for a reentry visa, an act of desperation that would allow Herschel to reunite with his parents if he were unable to remain in France. The Grynszpans, after all, attributed Herschel's intermittent bouts of illness to his homesickness and figured that he might benefit from the care of his family in Hanover if his health deteriorated. None of these sentimental concerns, however, made the least impression on the German consular staff; indeed, one efficient attaché went to the trouble of contacting the police in Hanover and confirming that Herschel's stated reason for leaving Germany back in 1936 had been to await a certificate for Palestine and not to study in France. For that reason, the request for a reentry visa was turned down, and a subsequent letter of appeal from Herschel's father on January 4, 1938, was also rejected.

Herschel found himself trapped for the next several months in a bureaucratic labyrinth that even Kafka could not have conjured up. By a certain grim irony, the French government finally bestirred itself to clarify the legal status of the troublesome young refugee just as the diplomats at Evian were debating the destiny of Jewish refugees from the Third Reich in their hundreds of thousands. The decision in the Grynszpan matter was a catastrophe.

On July 8, 1938, two days after the opening of the Evian conference, the prefect of police in Paris rejected Herschel's request for a

French residency permit, and the decision produced a formal decree of expulsion that was issued on August 11 and went into effect on August 15. The French Republic, in other words, afforded seventeen-year-old Herschel Grynszpan exactly four days in which to leave France. After August 15, he was subject to arrest and deportation if he remained in the country, but neither Germany, his country of birth, nor Poland, his country of citizenship, would allow him to enter because his German visa and his Polish passport had both expired.

His plight was hardly unique. Among the three million foreigners who found refuge of one kind or another in France in the 1930s, only 5 percent or so were Jewish. The Jewish population of France, however, grew steadily in absolute numbers, starting at 90,000 at the beginning of the twentieth century and reaching a peak of 300,000 in 1939. Significantly, fully half of the Jews in France were foreigners, and even among the Jews who held French citizenship, half of them were foreign born. Two-thirds of the Jewish population in France was concentrated in Paris and its environs, while 80 percent of the Jews living in Paris traced their origins back to Poland and other countries of eastern Europe. Troubled by its own population of *Ostjuden*, France resolved to send back as many of them as it could.

Even the native-born Jews of France, who tended to be more affluent, regarded Jewish families like the Grynszpans with a certain hauteur, if not open hostility. Jacques Helbronner, who presided over the Jewish community organization known as the Consistoire, openly warned against welcoming "the rejects of society, the elements who could not possibly have been of any use to their own country." Rather, he favored a highly selective policy toward his fellow Jews: "If there are 100 to 150 great intellectuals who are worthy of being kept in France since they are scientists or chemists who have secrets our own chemists don't know," he argued when the Nazis came to power in 1933, "these we will keep, but the 7, 8, or perhaps

10,000 Jews who will come to France, is it really in our best interests to keep them?"[35]

A similarly harsh attitude was shared by the United States and Great Britain, neither of which was willing to expand the opportunities for immigration for the Jews who remained in the Third Reich in 1938. The U.S. quota for immigrants from Germany and Austria remained at 27,130 per year, for example, and yet the requirements for entry to the United States were so exacting that the quota went unfilled during the years when the rescue of Jews became literally a matter of life and death. Great Britain sought to limit the number of Jewish refugees who would be granted entry to Palestine—a white paper later issued in the spring of 1939 capped the number at 75,000 over a five-year period—and the rest of the British Empire was no more welcoming: "We have no real racial problem," the Australian delegate to the Evian conference had remarked, "[and] we are not desirous of importing one."[36]

Herschel Grynszpan was merely one of countless hundreds of thousands of Jewish men, women, and children who faced the existential threat of statelessness in 1938. When he was served with an expulsion order by the French authorities, he found himself in an excruciating but hardly unique dilemma: France would not allow him to stay, Germany would not allow him to come back, and his name was not even on the waiting list for entry into Palestine. So Herschel resorted to yet another desperate ploy to extend his stay in Paris; he moved out of Uncle Abraham's apartment and took refuge in a garret under the eaves of the roof on the sixth floor of the building, an attic room ordinarily used only as a maid's quarters but now conveniently vacant. His goal was to evade detection by the French police and to permit Uncle Abraham to say, truthfully if a bit evasively, that his nephew from Hanover had moved out.

Early in October 1938, Abraham and Chava Grynszpan vacated the building on rue Martel and took new quarters around the corner at 6 rue des Petites Écuries. Herschel remained behind in the maid's room, and—just as he had hoped—it turned out to be a secure hiding place. When the police showed up to search the apartment where the Grynszpans were believed to live, they found it empty, and when they tracked down Abraham Grynszpan at his new address, the young man was not to be found there. If any of the neighbors at 8 rue Martel knew or suspected that Herschel was still somewhere in the building, they said nothing, and the police gave up the search.

✦   ✦   ✦

A SUBTLE ADJUSTMENT IN the policy of Nazi Germany toward its Jewish population took place in 1938, although it went unnoticed amid the shocks and sensations that filled the world headlines in that tumultuous year. Until then, Nazi propaganda, policies, and practices had been designed to make life in the Third Reich so oppressive that Jews would take any opportunity to leave. At a meeting of high-ranking Nazi officials in the Ministry of the Interior on September 29—the same day that the newspapers announced the capitulation of the Western democracies at Munich—it was decided that the emigration of Jews out of Germany and Austria must be not only "complete" but also "compulsory."[37]

The problem, of course, was to find a place where the Jews could be compelled to go. Adolf Eichmann had already traveled to Palestine in 1937 in the hope of making contacts that would speed up the emigration of Jews, but his mission was frustrated by the refusal of British authorities to allow him to stay more than twenty-four hours; Eichmann was forced to content himself with a picturesque carriage ride around Haifa, where his ship had docked, and a view from the peak of Mount Carmel. More imaginative was Julius Streicher, editor of the anti-Semitic (and pornographic) propaganda sheet *Der Stürmer*, who actively promoted a scheme to ship European Jews in their millions to the French island colony of Madagascar. Hitler confided to Hermann Göring that he was considering "some other territory in North America, in Canada or anywhere else the rich Jews could buy for their brethren."[38]

The Nazi authorities, however, were not waiting for the Western democracies to welcome its Jews to the Yukon. Among the 700,000 or so Jews who resided in Germany and Austria, approximately 50,000 were *Ostjuden* who remained citizens of Poland, the Grynszpan family among them. From time to time, Nazis had openly threatened to expel these Jews from Germany since coming to power in 1933. An audacious plan was devised in 1938 to round up these Jews in a single sweep, possibly on a single night, and transport them by rail to the Polish border, where they could be marched en masse to the international boundary and driven at gunpoint into Poland.

Of course, the Polish government, which was already imposing restrictive measures of its own on the three million or so Jews who currently lived in Poland, was hardly ready to welcome more indigent Jews. To prevent Germany from dumping its unwanted *Ostjuden*, the Sejm—the Polish legislature—enacted a law in March 1938 that empowered the government to revoke the citizenship of any Pole who had "resided abroad continuously for more than 5 years without maintaining any contact with Poland" and to prevent such expatriates from returning to Poland or even entering the country for a visit.[39] Zindel and Rivka Grynszpan, who had lived in Germany since 1911, were among the Polish Jews who were targeted by the new law, and so was their son.

Although the Polish government delayed in putting the law into effect, the Polish Jews in Germany were aware that yet another threat from yet another source now hung over their heads. Rivka Grynszpan traveled to Radomsk on two occasions in 1938, perhaps to establish the kind of contact that might exempt her from the new law and, almost certainly, to visit her relatives in her hometown and to find out for herself whether her own family might safely and securely return to Poland on their own initiative. While Rivka was in Radomsk in April, Salomon Grynszpan and his wife showed up on a brief visit from Paris, which gave her an opportunity to hear some firsthand news about how her son Herschel was faring in his Paris exile.

Rivka returned to Radomsk in August, and she extended her sojourn when she fell ill with influenza and symptoms of stomach distress that were not unlike the ones that occasionally afflicted her son. Now that she was beyond the reach of the Nazi censors who meticulously reviewed all outgoing mail, Rivka sent a postcard to Herschel in care of his uncle Abraham on August 14. She disclosed a plan to smuggle out a monthly remittance in the amount of ten reichsmarks and charged him with the duty of putting aside a portion of the money for their livelihood if they, too, managed to escape from Germany "because," she wrote, "it is clear that we cannot remain." To avoid alerting the German postal censors, Rivka adopted a subterfuge that was common among Jewish refugees; she instructed her son to use a code phrase in his return mail—"The food is good"—to confirm that Herschel had received the money in Paris.[40]

Such plans may have comforted both mother and son, but they were every bit as fanciful as enlistment in the Foreign Legion. Indeed, Rivka acknowledged in her correspondence that she knew of other Jewish refugees who had been refused a French residence permit, and she expressed her anxieties over his efforts to secure an all-important *permis de séjour*. Perhaps aware that the letter he had written to Roosevelt had gone unanswered, she inquired hopefully whether Herschel had made any progress in finding a way to reach the United States.

What Rivka Grynszpan did not yet know was that her own legal status in the Third Reich was about to change in a profound and perilous way. By a German police order of August 22, 1938, all residence permits previously issued to foreigners living in the Third Reich would be canceled not later than March 31, 1939. Applications for new residence permits would be considered but only if submitted by December 31, 1938, and permits would be issued only to applicants "considered worthy of the hospitality accorded them because of their personality and reason for their stay."[41]

Rivka Grynszpan and other members of what remained of her family in Hanover were all too familiar with the kind of "hospitality" that was available to the Jewish subjects of the Third Reich. They could not have held out much hope that the Nazi authorities would act favorably on any request for a new residence permit. Unbeknownst to them or to millions of other endangered European Jews, Reichsführer-SS Heinrich Himmler and his staff were already preparing to escalate the war on the Jews in a new and dramatic way long before the announced deadline. One tiny fraction of the Jewish Problem was about to be solved with the kind of brutal efficiency that would quickly come to be the hallmark of the Final Solution.

4

SPECIAL
HANDLING

T WENTY-NINE-YEAR-OLD ERNST VOM RATH WAS FINALLY discharged in the summer of 1938 from the sanatorium where he had been treated for the baffling maladies that he brought back from Calcutta. He promptly packed his bags and boarded a train for Paris, where he was to take up his new duties as third secretary of the German embassy at 78 rue de Lille. Immediately upon his arrival in August, he contacted his former tutor, Mlle Taulin, and arranged to resume his French lessons. After all, Rath realized how much more successful he would be as an emissary of the Third Reich if he possessed a ready command of the French language. Given the various tasks and duties that demanded the attention of the young diplomat in the months ahead, however, the teacher and her pupil agreed not to resume the lessons until November.

In the meantime, Rath settled into the daily routine of his new posting and renewed the social contacts he had cultivated on two previous sojourns in Paris. He especially valued the occasional invitation to dine in a French household where he could try out his French in a social setting, although the noisome odor of the Nazi regime and, especially, the mounting tension between France and Germany over the summer and early fall surely made such invitations ever rarer. At the same time, he also befriended a fellow embassy staff member named Auer, who served as private secretary to the German ambassador, Count Johannes von Welczeck, and the two young men spent time together out of the office, "but rarely at night, primarily due to vom Rath's poor health."[1] Herr Auer would later insist that his friend's "private life was without incident," a comment that he made only when pointed questions were being asked about exactly where and how Rath spent his off-duty hours during those days and nights in Paris.[2]

Auer assisted his new friend in finding both an apartment and a housemaid, a certain Mlle Ebeling, who was, as far as we know, the only woman who had an opportunity to see Rath in the unguarded setting of his lodgings. Mlle Ebeling apparently shared Auer's impression that her employer's private life "was quite proper." Rath "received only a few personal friends," she later told the authorities, "and in general led a very retiring life." Indeed, Mlle Ebeling detected only the finest qualities in the man who now employed her: "As far as character was concerned," she attested, "it would be difficult to find anyone kinder or more gracious than he was."[3]

The same high praise was bestowed on Rath by a French cavalry officer, "one of vom Rath's intimate friends," who met him during his earlier stay in Paris. The officer, who appears in the official records only by his surname Malavoy, was introduced to Rath by Freiherr von Watsdorf, another member of the German gentry who wanted to practice his language skills with a native speaker of the French tongue.[4] "His gentleness of character, his charm, and his air of distinction were such that I invited him on several occasions to my home, along with other students, mostly French," testified Malavoy. "Mr. vom Rath expressed himself in very good if not perfect French, and did not hide his pleasure in being received not only in a French milieu but especially in a French family."[5]

All of these affirmations were recorded by the French and German authorities in the course of the official investigation into the life of Ernst vom Rath that was occasioned by events that took place at 78 rue de Lille in November 1938, which may explain why a German diplomat, a French tutor, a cavalry officer, and a cleaning lady all seemed to express themselves with such polished and fulsome words and phrases. The same tone is found in the pronouncements of his fellow diplomats, all of whom depicted Rath as a saintly figure on the strength of less than three months of service at the embassy. "According to members of the staff of the Embassy, when callers appeared with complaints, it was customary to send them to vom Rath," writes Cuénot, "a young secretary who had a reputation for being humane in his approach and who greeted all visitors in a kindly and amiable way."[6]

✦   ✦   ✦

WHILE RATH INSINUATED HIMSELF into the lives of upwardly mobile Parisians and German expatriates, Grynszpan sought to remain invisible. Life in hiding in an attic room in the busy Tenth Arrondissement of Paris was not a terrible hardship for the wayward refugee. By now familiar with his environs, he was able to easily slip in and out of the apartment building by day or by night, and if the neighbors encountered the slender young man in the stairwells, the interior courtyards, or at the front door on rue Martel, they certainly did not think to alert the gendarmerie. After all, the district bustled with anxious Jewish immigrants, many of whom were facing the same difficulties in securing a lifesaving *permis de séjour* from the French authorities, and Herschel must have felt confident that he would not be betrayed by his fellow *Ostjuden*.

Still, Herschel tended to stay inside during daylight hours to avoid an awkward encounter with the police. Later, he claimed that he engaged in pious study of the Bible and the Talmud, but, given his well-founded concern about his own fate and the dire circumstances of his family in Hanover, he doubtless spent far more time poring over the news columns of the *Pariser Haint*. At the end of the day, he left the attic room to take dinner with Uncle Abraham and Aunt Chava at their new apartment around the corner on rue des Petites Écuries, where he would often encounter Chava's sister and brother-in-law, Basila and Jacques Wykhodz, who lived not far away at 9 rue Ernestine. He still spent his evenings with Nathan Kaufmann and Sam Schenkier, and managed to show up now and then at the Tout Va Bien, whether at an inside table, if he had a few francs in his pocket, or on the sidewalk along boulevard Saint-Denis, if he was broke.

Like any Jew in western Europe, footloose or otherwise, Herschel was tormented by the reports of each new act of aggression and every new anti-Semitic atrocity that emerged from Germany, all of which were the subject of much table talk at the Grynszpan apartment as well as the Tout Va Bien and the Aurore. The Nazi authorities had already announced their intention to cancel the residence permits of all Polish Jews who still lived in the Third Reich, including Herschel's family in Hanover, and the Polish government now checked the German move by enforcing the earlier decree that put the citizenship of Poles living abroad at risk of cancellation.

According to an order published in the official gazette of the Polish government on October 15, 1938, all such expatriates were allowed only fifteen days to present their passports to the nearest Polish consulates for validation; if the consulate declined to stamp a passport, its bearer would be considered stateless. As a result, any Polish Jew living in the Third Reich who showed up at the German–Polish frontier faced the prospect of being turned back by the border guards. After October 29, these Jews would be trapped in a diplomatic face-off between two stern and unyielding governments, neither of which had any sympathy for their plight.

Unbeknownst to the anxious residents of the Pletzel, but surely the subject of gossip inside the German embassy on the rue de Lille, the Foreign Ministry in Berlin put out a diplomatic feeler to its Polish counterpart: would Poland agree to suspend its decree and accept Jews who were expelled from the Third Reich after the deadline? The Polish diplomats rebuffed the German initiative on two separate occasions, and the Reich Foreign Ministry turned the whole matter over to another branch of the government—the various police agencies under the command of Reichsführer-SS Himmler. By October 26, 1938, three days before the Polish deadline, arrest lists had been expeditiously drawn up in Berlin, and the mass expulsion of 50,000 Polish Jews was set in motion. The first action targeted some 12,000 Jews in cities across Germany, including Hanover.*

Among the names on the arrest list for Hanover were those of Zindel and Rivka Grynszpan and their two adult children, Mordecai and Esther. Such was the bureaucratic efficiency of Himmler's "repression and terror system" that an officer of the Security Police (*Sicherheitspolizei*), colloquially known as a Sipo, showed up at the Grynszpan apartment at 9:00 p.m. on Thursday, October 27, 1938, and ordered the family to accompany him to the police station for the Eleventh Precinct.[7] "He assured us that we would be returning directly and that it was unnecessary to take our belongings with us," testified Zindel Grynszpan, who miraculously survived the Second World War, at the trial of Adolf Eichmann in Jerusalem in 1961. "When I arrived at the precinct with my family, we found many people there, seated and standing, and some of them in tears. A police inspector was shouting at them, 'Sign this paper. You are expelled.'"[8]

Thus began the first direct action of the authorities of the Third Reich to solve the Jewish Problem by arresting and expelling its

---

* The expulsion of Polish Jews from the Third Reich reached a total of 18,000 over the next few days, but 12,000 was the number that appeared in the early press coverage.

Jewish population rather than merely making their lives so unbearable that they would leave on their own initiative. Initially, the destination was a bleak no-man's-land on the German–Polish frontier, near the little Polish town of Zbąszyń, where the Jews would be herded like sentient cattle into Poland at gunpoint and under the blows of whips and rifle butts. Later, the destinations would be deeper inside Poland at places whose names are more familiar to us: Auschwitz, Birkenau, Sobibor, and Treblinka, among many others. Here and now, however, the Nazis experimented for the very first time with some of the techniques that would later be associated with an official euphemism—*Sonderbehandlung*, or "special handling."[9]

✦   ✦   ✦

A SEA CHANGE IN official Nazi policy toward the Jews manifested itself on the night of October 27, 1938. Until then, the Third Reich contented itself with the steady degradation of Jewish life with the goal of encouraging the Jews to leave on their own accord. Their destination was a matter of indifference; some Jews might prefer America, France, or England, and the more idealistic among them might aspire to go to Palestine, but some Nazis seriously entertained the notion that the Jews would end up in various less appealing settings around the world—Abyssinia, Angola, Haiti, and the Guianas in South America were all considered. This idea ran so deep in popular German culture that it found expression in a board game called *Juden Raus!* (Jews Out!), in which the goal of the players was to be the first to round up six Jews and hasten them *"Auf nach Palästina!"* (Off to Palestine!)[10]

Now, however, the Third Reich concluded that the Jewish Problem could be solved only through direct and decisive action. After all, the Evian conference had demonstrated just how hollow the expressions of sympathy for Jewish refugees actually were, and not a single country was willing to accept them in anything but token numbers. The Madagascar plan appealed to the utopian imaginations of some Nazi ideologues, but Hitler and his inner circle realized that it was ultimately untenable; the African island was, after all, a French colony, far from Europe and currently beyond the reach of Germany. While a few dutiful German bureaucrats still worked on the transfer of Jews and their money from the Third Reich to Palestine through the Ha'avara program, the strategic thinkers in Berlin pointed out that a Jewish homeland in Palestine (or, by the same reasoning, anywhere else in the world) would merely create a new and more dangerous Jewish Problem.

"The formation of a Jewish State or of a Jewish political entity under British Mandate is not in Germany's interest, given the fact that such a state in Palestine would not absorb all the Jews of the world but would give them a new power position, under the cover of international law, something comparable to what the Vatican represents for political Catholicism," declared the German foreign minister, Konstantin von Neurath, in a 1937 cable to diplomatic missions in London, Jerusalem, and Baghdad. "That is why it is in the interest of Germany to contribute to the strengthening of the Arab world in order to offset, if need be, the increased power of world Jewry."[11]

Deep inside the Reich Chancellery in Berlin, where the *Anschluss* and the dismemberment of Czechoslovakia had been first conceived and finally executed in 1938, even more-audacious and far-reaching plans were being made. What remained of Czechoslovakia after the Munich agreement would be divided up in March 1939, and the Wehrmacht had already been working on urgent plans for the conquest of Poland and longer-range studies for the invasion of the Soviet Union to provide lebensraum for the Third Reich. Hitler and his coterie understood with precise clarity that the so-called Jewish Problem would only be aggravated if Poland and Russia, each one with a Jewish population numbering in the millions, were to be absorbed into the ever-growing Nazi empire. "Special Handling," a term that would soon come to mean mass murder, was the only practical solution to the Jewish Problem if the Third Reich was to carry out its goal of world conquest.

Indeed, the inevitability—and, as Hitler saw it, the desirability—of another world war had figured in his ambitions from the outset. As early as 1935, a functionary in the Racial Policy Office of the Nazi Party recorded the instructions he had received directly from the Führer: "Vigorous emigration" would suffice for the solution of the Jewish Problem in the interim, but "in case of a war on all fronts, he would be ready for all the consequences."[12] Lest there be any misunderstanding about what he meant by "all the consequences," Hitler offered an unambiguous public explanation on January 30, 1939, when he addressed the Reichstag on the sixth anniversary of his assumption of absolute authority in Germany.

"And one more thing I would like now to state on this day memorable, perhaps not only for us Germans," he announced in a speech that was broadcast around the world.

I have often been a prophet in my life and was generally laughed at. During my struggle for power, the Jews primarily received with laughter my prophecies that I would someday assume the leadership of the state and thereby of the entire Volk and then, among many other things, achieve a solution of the Jewish problem. I suppose that meanwhile the then resounding laughter of Jewry in Germany is now choking in their throats. Today I will be a prophet again: If international finance Jewry within Europe and abroad should succeed once more in plunging the peoples into a world war, then the consequence will be not the Bolshevization of the world and therewith a victory of Jewry, but on the contrary, the destruction of the Jewish race in Europe.[13]

Hitler's open and unambiguous death threat against the Jewish people had not yet been uttered on the night when the Grynszpans were arrested in Hanover. Herschel Grynszpan, however, an attentive newspaper reader and a participant in anxious and deeply saturnine conversations around the tables at the Aurore and the Tout Va Bien, did not need to wait for any such public proclamation. He had already concluded that the Nazi intentions were both brutal and overtly murderous. In that sense, the seventeen-year-old boy, hiding in the garret room in Paris, was prescient in a way that so many other Jews were not. What he foresaw for his parents, himself, and his landsmen would turn out to be wholly accurate.

✦   ✦   ✦

TWO VERSIONS OF WHAT happened to the Grynszpan family in Hanover, and some 12,000 other Polish Jews across Germany, on the night of October 27, 1938, are preserved in the historical record. According to the Grynszpans, between 500 and 600 Jewish men, women, and children were held at the local police station for twenty-four hours. One man who refused to sign the expulsion order—"by the name of Gershon Silbery or Gerschl Silber," as Zindel Grynszpan recalled on the witness stand in Jerusalem during the Eichmann trial—was punished for his defiance by being made to stand in a corner of the station throughout the twenty-four-hour period. They were then herded en masse to a nearby concert hall that stood on the bank of the Leine River and loaded into police vans—"20 to a van"— for transport to the railroad station on Friday, October 28. "The street was full of people chanting, 'The Jews to Palestine,'" recalled Zindel.[14] In a scene that prefigured the *Endlösung* in full operation some two years later, they were loaded onto a sealed train and dispatched to the German–Polish frontier.

Esther Grynszpan, Herschel's sister, recorded the experience in a postcard that she was later able to send to her little brother in Paris.

"You undoubtedly heard of our great misfortune," she began, thus acknowledging that Herschel might have already read of relocation in the Yiddish papers. "I will describe to you what happened."

On Thursday evening rumors circulated that all Polish Jews had been expelled from a city. But we didn't believe it. On Thursday evening at 9 o'clock a Sipo came to us and informed us that we had to go to Police Headquarters. Almost our entire quarter was already there. A police van brought all of us right away to the Rusthaus. All were brought there. We were not told what it was all about, but we saw that everything was finished for us. Each of us had an extradition order pressed into his hand, and one had to leave Germany before the 29th. They didn't permit us to return home anymore. I asked to be allowed to go home to get at least a few things. I went, accompanied by a Sipo, and packed the necessary clothes in a suitcase. And that is all I saved. We don't have a Pfennig. More next time.[15]

Esther signed the postcard, "Best regards and kisses from all of us. Berta." Even at this point, forcibly expelled from the country in which she had been born, she clung to the German name that she had adopted and used in place of her Jewish name, and she continued to address her little brother as Hermann. Of course, she knew that the use of German names by Jews was now a criminal act in the Third Reich, and she realized, as she scribbled her message to Herschel, that "everything was finished for us."[16]

At 6:00 a.m. on Saturday, October 29, the train from Hanover reached the newly completed station at Neu-Bentschen, a riverside town on the Polish border whose population consisted largely of railroad workers. Other trains from all over Germany—Berlin, Leipzig, Cologne, Düsseldorf, Bielefeld, Essen, and Bremen—discharged a total of 12,000 *Ostjuden*, now officially stateless according to both

German and Polish law, at various points along the frontier. Each man, woman, and child was searched by the German guards, and if currency was found, all amounts over ten reichsmarks were seized. "When you arrived, you only had 10 RM," the guards taunted the Jews; "there's no reason for you to leave with more than that."[17]

The station at Neu-Bentschen was two kilometers from the official frontier, and a heavy rain was falling, but the German guards hastened their prisoners through the boggy woodlands on foot. More than twenty-four hours had passed since their arrest; by now, they were understandably hungry, weak, cold, and confused. Whatever luggage they had managed to bring out of Germany, they now carried through the forest. "The SS came with whips and struck us," testified Zindel Grynszpan. "Those who couldn't walk were beaten. There was blood on the road. Packages were snatched from their arms. The SS treated us in a cruel and barbarous manner. It was the first time in my life that I had suffered German brutality. We were made to run and they shouted at us, 'Run, run!' I was struck and fell on the side of the road. My son helped me get up and pulling me by the hand he said, 'Come, Papa, let's run, otherwise they will kill you.'"[18]

As these strange apparitions suddenly manifested themselves in the rain and fog on the horizon—thousands of Jews of various ages under the whips of their SS guards—the Polish frontier guard responded with alarm and bafflement. "The Poles had no idea why we were there," Zindel explained, "or why there were so many of us."[19] The Polish guards brandished rifles with fixed bayonets, and a few of them fired warning shots. "Some people sank to the ground, some fainted, others had heart attacks," according to Zindel. "Then a Polish general and some officers, astonished to see such a tremendous crowd, looked at our passports and found that we were Polish citizens. They decided then to let us enter."[20]

To accommodate the 12,000 Jewish refugees while the diplomatic confrontation between Germany and Poland was sorted out, the

Polish army transported them to a military base in the nearby town of Zbąszyń; the sheer number of arrivals compelled the Poles to lodge some of them in the stables as well as in the barracks.* Indeed, the number of refugees outnumbered the population of Zbąszyń by more than two to one. On Sunday, the Poles finally managed to bring in a few truckloads of bread, and the Jews were offered food for the first time since they were taken into custody in Hanover.

Quite another version of these events originated with the agencies of the Third Reich, all of which were deployed a few months after the fact to prettify the story for the world press. According to an official report by the German railroad in Hanover, the Grynszpans were among 484 Jews who were comfortably accommodated in two large rooms at the Rusthaus (Rustic House), as the restaurant and hostel at the railway station was quaintly named. Another, more ambitious report, crafted by an agent of the Ministry of Propaganda, maintained that the Jews were allowed to purchase food and other supplies for the journey to Poland.

The Nazi propagandist provides an astonishing inventory of the quantities of comestibles that were supposedly on offer that night, including "1400 to 1600 rolls, 20 to 30 loaves of white bread, 10 cakes of one-half or one pound, 30 to 35 loaves of white bread, 100 other pieces of pastry, 600 slices of lard, 500 slices of sausage, 550 to 600 quarts of pea soup with bacon, 300 to 400 quarts of coffee, 434 bars of chocolate, 700 packages of fruit cake, 150 bottles of mineral water, 15 pounds of fruit," plus a thousand cigarettes and assorted alcoholic

---

* Neu-Bentschen was founded after World War I, when border adjustments in favor of newly independent Poland deprived Germany of the rail facilities at Zbąszyń (known in German as Bentschen). During World War II, Neu-Bentschen was the site of a camp where prisoners of war and Jewish slave laborers were confined. When Poland's border was moved westward after the defeat of Nazi Germany, the town of Neu-Bentschen, now renamed Zbąszynek, once again came under Polish sovereignty.

beverages, and 500 kosher dinners that were thoughtfully provided for those who declined to eat non-kosher food, or so the Nazis insisted.

"When the Jews vacated the premises," wrote the author of the self-serving official report, "they left such a large quantity of food that it would have been possible to feed the same number of people over again."[21]

The train ride to the Polish border, as the Nazis portrayed it, was unremarkable and unobjectionable, almost as if 12,000 Jews had suddenly decided to embark en masse on a pleasure excursion to points east. "The police and the members of the SS made an effort to treat properly the Jews whom they were obliged to expel," the report insisted. Supposedly acting as porters, the SS "even helped as much as possible to carry their baggage which was considerable." The train, officially designated as *Train Sp IIan 4199*, was routed on the Berlin–Warsaw rail line and consisted of fourteen ordinary passenger cars, "averaging 55 seats each, with approximately 35–40 passengers per car." At the border, the Jews were transferred from the train to the crossing point "partly on foot and partly by bus," and the route consisted of "three regular roads." The only "disagreeable" conduct, as the Germans saw it, was on the part of the Poles, who detained the Jewish refugees at the border in bad weather. "Whenever the Polish frontier officials made things difficult, they were finally persuaded to be reasonable and do what was necessary," that is, they yielded to the will of the Third Reich and permitted the Jewish refugees to cross the border at last.[22]

So extensive was this skein of lies that the Nazi version did not even concede that the Jews had been forcibly expelled from Germany; rather, they were "made available to Poland," according to the official report of the Ministry of Propaganda. "The matter was handled in the most proper and humane fashion." Indeed, the Nazis characterized the Grynszpans as the ungrateful beneficiaries of German largesse: "The Grynszpan family arrived in their country, where they were reunited with their relatives and friends," the report stated. And the author of the report included an ironic crack that acknowledged the plight of all Jewish refugees from the Third Reich: "They could leave for America as easily from Gdynia"—a Polish port city on the Baltic Sea—"as they could from any city in Germany."[23]

✦   ✦   ✦

NONE OF THESE PARTICULARS were known to Herschel Grynszpan in the last few days of October. Yet dramatic newspaper and radio reports soon began to come from the German–Polish frontier—12,000 Jews trapped in no-man's-land in the rain and cold, deprived of food and shelter, unable to enter Poland or return to Germany—and they were sufficient to stoke his anxieties for his own little family and his anger toward their Nazi tormentors.

Watchful for the latest evidence of German aggression, the world press continued to run stories about the expulsion on the front pages. REFUGEES DESPOILED IN GERMANY was the headline in the *Times* of London, which emphasized the brutality of the Nazi troops and the sufferings of the Jewish victims. "They declare that they were driven by soldiers with a machine gun, which now and then fired a few rounds into the air to make the crowd hurry," reported the *Times*. "Disease has broken out among them, especially among the children."[24]

Esther Grynszpan's postcard was dated and mailed on Monday, October 31, 1938—the day after the family reached Zbąszyń. The card arrived at Uncle Albert's apartment in Paris the following Thursday, November 3. The mere sight of his sister's words, written in her own hand and signed with the name by which he had always known her—"Kisses from all of us, Berta"—were enough to trigger a new upwelling of the anxieties that always churned inside him. Herschel had fretted openly about the fate of his family with Nathan and Sam, Uncle Abraham and Aunt Chava, ever since his arrival in

Paris, but now Esther's card confirmed that his worst fears were all too real. Herschel was agitated, inconsolable, and ready to explode.

On the next day, Herschel opened the *Pariser Haint* to find an urgent dispatch from Zbąszyń that reinforced some of the details in the postcard and added some new ones. "Their living conditions are uncomfortable and distressing," wrote the correspondent from the town where the refugees were being held. "Twelve hundred of them have fallen ill and several hundred are without shelter." The Red Cross doctors who had rushed to the site of the emergency at the invitation of the Polish government administered typhus vaccinations and handed out ten thousand aspirin tablets, according to the *Pariser Haint*, but some of the victims were beyond medical assistance: "A number of cases of insanity and suicide have been reported."[25]

The Grynszpans were always prone to engage in bickering and recrimination, and now it was Herschel who lashed out at the relations who were closest at hand and, paradoxically, who were his sole source of support as an illegal alien in Paris. The flash point was a sum of money that would soon figure crucially in the various mysteries that attached themselves to Herschel Grynszpan—some 3,000 francs that supposedly had been smuggled out of Germany by Herschel's father to provide for his son in exile. The money, Herschel now insisted, should be sent immediately to his parents in Zbąszyń because they needed it more than he did. Abraham apparently disagreed with the impulsive young man and insisted on holding on to the money while waiting to see how the family fared in Poland.

Herschel promptly wrote back to Esther and the rest of the family in Zbąszyń, and his sister and his father scribbled out a hasty message in reply. The second postcard would have only served to sharpen the dispute between uncle and nephew if Herschel had seen it. "We are in a very sad situation," Zindel wrote to his brother. "We are poor and in misery. We don't get enough to eat. You, too, once were in need. I beg you, dear Brother, to think of us. We don't have the strength to endure this. You mustn't forget us in this situation."[26] On the same card, Esther added to her earlier description of their woes: "Believe me, Hermann, we won't be able to stand this much longer," she wrote. "We haven't yet received money from you. What do they say there about what will happen to us? We can't go any further."[27]

As it turned out, the second postcard from Zindel and Esther arrived in Paris too late for Herschel Grynszpan to see it. On Sunday, November 6, while the postcard was still en route, the mounting resentment that Herschel harbored toward his uncle reached a breaking point. Herschel slipped out of his attic room and walked around the corner to Abraham and Chava's apartment, where he planned to visit with his uncle as well as Chava's sister-in-law, Mina Berenbaum, and her sister and brother-in-law, Basila and Jacques Wykhodz. Herschel's best friend, Nathan Kaufmann, also showed up at Abraham's apartment, and the two boys planned to go out together and join their friends at the Aurore.

Something was said in the Grynszpan apartment on that Sunday afternoon that provoked an angry confrontation between Herschel and Abraham. Like so many other crucial details in the Grynszpan affair, the exact nature of the argument was never fully disclosed by the members of the family, although the Nazis later came up with their own, self-serving version of the story. The conventional account of the family argument, however, is a reprise of the earlier dispute about sending money to Herschel's father in Zbąszyń. Nathan, for example, later recalled an exchange that he overheard between Herschel and his uncle after his arrival at the apartment on that Sunday evening.

"You don't appreciate the misfortune that has befallen them," cried Herschel, close to tears.

"I've already done just about everything I could for you," replied his exasperated uncle, "and if you're not satisfied, you are free to go."

Herschel rose abruptly from the table and struggled into his overcoat. A sobbing Aunt Chava now joined in the fray; she clutched his coat to keep him from stalking out of the apartment. Nathan said what he could to soothe his distraught young friend, and Herschel relented for a moment. Then his adolescent temper flared up again, and Herschel renewed his angry exchange with Abraham. How could they sit in comfort in Paris while his mother and father, sister and brother, suffered the outrage that Esther described in the postcard that he found so heartrending?

"I am leaving," Herschel finally announced. "Goodbye!"[28]

Abraham, no less distraught, fumbled with a fistful of currency and thrust it on Herschel as he pushed toward the front door—not the 3,000 francs that would figure so importantly in the historical postmortems, but only two 100-franc notes. Chava again broke down in tears and sobbed helplessly as Herschel, red-faced and perhaps tearful himself, turned and headed for the front door. Abraham, now in a towering rage of his own, glowered at the boy but made no effort to stop him. Then, abruptly, the door slammed and Herschel was gone.

✦   ✦   ✦

THE GRYNSZPANS AND THEIR in-laws turned to Nathan Kaufmann and implored him to go after Herschel and bring him back. By then, two years after meeting and befriending Herschel in Paris, Nathan may have acquired a certain expertise in coping with the temperamental spikes that he observed in his best friend. Certainly he was the calmest one in the confines of Maison Albert on that Sunday afternoon, and if anyone was able to catch up with Herschel, calm him down, and persuade him to return, it was his friend rather than his relations. This Nathan vowed to do.

Nathan quickly found Herschel on the street not far from Abraham's apartment, but he did not bother to press the demands of Uncle Abraham and Aunt Chava on Herschel in his current state of

agitation. Rather, the two young men strolled through the boulevards and side streets of Faubourg Saint-Denis, still bustling with
Sunday pleasure-seekers, in the direction of the Aurore, where they
had already planned to meet their friends and attend a dance. They
threaded their way through the crowd on the sidewalk outside the
Cirque d'Hiver, a Paris landmark and another lively entertainment
venue, and made their way around the corner to the sports club,
where their friends waited.

Herschel was calmer now, but he remained sullen and aloof for
the rest of the evening. They quickly found the rest of their friends in
the hectic and noisy hall, but Herschel did not join in the chatter
among his cronies, and he hung back from the games and amuse-
ments in progress around the club. Perhaps his friends were accustomed to Herschel's moods, or maybe Nathan explained to them in
a whispered aside what had just happened at the Grynszpan apartment, but nothing in the historical record suggests that Herschel
revealed to any of them what he was planning to do now that he had
broken with his uncle.

At 7:00 p.m., Herschel and Nathan walked back to the corner of
rue du Château d'Eau and rue du Faubourg Saint-Denis and idled
there for a few moments under the lights of the ornate building that
housed *la mairie*, the municipal offices of the Tenth Arrondissement.
The city hall was dark and empty on a Sunday evening, and so were
the shops and offices that lined the streets around them. Now and
then, a pedestrian wandered past them, heading for the cafés and
cinemas on the nearby boulevard de Strasbourg, but the two were
able to talk in confidence about the family fight that Nathan had
witnessed a few hours earlier.

Only now did Nathan honor the promise he had made to the
Grynszpans, and he gently encouraged his friend to return to Abraham and Chava's apartment, if only to reassure them that he was all
right. Herschel was still agitated, however, and his anger flared up

once again. His uncle's stubborn and stingy refusal to come to the rescue of the family in Zbąszyń was a point of honor for the excitable boy, and nothing would persuade him to defer to Abraham.

"I will not go back," he vowed to his friend. "I'd rather die like a dog from hunger than go back on my decision."[29]

Herschel was carrying a wad of cash, including the money that Uncle Abraham had thrust upon him, and he told Nathan that he intended to treat himself to dinner at the Tout Va Bien—perhaps they would meet there later in the evening, he allowed—and then Herschel would find a cheap hotel in the neighborhood where he could spend the night. If he had plans for the next day, Herschel did not reveal them to his friend. So Nathan could do no more than to shrug, clap Herschel on the back, and head back to his own family apartment. Herschel remained on the corner in front of *la mairie* and pondered what lay ahead in the coming hours and days. Yet he could not linger there very long; if a passing gendarme asked to see his identity papers, Herschel would be spending the night in jail.

Glancing in one direction, he could see the lights of the Gare de l'Est, the vast neoclassical depot—"with its immense arched window and aristocratic arcade," as Victor Brombert recalls—from which trains departed for various points in Germany, including his own hometown of Hanover, but his family, as Herschel now knew, was no longer there.[30] Turning in the opposite direction, Herschel's eye fell on the window of a shop on the far side of the street—À la Fine Lame (At the Sharp Blade)—a place where someone in need of weaponry might buy a gun or a knife. He crossed the intersection, walked half a block down the rue du Faubourg Saint-Denis, and stopped in front of the shop, now closed and dark. A nearby streetlamp cast enough light to enable Herschel to inspect a selection of revolvers on display in the front window.

"And so it was that this emotional young man, torn from the family he loved, persecuted for his heritage of which he was proud," explains Gerald Schwab, "apparently decided to become an avenger for his people."[31]

✦   ✦   ✦

ONLY A FEW BLOCKS away from Á la Fine Lame, the Grynszpans were still fretting about the whereabouts of young Herschel in the apartment on rue des Petites Écuries. During the angry and hurtful exchanges that had taken place earlier in the day, Herschel had threatened to take his own life if Uncle Abraham did not act to save the lives of his parents. Abraham and Chava were familiar with such outbursts by their nephew, who was given to moments of high drama, but now—as the sky darkened and the night air grew chill—they could have easily imagined his lifeless body floating in the Seine.

By 8:30 p.m., they could no longer contain their own anxiety. Abraham Grynszpan and Jacques Wykhodz, his brother-in-law, vowed to search the neighborhood for the missing boy, and the rest of them would stay behind in case Herschel showed up. They headed first to the nearby apartment building where Nathan Kaufmann lived, and then planned to check all the places where Herschel was known to spend his time, including the café Tout Va Bien and the Aurore. Under no circumstances, of course, could they alert the police, since they were all too painfully aware that Herschel, as an illegal alien, was subject to arrest and expulsion for lack of a *permis de séjour*.

When Abraham and Jacques knocked on the door of the Kaufmann family's apartment, Nathan rose from the dinner table and quickly revealed what Herschel had told him about dining at the café and taking a hotel room for the night. They rushed off in the direction of the Tout Va Bien, but Nathan was detained by his own family, who demanded that he finish eating supper with them. So it was not until after 9:00 p.m. that Nathan, too, showed up at the café. Herschel, however, was nowhere to be found.

PART II

INCIDENT ON THE RUE DE LILLE

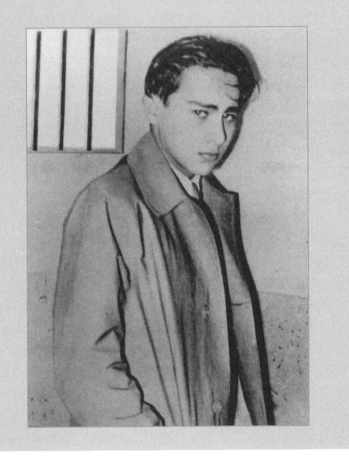

5

"SO THAT THE WORLD WOULD NOT IGNORE IT"

Even as Nathan Kaufmann was cruising through the Faubourg Saint-Denis in search of his missing friend, glancing into the faces of the young men on the sidewalk in front of the Tout Va Bien, Herschel Grynszpan was checking into the hotel where he planned to spend the night—the Hôtel de Suez, a grandly named but exceedingly modest stopping place for tourists and business travelers, located over a movie theater at 17 boulevard de Strasbourg, only a few blocks from his uncle's apartment and not far from the Gare de l'Est.[1]

Herschel mounted the stairs to the front desk, one floor up from the street, and encountered the young woman who was serving as the night clerk—Mlle Laurent, the daughter of the hotel owner and a careful custodian of her father's business. She noticed immediately that the young man carried no luggage, demanded to be paid in advance for a one-night stay, and watched as Herschel counted out 22.50 francs from the stash of French currency in his wallet. The clerk readily marked him as a *métèque*, a term applied to those whose imperfect command of French identified them as foreigners—

"Jewish refugees from Hitler," explains Alice Kaplan, tended to mis-
pronounce French words by "substituting z's' for s's"—and so she
asked to see his identification papers. She did not turn him away
when he shrugged and said he had none, but she began to interrogate
the oddly handsome youth, whether out of caution or curiosity or
maybe just to pass the time on a quiet Sunday night.[2]

Readily identifying his country of origin, Mlle Laurent shifted
seamlessly into German—a tool of the trade for any hotelier whose
premises were located so close to the Gare de l'Est and the Gare du
Nord, the two major railroad terminals in the Tenth Arrondissement. Now the young man was considerably more fluent, if still nervous and guarded, and she managed to elicit a few biographical
details: he had been born in Hanover, he was eighteen years old, he
was a salesman by occupation, and his name was Heinrich Halter—
one fact and three lies. At last, the guest posed a question that
betrayed his awkwardness and naïveté.

"Would it be all right," he meekly asked the woman behind the
counter, "if I went out?"[3]

The porter, who watched from a few feet away in the cramped
hotel lobby, overheard the exchange and figured that the guest was
heading back to the Gare de l'Est to pick up his luggage. The porter
was familiar with the train schedules, and he knew that the young
man's appearance at the front desk coincided with arrival of a nightly
train from Germany. But when the youth finally returned to the
Hôtel de Suez later—shortly before midnight—he still had no luggage. But, then, the lack of luggage was hardly unusual at a small
hotel like the Suez, especially when the room was to be used merely
for an assignation. So the porter conducted the young man to his
room and returned to the lobby to resume his long nightly vigil.

Where had Herschel Grynszpan spent the three hours between
check-in and bedtime at the Hôtel de Suez? Perhaps the porter gave it
no further thought; Paris, after all, offered an infinite variety of

diversions after night fell. In any event, the little hotel was equipped with a newfangled control board that allowed him to monitor the use of room lights throughout the hotel, and he noticed that the guest did not leave his room again or dim the lights for the rest of the night. So passed the first and last night that Herschel Grynszpan spent alone, on his own and on the run.

✦ ✦ ✦

HERSCHEL SLEPT BADLY THAT night. Perhaps it was because he was occupying an unfamiliar bed in a musty little hotel room or because he was still agitated by his fight with Uncle Abraham. Maybe it had something to do with what happened during the last few hours when he was at large in the streets of Paris. Or perhaps Herschel stayed awake because his mind was occupied with what he planned to do the next day. To hear Herschel tell it, and quite believably, he spent "a very restless night" in the Hôtel de Suez because he was tortured by nightmares that were inspired by what had happened to his family in Nazi Germany and what they were enduring at that very moment in a refugee camp on the German–Polish frontier.

"In my dreams, I saw my parents mistreated and beaten and the dreams made me suffer," he would later testify. "In my dreams I also saw Hitlerites who grabbed me by the throat to strangle me. I also saw boycott demonstrations such as those I had experienced in Hanover where, for example, I saw Germans mistreated and spit at when they went into a store owned by a Jew.* Demonstrators screamed at them, 'You are damned! You are selling the German people to the Jews!' I was obsessed by that question. Again and again I asked myself, 'What have we done to deserve such a fate?' And I couldn't find any answer to the question."[4]

---

* Germans who insisted on patronizing Jewish-owned businesses in defiance of the Nazi boycott were at risk of verbal abuse and worse by their fellow Germans.

The newsreel quality of Herschel's dreams—and the explicit reference to the core moral and historical issue of the Jewish Problem—seems far too calculating to be taken at face value. Yet Herschel also frankly recalled that he was already considering the deed that he was planning for the next day—a plan that may have been suggested to him by the weaponry he had seen on display in the shop window of À la Fine Lame the night before. "I saw myself going into the gun shop," he recalled. "I also had visions of my family's plight. I woke up three times during the night. Each time my heart was beating fast. To make it calm down, I put my hand on my chest."[5]

Herschel, according to his later account, finally drifted off to sleep, and he did not rise again until 7:30 a.m. on Monday, November 7, 1938, an unremarkable day except for the unusually mild weather for Paris in autumn. His stay at the Suez may have been his first night alone in a hotel of any kind, and he took advantage of the unaccustomed services that were now available to him by ringing the front desk at 7:45 a.m. and ordering a *café complet* to be delivered to his room. Herschel's stomach, however, tended to betray him in times of anxiety and stress, and so he contented himself with a few sips of black coffee and a bite of bread. Then he began to prepare himself for the mission that he had resolved to carry out in the hours ahead.

First he took out a pen and a blank postcard imprinted with a photograph of himself in a tie and a three-piece suit, jauntily holding a cigarette in his left hand, his right hand behind his back, and his left foot pointed in an almost dancerlike pose, all against a painted canvas scrim that depicts a village scene—a novelty he had probably purchased from an itinerant photographer at a street fair. The camera seemed always kind to Herschel, and he appeared to take pleasure in striking a pose even if he remained stern and unsmiling. Then he began to scribble out an anguished message to his family on the back of the postcard.

"With God's help," he began, writing the words in Hebrew, and then he continued in German, composing the message too hastily to notice his spelling and grammatical errors or deciding that he had more urgent things to do than to correct them. "My dear parents, I couldn't do otherwise," wrote Herschel. "God must forgive me. My heart bleeds when I think of our tragedy and that of the 12,000 Jews. I have to protest in a way that the whole world hears my protest, and this I intend to do. I beg your forgiveness." And he signed the postcard with the German name by which he was known to his friends and family: "Hermann."[6]

Herschel addressed the postcard to Maison Albert, put the postcard back in his wallet, and dressed himself in the three-piece pinstriped suit and the light overcoat he had worn the day before. Then he assembled his belongings and headed for the lobby, where he settled his account for the night by paying a room service charge of 2.75 francs. He took the short staircase to the street level, stepped out of the hotel, paused momentarily on the boulevard de Strasbourg, a principal north–south axis that was already bustling with both pedestrian and vehicular traffic on the first day of the workweek. Thanks to the Indian summer that had hung over Paris for the last week or so, he realized that his overcoat would be unnecessary and even uncomfortable, but he also knew that it would be convenient to conceal the items he was about to acquire at the gun shop around the corner.

Herschel turned left, walking past the corner where the Tout Va Bien was already open for breakfast but not bothering to check for any familiar faces. He was so intent on what lay ahead that he even neglected to drop the postcard into a mailbox; it would be found in his wallet at the end of the day.

✦   ✦   ✦

By 8:35 a.m., barely an hour after waking, Herschel was already approaching 61 rue du Faubourg Saint-Martin, where he encountered a middle-aged woman who was cranking open the iron shutters of À la Fine Lame. He appeared to be calm and composed, as she later told the authorities, but he immediately announced to the woman on the sidewalk that he wanted to buy a gun. She glanced at the slight but intense figure in the suit and overcoat and then called to her husband inside the shop, a stocky, mustachioed man whose name was Carpe. The proprietor beckoned to the young man to enter the narrow little store, which was only now filling with light as Mme Carpe finished opening the shutters.

"Why do you need a gun?" Carpe asked the youth, who certainly looked rather too young to be buying a firearm and was clearly agitated by the display of weaponry around the shop.

"I often need to carry large sums of money for my father," explained Herschel, speaking as best he could in French and pulling the wallet out of his coat pocket as if to demonstrate the truth of his excuse. "I want a gun for protection."[7]

Then as now, and in France as in America, gun dealers are not fussy about their customers. Under French law, the only grounds on which to deny the young man a gun was lunacy, and the law entrusted the gun shop owner, perhaps not the most reliable detector of psychiatric aberration, with the power to decide whether or not the customer was of unsound mind. Otherwise, Carpe needed only to confirm the customer's identity and enter the transaction in his records, and then it was up to the buyer to register his new weapon with the local police. So the proprietor set a few handguns on the counter for inspection by the customer, who plainly knew nothing about firearms and looked in confusion from one to another. At last, according to one account, Herschel asked for a .45—the only caliber he knew, and only because it was ubiquitous in the American movies that he watched with his friends at the local theaters.[8]

M. Carpe sought to dissuade the young man from choosing a .45-caliber handgun, a large and heavy weapon, and instead recommended a five-shot 6.35-millimeter revolver, small and light and designed to be carried as a concealed weapon. The revolver was known as a "hammerless" model because the hammer mechanism was contained within the external frame of the weapon and for that reason would not snag on the lining of a pocket when it was being drawn out for use. Although the weapon was a bit cumbersome to empty and reload after firing, it would not matter to Herschel, who did not expect to find himself in a running gun battle. Clearly, the hammerless revolver was perfect for what Herschel intended to do with the gun, although he had told yet another lie when he explained to Carpe why he needed one.

Herschel watched attentively as Carpe obligingly demonstrated how to load, fire, and unload the revolver. After all, Herschel was intrigued with mechanical devices, and he must have quickly grasped the workings of the firearm. Indeed, an industrial sewing machine of the kind that was in use at Maison Albert was a more complex mechanism, and—in any event—Herschel did not need a gunsmith's mastery of the weapon in order to do what he now planned to do. The young man agreed to take the weapon that the proprietor had recommended, and so Carpe put a box of twenty-five 6.35-millimeter cartridges on the counter next to the revolver and asked the young man for his name, address, and identity papers.

Herschel pulled out his Polish passport and told Carpe that he resided at 8 rue Martel. None of the irregularities that now attached to these particulars were apparent to Carpe, of course, and Herschel had no intention of registering the weapon with the police, who would have quickly identified him as an illegal alien. Carpe dutifully filled out the registration form, handed it to Herschel, and instructed him where to find the police station. Then Carpe collected 210 francs for the weapon and another 35 francs for the shells, which the young man paid in 100-franc notes that he extracted from his wallet—the same banknotes that Uncle Abraham had pressed on him the night before. Finally, Carpe wrapped the revolver and the box of cartridges in brown paper, secured each package with rubber bands, and handed both to Herschel.

As he left the gun shop, Herschel was careful not to excite the curiosity of the proprietor: he turned in the direction of the police station and continued walking until he was out of sight. Then he turned off the rue du Faubourg Saint-Martin, circled back to the boulevard de Strasbourg, and headed instead toward the Tout Va Bien, only three blocks away at the intersection where the busy thoroughfare crossed the boulevard Saint-Denis. By 8:55 a.m., he was already in the sour-smelling lavatory of the café, alone and undetected by any of his friends or acquaintances who might have been taking a morning coffee at one of the tables.

Now Herschel hurriedly unpacked his purchases, inserted five rounds into the cylinder, and slipped the loaded weapon into the inside left pocket of his expertly tailored suit jacket. In his haste, Herschel neglected to remove the price tag, which was still tied to the trigger-guard on a red string. But the weapon itself, just as M. Carpe had assured him, was undetectable.

✦   ✦   ✦

HERSCHEL HAD BECOME A boulevardier—"a kind of stroller of streets," according to Schwab—and he could easily have reached the Left Bank by continuing on the boulevard de Strasbourg in the direction of the Seine.*9 On a fair day like that one, it would have been an especially pleasurable ramble of less than an hour. Herschel was not out for a stroll, however, and when he left the Tout Va Bien, he walked directly to the Strasbourg Saint-Denis station, boarded the Line 8 Métro train and rode as far the Madeleine station, where he transferred to the Line 12 train. He exited at the Solférino station,

* As laid out by Baron Haussmann in his renovation of Paris in the mid-nineteenth century, the boulevard de Strasbourg turns into the boulevard de Sébastopol and then, after crossing the Seine, the boulevard Saint-Michel.

climbed the stairs to the street, and walked briskly past the sprawling Orsay train depot. At 9:35 a.m., he arrived at the German embassy at 78 rue de Lille.

The embassy was housed in the Hôtel Beauharnais, a stately pile that had been erected in 1713 in the style of late baroque classicism that was the specialty of the architect Germain Boffrand, whose clientele included both French and German aristocrats. The property had been a German diplomatic venue since its purchase by the king of Prussia in 1817 after the final defeat of Napoleon. Many of the elegant interior rooms were subdivided into a warren of smaller offices, where functionaries of the Foreign Office attended to the various undertakings of the ascendant Third Reich—diplomacy, commerce, propaganda, and intelligence. So many importuning visitors sought entry to the embassy that armed French gendarmes were always stationed at the portal on the rue de Lille.

Herschel Grynszpan presented himself at the guard post outside the arched gateway. He had previously called several times at the German consulate on the rue Huysmans, which was located near the Jardin du Luxembourg, when he was struggling to put his papers in order, but this was Herschel's first visit to the embassy itself. Among the several gendarmes who were gathered at the post, he approached an officer named François Autret.

"What is the purpose of your visit?" asked Autret in French.

His inquiry was strictly routine. Nothing in the appearance or demeanor of the intense young man alarmed the gendarme. After all, many of the callers at the German embassy in those troubled times were ill at ease, or openly anxious, or even distraught, and Herschel himself was capable of maintaining his composure when it was necessary to do so. Indeed, he would later reveal that he was, at that moment, making "a giant effort to control himself and give no sign of his great nervousness," and he was entirely successful in doing so.[10]

"I wish to obtain a German visa," Herschel lied coolly.

"In that case, you should address your request to the consulate instead of the embassy," instructed Autret, but he nonetheless pointed out the door for public entry—one of several doors opening onto the rue de Lille—and left it up to the visitor to find his way to the proper office.[11] Then Autret turned back to his fellow officers and thought nothing more about the young man, one of the countless daily visitors to the embassy, each with his own little melodrama to play out, and none of them of any concern to him.

Herschel now approached the door that Autret had indicated. As Herschel pulled it open, a middle-aged gentleman in street clothes was on his way out of the building, and the man strode past Herschel without addressing or even acknowledging him. The distinguished and distracted figure, as it turns out, was Count Johannes von Welczeck, the German ambassador to France, who was leaving the embassy to take his customary morning walk around the neighborhood. Much would later be made of the apparent chance encounter between the armed Jewish refugee and the titled German diplomat, as we shall see, but if there was any irony in their near-miss, it was wholly unknown to either of them at that moment.

After brushing past the highest-ranking diplomat in the embassy, Herschel next ran into one of the humbler members of the staff—Mme Mathis, the wife of the Frenchman who served as concierge for the embassy building. Here was another chance encounter: her husband was momentarily out of sight because he was changing his dirty clothing after making a repair to the furnace in the basement, and so Herschel was compelled to address the man's wife instead. Exactly what words he spoke turned out to be of considerable consequence in solving the mystery of *l'affaire Grynszpan*, however, and they were to be much debated in the months and years ahead. According to one version of the story, the request that Grynszpan addressed to the concierge's wife was quite different from the one he had used to gain entry to the embassy a few moments before.

"I need to see a gentleman from the embassy," Herschel suppos-edly said, speaking in French and telling a second and different lie. "I wish to submit some important papers to him."[12]

The young man's urgent request was a matter of indifference to the concierge's wife, whose duties included washing her husband's dirty clothing but not handling "important papers," and she merely directed him to the staircase—the receptionist on duty, Herr Nagorka, was one flight up. Herschel ascended the stairs, presented himself to the German official at the desk, and repeated his request to see someone in order to deliver "a confidential and very important document." Now he spoke in German, and he supposedly specified that he wanted to see "one of the embassy secretaries."[13]

Nagorka apparently saw nothing unsettling or even unusual in the fact that an unannounced stranger had appeared at the embassy with an offer to turn over an "important document," which lends some credibility to the French newspaper account that characterized the German embassy as a nest of spies: "One had only to be announced as an intelligence agent to be received without diffi-culty."[14] Another, equally plausible explanation is that enterprising or desperate people in need of favors commonly offered blandish-ments of various kinds to the embassy staff, including the promise of secret papers, and Nagorka merely shrugged off the latest such ploy. Nagorka, in any event, offered to take the document and pass it along, but the young man declined.

"It is too important," Herschel insisted. "I wish to submit it myself."[15]

More intriguing is the question of exactly whom Herschel sought to see in order to turn over his nonexistent papers. Did he ask to see the ambassador himself, the man he had just unwittingly passed in the doorway a few moments before? Would he have been satisfied with an "embassy official" of any rank? Or did he specify that he needed to see a *Legationssekretär* (legation secretary), a job title that applied to three individuals in the German embassy at 78 rue de Lille, only one of whom was present on that morning? Later, both the German and French authorities would have reason to consider all of these questions, and so will we.

Nagorka, for his part, regarded the whole encounter as unremark- able. He invited the insistent young man to take a seat in the waiting room, and he returned a few minutes later to escort the visitor to the office of the embassy staff member who had agreed to see him—the newest and lowest-ranked of the three legation secretaries, an ami- able twenty-nine-year-old diplomat who was known among his col- leagues for his willingness and ability to cope with even the most overwrought callers at the embassy.

✦   ✦   ✦

ERNST VOM RATH WAS seated behind his desk, with his back to the door and his face toward the window, when Nargorka delivered the caller to his small office at 9:45 a.m. The handsome young diplomat gestured at one of the two overstuffed leather guest chairs that faced the desk, and the caller seated himself in one of them. Nagorka turned, pulled the door shut behind him, and returned to his post at the reception desk, leaving Rath and Grynszpan alone behind closed doors.

What happened next is known only because Herschel Gryszpan himself—the sole surviving eyewitness—readily revealed the details, although he would offer more than one version of the crucial account in the months and years ahead.

Rath moved his chair a quarter turn to the left so that he was now facing his young caller.

"So," he said, "let me see the document."

"You're a *sale boche*," said Grynszpan—the phrase is colloquial French for "a dirty Kraut"—as he reached into the inside left pocket of his suit jacket and smoothly drew out the loaded hammerless revolver, "and in the name of 12,000 persecuted Jews, here is the document!"[16]

Herschel now pointed his new weapon, the price tag still dangling almost comically from the trigger guard, and Rath rose from his chair in alarm as Herschel fired all five shots in the cylinder. The two men were only a few feet apart from each other, and Herschel was firing from a stationary position, and yet he managed to put only two of the five bullets into his target. By a certain irony, one lesson that Herschel Grynszpan learned at that moment was how damnably hard it can be to kill a man with a gun, especially for a novice shooter who had never fired a weapon before and who was using a small-caliber and low-velocity firearm of the kind that the helpful M. Carpe had urged upon him. The *Legationssekretär* was still alive when Herschel dropped his empty weapon to the floor.

The sound of gunshots from a small handgun fired behind a heavy wooden door would have reached the ears of the embassy staff as nothing more than the sound of faint popping. Still, it would have been readily identifiable as gunfire, and especially among men who were familiar with the use of firearms, whether because of their service in World War I or their postwar training in the Brownshirts. Only moments later, the door to Rath's office opened, and the injured man stumbled into the corridor and cried out. Nagorka, sitting at his desk some thirty yards away, rose immediately and hastened to his colleague, who was now bracing himself in his office doorway and clutching his stomach with both hands. When Rath saw Nagorka, followed by an embassy staff member named Krüger, he managed to utter a wholly unnecessary explanation: "I am wounded."[17]

When Nagorka looked past his injured colleague, he saw that the young man with the "important document" was now sitting impassively in the empty office, a handgun on the floor next to him. Nagorka and Krüger seized him forcefully, but he offered no resistance. As they hustled him roughly down the corridor, leaving the wounded man in the care of an embassy attaché whose office was adjacent to Rath's, the young man assured his captors that he did not intend to escape but audaciously demanded to be placed into the custody of the French police.

His captors promptly complied with his demand. Perhaps because these low-ranking German diplomats were mindful of international protocol—and because they were well briefed on Hitler's current and highly successful policy of courting French appeasement—they did not mistreat the shooter or hold him as a prisoner on the embassy grounds. Rather, only moments later, the two German staff members and the shooter were back on a sunny stretch of the rue de Lille, where Nagorka approached the French guard post and pushed the young man toward the same police officer who had sent him into the embassy a few minutes earlier.

"*Sales boches!*"—Dirty Krauts!—shouted Grynszpan, who was surely emboldened by the fact that he was standing once again on French soil and beyond the reach of the Third Reich.

Autret surveyed the little assemblage of agitated men who now stood in front him and calmly asked what had happened. Nagorka and Krüger breathlessly recounted the events that had just taken place inside the embassy and concluded with the report that the victim of the shooting was badly wounded but still alive.

"It's a shame that he isn't dead," said Herschel, at least according to the subsequent testimony of Krüger (but not Nagorka).

Autret placed the young man under arrest. "Don't worry," Herschel reassured his new captor, "I will come with you." The officer searched him for weapons, found none, put him in handcuffs, and then conducted the willing, even effusive young prisoner in the direction of the local precinct house at 2 rue de Bourgogne. On the short walk to the police station, only fifteen hundred feet away, Herschel continued to speak unguardedly about his crime.

"I have just shot a man in his office," said Herschel. "I do not regret it. I did it to avenge my parents who are miserable in Germany."[18]

✦   ✦   ✦

ONCE AUTRET TURNED HIS prisoner over to his fellow officers at the Commissariat de Police, the young man was more thoroughly searched. Only 38 francs in bills and coins remained in his wallet and pockets. He also carried the registration form for the gun he had purchased earlier in the day, the box of ammunition (now reduced by five cartridges), a Polish passport, three invitations to a dance at the Aurore sports club, and two handwritten postcards—the one that Esther had composed in the refugee camp at Zbąszyń on October 31, and the one that Herschel had scribbled in his room at the Hôtel de Suez earlier that day but neglected to mail on his way to the embassy. Herschel's postcard, of course, was an admission of guilt in itself: "I have to protest in a way that the whole world hears my protest, and this I intend to do."[19]

The prisoner was conducted to the office of M. J. Monneret, police commissioner for the Invalides and École Militaire precincts, and he was asked to formally identify himself. The young man gave his name as Herschel Feibel Grynszpan, born March 28, 1921, the son of Zindel and Rivka Grynszpan. For the very first time in the past twenty-four hours, Herschel had told the complete truth to one of his interlocutors, and the details were duly set down in the opening pages of an official record that would quickly reach heroic proportions.

"From the moment I read my sister's postcard on Thursday, November 3," he readily announced to his interrogators, "I decided to kill a member of the embassy."[20]

Herschel himself was suddenly transformed from a wholly obscure Jewish adolescent refugee, one of tens of thousands of nameless and faceless *Ostjuden* in Paris, into the object of intense and ongoing investigation by several governments, and a figure of fascination for the international press. Starting immediately upon his arrest outside 78 rue de Lille, his private tendency toward grandiosity was confirmed by his captors, and the boy who once wrote a letter to the president of the United States would soon be known by name to the prime minister of France and to the Führer, too.

Not more than an hour had passed after the shooting, for example, before Ambassador Welczeck dispatched an embassy staff member named Lorz to monitor the investigation on behalf of the Third Reich. The French police commissioner readily assented to the direct questioning of the suspect by the German emissary, who asked Herschel—yet again and in French—why he had shot Rath. "I am Jewish," Herschel responded bluntly, "and I wanted to avenge the great wrong which has been visited upon my fellow Jews in general and on my family in particular."[21]

Indeed, the fact that Herschel had entered the embassy of the Third Reich and shot a Nazi diplomat elevated the case from an ordinary crime into an international crisis. The breaking news of the Grynszpan case, which was soon broadcast on the radio and featured in the headlines of the afternoon papers in Paris, was recognized by everyone in the French government, ranging from Prime Minister Daladier and Foreign Minister Bonnet all the way down to the gendarmes who now guarded their young prisoner, as a provocation that might send Nazi Germany to war against France.

"Jewish Murder Attempt in Paris – Member of the German Embassy Critically Wounded by Shots – The Murdering Knave a 17-Year-Old Jew" ranted one of the headlines in the official Nazi newspaper, *Völkischer Beobachter*. "The Shots in Paris Will Not Go Unpunished!"[22]

So members of the gendarmerie, whether on their own initiative or according to instructions from on high, conducted the initial investigation at high speed. By noon, Herschel Grynszpan had already been formally deposed by Commissioner Monneret, with the assistance of the Nazi emissary, and he was transported by the detectives in the early afternoon to the room he had occupied at the Hôtel de Suez and his hiding place in the attic at 8 rue Martel, both of which were thoroughly searched. Herschel was also taken to the scene of the crime, but he refused to set foot on the grounds of the German embassy, out of fear that the aggrieved diplomats of the Third Reich would abduct or maybe even murder him. So Monneret entered alone, took note of the bullet holes that could be seen behind Rath's desk, and returned with the revolver he had found on the office floor, five spent cartridges in the cylinder and the price tag hanging from the trigger guard on a red string.

Several persons of interest in the case were also questioned on the day of the shooting, some of them in Herschel's presence: the gun shop owner, M. Carpe; the night clerk at the Hôtel de Suez, Mlle Laurent; various members of the German embassy staff; and even Abraham Grynszpan, who now understood what had happened to his nephew after the young man stormed out of his apartment. Laurent and Carpe were asked to identify Herschel as the young man who had entered their places of business, and Abraham Grynszpan was required to formally confirm that Herschel was his nephew and his dinner guest on the night before the shooting. All of the witnesses complied.

Abraham and Chava Grynszpan discovered that they were suspects in their own right, not only because they had harbored an illegal alien but also because the police entertained the suspicion they had known in advance of Herschel's plan and perhaps even participated in a conspiracy to put him inside the German embassy—a notion that was raised at the outset in both French and German circles and was never fully erased. Indeed, the case against the Grynszpans would proceed at a far faster pace than the one against their embattled nephew.

At 11:00 p.m. on November 7, Grynszpan was taken by car from the precinct house to the offices of the Sûreté, the criminal investigation unit of the Paris police, at the Quai des Orfèvres on the Île de la Cité, where he was formally interrogated yet again by a police inspector. Now that he was the target of a full-scale investigation at the highest level of French law enforcement, Herschel seemed to enjoy the attention he was receiving. Indeed, the experience only served to validate the historic role that he had imagined for himself when he was still living in hiding, isolated and obscure.

Herschel also began to polish up his version of what had happened behind the closed doors of Rath's office earlier that day. Physically exhausted but charged up by the constant questioning, he carefully revised the account he had given to Officer Autret by dropping any reference to the vulgarism *sale boche* and by emphasizing the impact of the heartrending postcard that he had received from his sister. Above all, he spoke of himself and his deed in elevated terms, as if he were conscious that whatever he told the police would end up in the newspapers, too.

"After I received the card, I planned an act of vengeance and protest against a representative of the Third Reich," he explained. "I wanted to create a stir great enough so that the world would not ignore it because Germany's conduct provoked me beyond measure." Intriguingly, Grynszpan did not mention Rath's name and may not have known it: "The person himself," he said of his target, "was of slight importance." Once he had been escorted into one of the embassy offices, "the official in question asked me to present the papers which I had indicated I had," Herschel told Commissioner Badin. "I then took out my revolver from my suit coat pocket and, before firing, I said, 'Isn't it enough that Jews have to suffer so severely from German persecution, and that they are thrown into concentration camps? Now they're being expelled as if they were nothing but stray dogs.'"[23]

Herschel also added a significant detail that he had omitted when he was interrogated earlier in the day by Commissioner Monneret.

"Wounded by the bullets, the official put both his hands on his abdomen, and he still had the strength to give me a punch in the jaw, calling me, at the same time, 'dirty Jew' [*dreckiges Judenvolk*],'" declared Herschel. "He made a rush for the door of his office crying out, 'Help!' I wanted then to avenge myself further for the epithet that he had bestowed on me, and I tried to hurl the weapon at his face but I missed him."[24]

✦   ✦   ✦

AT THAT MOMENT, Ernst vom Rath lay unconscious in a hospital bed as a hastily assembled medical staff from across Europe struggled to save his life.

Rath had been given first aid under the supervision of Ernst Achenbach, the attaché who tended to the victim while Krüger and Nagorka took custody of the shooter, and Achenbach later reported that "Rath managed to tell him that the assailant had fired almost immediately upon entering the office, saying that he wished to avenge the Jews."[25] One of the physicians on the embassy staff, a certain Dr. Claas, was called to the scene of the shooting, and he summoned an ambulance to transport Rath to a nearby private hospital, the Clinique d'Alma on the rue de l'Université. Another physician who was affiliated with the embassy, a French surgeon named Dr. Baumgartner, met the patient at the hospital and examined his wounds.

Rath had been hit by two bullets from Herschel's revolver, both traveling upward from the entry wounds since he was standing and Herschel fired from a seated position. One bullet had entered the left side of Rath's torso, passed through his body without striking any internal organs, and was now lodged safely in his shoulder. The other bullet, however, entered lower on the left side and penetrated deeply into the organ cavity. A more meticulous examination later confirmed that the second bullet, as it tumbled through Rath's body, ruptured his spleen, tore up his pancreas, and punched a hole in his stomach before finally planting itself near his thorax. Dr. Baumgartner and the other physicians who were gathered around Rath's bed briefly debated whether it would be prudent to transfer the patient to the American Hospital, in the suburb of Neuilly, but they decided that severe internal hemorrhaging demanded emergency surgery.

Rath's spleen, the site of the hemorrhage, was removed, and the stomach wounds were sutured. The internal blood clots were cleaned out, and several direct blood transfusions were administered by a French specialist named Dr. Jubé. The blood donor was a decorated war hero named Thomas, a man who had famously given his blood to his fellow citizens of France more than a hundred times over the last several years, but who now offered his blood to a wounded German diplomat. Every detail of the case, including the identity of the blood donor, was quickly exploited for its propaganda value; according to the Nazi Ministry of Propaganda, the donor's act of generosity served to promote amity between France and Germany, a relationship that others—including Herschel Grynszpan—were seeking to poison.

Adolf Hitler himself, on receiving the first news of the shooting, apparently consulted his inner circle to decide how to use the incident to best advantage. In the days ahead, the shooting of Rath would be exploited as the pretext for an escalation of the war on the Jews. For now, however, the Führer contented himself with the showy gesture of dispatching his personal physician, Dr. Karl Brandt, to Paris to attend to the wounded diplomat—yet another early indication that the Nazi propaganda apparatus intended to exploit the case for its own purposes.

Brandt was fated to die on the gallows for his crimes during World War II, which included the gassing of disabled German civilians and the performing of gruesome medical experiments on concentration camp inmates. His criminal tendencies, however, were not yet known to the world when Brandt set off for Paris by air in the company of Dr. Georg Magnus, director of the Surgical Clinic of the University of Munich. The two German doctors arrived at Le Bourget airport less than twenty-four hours after the shooting and appeared at the Clinique d'Alma to make a show of examining the wounded diplomat. As it turned out, Brandt was far more accomplished at torture and murder than at healing; he pronounced the patient's condition to be "extremely serious," agreed to Dr. Baumgartner's recommendation to administer another transfusion of French blood, and retreated to his hotel for the rest of the day. By the time Brandt returned to the hospital at the end of the day, Rath's fever was elevated and his condition was deteriorating.

Next to reach Paris were Rath's father and brother, who arrived at the Gare du Nord in the Tenth Arrondissement on an express train from Cologne on Tuesday, November 8. His mother later joined them, and when she showed up at the Clinique d'Alma the next day, she carried a small suitcase—a sign that she intended to keep a vigil by the bed of her wounded son. Rath apparently recognized his parents and his brother, and he "was very much moved by their presence," reports Cuénot, a physician, but "unnecessary exertion was forbidden due to his greatly weakened state and the parents, therefore, urged him not to talk."[26] Rath, in fact, was slipping into a state of shock.

Another and entirely different vigil was being maintained by the reporters who staked out the hospital, the police commissariat, and the embassy. Dr. Baumgartner, for example, was set upon by the French news hounds when he emerged from the Clinique d'Alma around noon on Wednesday, November 9, and announced that the young diplomat's condition was critical. One reporter asked whether Rath's youth and strength did not bode well for his recovery, but Dr.

Baumgartner offered no hope. "If there had been only one wound," he shrugged, "but there are three!"[27]

The only good tidings came from Berlin, where the Propaganda Ministry announced that the Führer had honored the young diplomat by raising him to the rank of *Gesandtschaftsrat* (legation counselor), a gesture that turned out to be a deathbed promotion. As Rath's mother and father were joined at his bedside by the Nazi doctors from Berlin—and as the world press monitored and reported his deteriorating condition—the patient slipped into a final coma shortly after 3:00 p.m. on the afternoon of November 9. "Pancreatic injury alone was the determining factor," reports Dr. Cuénot, since it caused an "overflow of a digestive juice which, when unleashed, is capable of consuming all the surrounding tissues." By 4:25 p.m., Ernst vom Rath was pronounced dead.[28]

Only an accidental intersection between physics and anatomy, in other words, caused the death of Rath. The first of the two bullets that struck him inflicted a survivable wound. The second bullet damaged the stomach and spleen, but neither of these injuries killed him. When the same bullet nicked the pancreas, however, the damage was beyond the power of mid-twentieth-century medicine to repair. With the death of Rath, the charge against Herschel Grynszpan was now formally elevated to murder in the first degree.

6

THE BLOOD FLAG

AT THE MOMENT OF ERNST VOM RATH'S DEATH IN PARIS, Adolf Hitler and his earliest comrades—the *Alte Kämpfer* (Old Fighters)—were gathered in Munich to celebrate the anniversary of an event in the history of the Nazi Party that had taken on the trappings of a creation myth, the so-called Beer Hall Putsch of 1923.

The fact that Rath had joined the party a few months before the Nazis assumed power in Germany in 1933 entitled him to be called an Old Fighter, too, but it was strictly an honorific when applied to the young diplomat. By contrast, the men who gathered around Hitler in the smoke-filled hall in Munich on the night of Rath's death included authentic veterans of the bloody uprising, and Hitler invariably addressed them with special fervor at each year's celebration.

Like so much else in the hagiography of Hitler offered by Nazi propagandists, the Beer Hall Putsch was, in fact, an abject defeat. Hitler and some six hundred Brownshirts had launched the uprising at the Bürgerbräukeller, a Munich beer hall, on the evening of November 8, 1923, where Hitler announced that "the National Revolution has begun." At dawn on the next day, he marched with his followers—an assortment of embittered veterans of the First World War, desk workers with a penchant for dressing up in uniforms, and bullying street brawlers—toward the offices of the Ministry of War.[1] Hitler's ambition was to seize the government by force of arms, but his little army was turned back by a hundred or so police officers with carbines at a colonnaded structure in the Odeonsplatz called the Feldherrnhalle.

Gunfire was briefly exchanged, and sixteen Nazis and three policemen were killed in the moments of mayhem. A slightly injured Hitler and the rest of his followers turned and ran. Hitler was arrested, tried, and sent to prison, where he took advantage of his confinement by dictating *Mein Kampf* to another veteran of the Beer Hall Putsch, Rudolf Hess. Another ten years would pass before the Nazis came to power, and when they did, victory was achieved by campaigning for the votes of their fellow Germans. Meanwhile, history was rewritten by the Nazi Party propagandists to turn the Beer Hall Putsch into "the holiest day in the entire Nazi calendar."[2]

The anniversary of the Beer Hall Putsch, an event known in Nazi usage as the *Tag der Bewegung* (Day of the Movement), was observed on November 9 of each year as an official holiday. Nazi Party promotions and honors were announced, and the proud recipients wore their gleaming new badges and medals at the festivities that took place on that day. Each year, the march from the Bürgerbräukeller to the Feldherrnhalle was reenacted, wreaths were laid in memory of the fallen comrades, and the flag that the Old Fighters had carried— a Nazi relic known as the blood flag—was displayed.

Then Hitler spent a "comradely evening" at the Old Town Hall with five hundred or so of the highest-ranking members of the Nazi Party, including the leadership of the SA, the SS, and the Hitler Youth.[3] The day ended with the midnight ceremony at which new recruits to the SS took their blood oaths in the presence of the Führer. Adolf Hitler, an impassioned speaker and never more so than when surrounded by the *Alte Kämpfer*, was always capable of moving an audience to both rage and rapture, but his remarks on the *Tag der Bewegung* were especially well received by men who were full of beer and memories.

On Wednesday, November 9, 1938, the fifteenth anniversary of the Beer Hall Putsch, Hitler joined his comrades at the Old Town Hall for the customary festivities. Shortly after 7:00 p.m., however, a messenger was observed to enter the hall, discreetly approach the Führer, and whisper something to him. Then Hitler turned to Joseph Goebbels, and the two men engaged in an "intense conversation" in such hushed voices that only a single phrase was overheard: "The SA should be allowed to have its fling."[4] Goebbels was delighted: "For once," he later confided to his diary, "the Jews should feel the rage of the people."[5]

Hitler had apparently already known about the latest events in Paris even before he arrived at the Old Town Hall. Karl Brandt had telegraphed the Reich Chancellery in Berlin within fifteen minutes after the death of Rath, and he may have also placed a personal telephone call to Hitler at his apartment in Munich. The news was released to the world by the DNB press agency forty-five minutes later. One eyewitness reported that Hitler, en route from his apartment to the Old Town Hall in the company of Goebbels, told an SA officer that the "outraged people" of the Third Reich should not be restrained by the police from expressing their righteous anger.[6] In any event, once he had finished his conversation with Goebbels at the Old Town Hall, Hitler abruptly left the hall—a sight that was recognized by the crowd as something unusual and unsettling. The task of announcing the order was left to Goebbels.

The minister of propaganda, in fact, was obsessed with "the Jew Grynszpan," as he called Herschel Grynszpan, and relished the opportunity to make the most of the assassination of a diplomatic subaltern.[7] Goebbels had motives of his own for focusing attention on the case: the prudish Hitler disapproved of his much whispered-about affair with a Czech actress, Lida Baarova, and Goebbels may have seized upon the Grynszpan affair as a high-profile project that would distract Hitler from the scandal and put Goebbels back into his good graces. Goebbels urged the Führer to "unleash the wrath of the people," and the Führer assented.[8] Now it was Goebbels who took the podium at the Old Town Hall and addressed the watchful crowd.

"I have news here for you tonight, to demonstrate what happens to a good German when he relaxes his vigil for one moment," declared Goebbels. "Ernst vom Rath was a good German, a loyal servant of the Reich, working for the good of our people in our embassy in Paris. Shall I tell you what happened to him? He was shot down! In the course of his duty, he went, unarmed and unsuspecting, to speak to a visitor at the embassy, and had two bullets pumped into him. He is now dead."[9]

Goebbels, of course, was second only to Hitler in the manipulation of crowds, and he put his rhetorical skills to expert use on that night. The directives issued to the German press had already exploited the incident on the rue de Lille as a rationale for the official persecution of the Jews. The death of Rath, however, provided him with an even more provocative denouement. Many of the high-ranking party officials in the audience must have already known the news out of Paris, but they responded with angry murmers and shouts just as he had intended.

"Do I need to tell you the race of the dirty swine who perpetrated this foul deed?" ranted Goebbels. "A Jew! Tonight he lies in jail in Paris, claiming that he acted on his own, that he had no instigators of this awful deed behind him. But we know better, don't we? Comrades, we cannot allow this attack by international Jewry to go unchallenged!"[10]

Here was the first note of the leitmotif that runs through all of the Nazi propaganda about the Grynszpan case—the boy who pulled the trigger was merely the cat's-paw of an international Jewish con-

spiracy. Goebbels next articulated the party line on the proper punishment of the Jewish population for the act of a single Jew. When
Wilhelm Gustloff was felled in Davos by David Frankfurter in 1936,
the Nazi regime was reluctant to taint the Olympics with official
acts of violence against the Jewish community, and it restrained
party members and the populace at large from doing so. Now, however, nothing prevented the Nazi authorities from imposing collective punishment on all of the Jews who were still trapped inside the
Third Reich.

"Our people must be told, and their answer must be ruthless,
forthright, salutary!" continued Goebbels. "I ask you to listen to me,
and together we must plan what is to be our answer to Jewish murder and the threat of international Jewry to our glorious German
Reich!"[11] Goebbels acknowledged that incidents of anti-Semitic violence had already taken place in Magdeburg-Anhalt and Kurhessen,
and he offered the thin excuse that would be used to justify a night
of orchestrated violence across Germany and Austria: "The Führer
has decided that such demonstrations should not be prepared or
organized by the party," declared Goebbels, "but insofar as they
erupted spontaneously, they were not to be hampered."[12]

Thus began the officially sanctioned pogrom that the Nazis
referred to, cheekily and dismissively, as Kristallnacht (Crystal
Night). In some towns and cities around Germany, as Goebbels
noted, German mobs had already carried out acts of violence against
Jewish targets on their own initiative; on the Unter den Linden in
Berlin, for example, Jews who were queued up outside the French
tourist office were set upon by a mob: "Down with the Jews!" they
chanted. "They are going to Paris to join the murderer!"[13]

Even these incidents, however, owed something to the propaganda
blitz that Goebbels had unleashed at 8:37 p.m. on November 7, less
than twelve hours after the shooting, when a directive was circulated
to newspapers across Germany. Coverage of the shooting in Paris

"should dominate the front page," the editors were instructed, and editorials should emphasize that the attack on Rath "must have the most serious consequences for the Jews."[14] Now those consequences would be revealed to the German people and played out as a kind of monstrous street theater for a worldwide audience.

"I immediately give the necessary instructions to the police and the Party," Goebbels recorded in his diary after his address in Munich. "Then I briefly speak in that vein to the Party leadership. Stormy applause. All are instantly on the phones. Now people will act."[15]

By midnight on November 9, a set of detailed orders was issued systematically by teletype and telephone from Munich to party offices and police, army and SA units across Germany and Austria, to make sure that "spontaneous" acts of violence were carried out precisely according to the official specifications. All Jews, and not merely *Ostjuden*, were to be disarmed, according to one such order. "In the event of resistance, they are to be shot immediately." Synagogues were to be set afire, and Jewish-owned shops were to be vandalized by the Brownshirts, but firemen and policemen were to make sure that the fires did not spread to "Aryan" property and the Jewish shops were not looted.[16]

So meticulous were the planners of Kristallnacht that they even issued a list of phrases that were to be scrawled on the windows and walls of Jewish-owned buildings. "Death to international Jewry" was a beloved old trope of Nazi propaganda. "No understanding with nations under the sway of Jews" was on the list of approved graffiti even if it was rather wordy for the Brownshirts who were actually wielding the paintbrushes. The single most telling phrase of all was short, unvarnished in its meaning, and hot-wired to the headlines: "Revenge for the murder of vom Rath!"[17]

✦   ✦   ✦

AMONG THE OLD FIGHTERS who marched alongside Adolf Hitler in the front rank of the Beer Hall Putsch was the notorious Julius Streicher. He is best remembered as the publisher of the anti-Semitic newspaper *Der Stürmer*, but he was also a regional leader (*Gauleiter*) of the Nazi Party in a portion of Bavaria that was first designated as Nuremberg-Fürth and later as Franconia. Since Streicher was a Jew-hater whose vileness and vulgarity were capable of astonishing even Hitler himself—and since Franconia had already been the site of atrocities against its Jewish residents—no one in the Third Reich was surprised when the so-called King of Franconia put himself in the front rank of Jew-bashing during the spasm of violence called Kristallnacht.

Within a few hours after the orders had been issued from Munich on the night of November 9–10, the Brownshirts in the town of Fürth, considered a suburb of Nuremberg, were already ranging through the streets in search of Jewish victims. Fürth, ironically, was renowned for its early acceptance of Jews, a rare example of toleration in the southeastern state of Bavaria, which was predominantly Catholic and even more overtly anti-Semitic than other regions of Germany. Significantly, members of the Sturmabteilung in Nuremberg, only seven kilometers away, had already laid in a supply of crowbars and iron rods in anticipation of an order to spill Jewish blood. Now their fellow storm troopers in Fürth followed their example in an atavistic spasm of violence for which the local Jewish populace was wholly unprepared.

The Jewish residents of Fürth, ranging in age from newborns to septuagenarians, were dragged out of their homes and even the beds at the Jewish hospital and marched under guard to the town square—the Schlageter Platz, named in honor of a German soldier who had been shot by the French army of occupation in 1923 for blowing up French rolling stock. They were made to stand at attention in the chilly darkness, and if a toilet was needed, they were ordered to uri-

nate or defecate where they stood. Such outrages were a wholly new
experience for the Jewish burghers of Fürth, a place sometimes
called the Franconian Jerusalem precisely because it had sheltered an
accomplished Jewish community that dated back to the sixteenth
century.

Meanwhile, members of the SA headed for the seven synagogues
in Fürth, including the four *shuls* that were arrayed around a large
courtyard along with the ritual bath and a kosher butcher's shop—
the Neuschul, the Mannheimer Shul, the Klaus Shul, and the Reform
Temple. All were set afire, and the Jews being held in Schlageter
Platz "were ordered to execute a smart about-face in the direction of
the Schulhof," according to survivor Edgar Rosenberg. "The sky had
turned crimson." Then the storm troopers unfurled a Torah that had
been seized from one of the synagogues, and the chief rabbi of Fürth
was ordered to trample upon the sacred scroll, all to "the vast amuse-
ment and hoots of delight by the citizen spectators," as the local
newspaper reported the next day.[18]

After dawn on November 10, the Jewish women, children, and
elderly men in Schlageter Platz were finally sent home, while the rest
of the Jewish men were driven into a community hall that was ordinarily used for concerts and lectures. As they were marched through
streets "littered with glass splinters, torn overcoats, unhinged type-
writers, beheaded teddy-bears, and the Dali-esque picture of half a
pianola lying athwart our busy main street," according to Rosenberg's account, the Jewish men were beaten, spit upon, and taunted:
"*Saujuden!*" (Jew Sows!) was taken up by the crowd in chorus. A
few of the Brownshirts set upon "the Jew Kahn" and tore out his
long beard, a torture favored by German police and soldiers when
dealing with an observant Jewish man for whom a beard was a symbol of piety.

Once confined in the community hall, Jewish men were singled
out at random for beatings and whippings. A rabbi was threatened

with death by *Genickschuss*—a gunshot in the neck—unless he revealed the whereabouts of a synagogue that was supposedly hidden in the woods on the outskirts of the town, but was unable to comply because no such place existed. A few of the men reacted to the abuse with indignation and even open defiance; Rosenberg's father, a combat veteran of World War I whose decorations included an Iron Cross, confronted one of the Brownshirts by pointing to the man's battle ribbons: "Ah, I see you've got the same medals I've got!"[19] By nightfall, when the last embers of the torched synagogues were burning out, the Jews who had been selected for further persecution were trucked to Nuremberg, locked up in the same public building where Nazi war criminals, including Streicher himself, would later be put on trial, and then transported to Dachau. The rest were released—for the time being.

What happened in Fürth on Kristallnacht was repeated throughout the Third Reich—"more than a thousand cities, towns and villages," according to historian Martin Gilbert—and all according to the same set of orders that were dispatched by teletype and telephone from Munich within a few hours after the death of Ernst vom Rath.[20] The orders originated with Reichsführer-SS Heinrich Himmler and were circulated by his deputy, Reinhard Heydrich, and Gestapo chief, Heinrich Müller, the three men who commanded the elaborate security apparatus of the Third Reich.

"As soon as the events of this night make it feasible for the officials concerned, they are to arrest as many Jews—especially wealthy ones—in all districts as can be accommodated in existing cells," or so went the directive titled "Measures Against the Jews This Night." "For the time being, only healthy male Jews of not too advanced age are to be arrested. After the arrests have been carried out, concentration camps in the region are to be contacted immediately, to make arrangements for the transfer of the Jews to the camps as quickly as possible."[21] Another order, issued even earlier in the evening by Müller, specified an arrest quota of no fewer than 25,000 to 30,000 Jewish men for the night ahead.

The detailed specifications for what was to take place in the Third Reich on the night of November 9–10, and the speed with which the orders were circulated and carried out, are the best evidence that Kristallnacht was hardly a spontaneous eruption of righteous wrath. Indeed, just as the Sturmabteilung in Nuremberg was already supplied with iron bars, some intriguing suggestions have been made that an escalation of anti-Semitic violence was being planned long before Herschel Grynszpan bought a revolver and presented himself at the German embassy in Paris. Sooner or later, and with or without a high-profile pretext like the one that Grynszpan unwittingly provided, the Nazi machinery of violence would have been set into motion against the Jews.

As early as February 1938, for example, "a very reliable private source—one which can be traced back to the highest echelons of the SS leadership"—alerted the Zionist leadership in Palestine of "an intention to carry out a genuine and dramatic pogrom in Germany on a large scale in the near future."[22] According to the memoirs of Harry Naujoks, a German political prisoner in the concentration camp at Sachsenhausen, orders were issued in July 1938 to the unit in charge of prisoner uniforms to increase its inventory and, in particular, to manufacture "several hundred uniforms for heavy-set individuals"—an indication that wealthy (and presumably well-fed) Jewish men were expected soon. Naujoks, the foreman of the supply unit, also received extra bolts of yellow cloth to be used for fashioning the badges in the shape of a Star of David that were applied to the uniforms of Jewish prisoners. When he put the cloth into storage, he was "reprimanded and told immediately to prepare the identifying patches."[23]

Such preparations paid off, and the supply of uniforms and yellow Stars of David were soon put to use. The Gestapo's arrest quota was fulfilled with characteristic precision: 9,845 Jews were incarcerated in Buchenwald, 10,911 in Dachau, and approximately 9,000 in Sachsenhausen.*[24] A transport from Hanover, where the Grynszpan family had resided until the last days of October, contributed 316 Jewish men to the Jewish population of the camp at Buchenwald. Just as anticipated, the inmates included men who needed uniforms in larger sizes, and the SS guards singled out the overweight prisoners for verbal abuse and for physical ordeals that occasionally led to their deaths.

The Nazis themselves confirmed that 91 Jews were killed on Kristallnacht, and scholarship suggests that the death toll may have reached 236 men, women, and children. Some 2,000 more Jewish men died in the camps in the following months.[25] Some of the concentration camp inmates died of beatings or torture or exposure, some suffered heart attacks after the exertions of hard labor, some were deprived of essential medications, and some took their own lives by throwing themselves on the electrified wires that enclosed the camps. Back at home, other Jewish men and women, including a few Jewish families in their entirety, resorted to suicide out of despair over the sudden escalation in violence.

✦   ✦   ✦

AT LEAST 1,300 SYNAGOGUES were burned down, and some 7,500 Jewish-owned shops were vandalized. Indeed, it was the sight of glass shards in the streets of towns and cities across the Third Reich that inspired the term "Kristallnacht," which is conventionally rendered in English as "Night of Broken Glass." The word was probably

---

* These three concentration camps, already notorious even before Kristallnacht, had been established for the confinement, punishment, and murder of political enemies of the Nazi regime. Dachau, located near Munich in the state of Bavaria, opened within weeks after Hitler came to power in 1933, Sachsenhausen in 1936, and Buchenwald in 1937. Now, for the first time, the camps were repurposed for use in the war against the Jews.

invented by the burghers of Berlin, "who have long been known for their sardonic wit," rather than Joseph Goebbels, who is often credited with the coinage.[26] But the euphemism only serves to encourage "a discounting of grave reality," according to historian Walter Pehle, thus transforming "manslaughter and murder, arson and robbery, plunder and massive property damage [into] a glistening event marked by sparkle and gleam."[27] For that reason, some historians insist on calling Kristallnacht by other and blunter names: the "November pogrom" or the "Reich pogrom."[28]

The men of the SA were in the vanguard in the acts of violence that took place after the shooting of Rath, but the German populace soon followed their example. In the town of Bebra, for example, an SA member whose name is given in the postwar court records as Otto R. joined his comrades on the night of November 7 as they broke into the home of an elderly Jewish man identified as Siegfried A. and demanded that he "read and translate a Hebrew text that was held in front of him upside down."[29] But a middle-aged railroad conductor identified as Johannes L., who did not belong to the Nazi Party or the SA or any other Nazi organization, also joined the mob and participated in pouring a chamber pot over the head of a Jewish man identified as Herr K.

The violence escalated sharply over the night of November 9–10, when the formal orders were issued by Himmler, Heydrich, and Müller, and during the daylight hours of November 10, when the pogrom reached its peak. Some owners and managers of German businesses released their employees from work and sent them into the streets en masse to join in breaking and entering Jewish homes, beating up Jewish men and women, and torching synagogues. Kristallnacht also provided an opportunity for the children and adolescents of the Hitlerjugend (Hitler Youth) to put what they had been taught about Jew-hatred to practical use. "Similarly, classes of schoolchildren were marched from their schools," reports historian

Alan E. Steinweis in *Kristallnacht 1938*, "and set loose on Jewish targets, egged on by their teachers."[30]

The catalog of brutality and cruelty that constituted Kristallnacht is modest when compared with what was shortly to come, but it still managed to astound a world that had re-accustomed itself to the medievalism of the Third Reich. The 12,000 Polish Jews who were expelled from Germany in October, for example, had been allowed to dress, pack a few belongings, and—if Nazi propaganda is to be believed—dine on a rich array of delicacies before their train ride in passenger cars to the international border. By contrast, the Jewish victims of Kristallnacht were dragged out of their homes in their nightclothes, forced to walk barefoot on broken glass, and ordered to sing obscene songs in front of burning synagogues. Children at a Jewish orphanage were rousted from their beds and the building was set afire, and other children were arrested en masse as they sat in their classrooms. An old-age home was set afire with its occupants still inside. Ritual objects were piled up and burned, and beards were plucked out, hair by hair, or torn out in clumps. A rabbi was ordered to repeatedly recite the Kaddish—the mourner's prayer—in a holding pen full of Jews who had been told that they would all be shot at 4:00 a.m.

"Tonight it's a free-for-all," said the SA leader in Ober-Mockstadt to the young men under his command. "Tonight you can all let loose."[31]

Now and then, a random act of kindness apparently took place amid the carnage. "Dozens of Brownshirts displayed a certain embarrassment—to the point of developing an alarming stutter—at having been picked to knock up at five in the morning a family who for years had patronized their bakeries or tobacco shops," recalls Edgar Rosenberg about the events in Fürth. "Everybody liked Dr. Einhorn, the pediatrician—so much so that one of the Brownshirt gangsters, whose child Dr. Einhorn might have cured of the scarlatina or a whooping cough, said, 'Don't mind us, Dr. Einhorn, but they told us to smash something here. Anything in particular you wouldn't mind us smashing?'"[32]

Other Germans, however, took advantage of the chaos to avenge themselves upon the Jewish neighbors against whom they held petty grudges, sometimes more imagined than real. A thoroughly unfortunate Jewish cattle trader whose name is recorded as Max R. was carried by the mob in Abterode to the second floor of the local synagogue and dangled over the balcony railing; one of the rioters, who had a longstanding dispute with Max R. over the sum of thirty reichsmarks, chose that moment to collect the debt out of the pocket money that the terrified man was carrying. When he was finally released, Max R. hastened to the street and collapsed on the ground in exhaustion. Along came a young German woman called Martha S., whose family had settled a long-running lawsuit with Max R. on terms that still aggrieved them. "When she saw him on the street, she approached him, announced, 'This is for then,' and struck him hard on the side of the head."[33]

As the abuses and atrocities of Kristallnacht continued to play out across the Third Reich on Thursday, November 10, Adolf Hitler enjoyed a leisurely lunch at the Osteria in Munich—the same Italian restaurant where, five years earlier, Friedrich Reck-Malleczewen once pondered putting a bullet in the head of "the raw-vegetable Genghis Khan."[34] On that day in 1938, however, Hitler dined safely and sedately in the company of Joseph Goebbels, and the Führer issued a new set of orders about what was to happen now that the Jews had been given a taste of Nazi violence.

Hitler assured Goebbels that his plans for the solution of the Jewish Problem were "entirely radical and aggressive," or so Goebbels wrote in his diary, but the arson, looting, beatings, and killings must stop. Goebbels promptly issued a new directive through the DNB news service to implement the latest decision by the Führer.

"The justified and understandable outrage of the German people against the cowardly Jewish assassination of a German diplomat in Paris vented itself on a large scale last night," Goebbels announced. "A strict order is now being issued to the entire population to desist from all further demonstrations and actions against Jewry, regardless of what type. The definitive response to the Jewish assassination in Paris will be delivered to Jewry via the route of legislation and edicts."[35]

✦   ✦   ✦

A CERTAIN AWKWARDNESS VEXED the leaders of the Third Reich in the aftermath of Kristallnacht. Hundreds and perhaps thousands of "excesses" had taken place, as the Nazis themselves were forced to admit, and the fussier officials in the police and the courts felt obliged to do something about these wrongdoings.[36] The "excesses" included the brutal murder of at least ninety-one Jews, of course, but the Nazis were far more troubled by the acts of looting and, above all, the rape of Jewish women by men who belonged to the Nazi Party. After all, sexual contact of any kind between Germans and Jews had been a criminal act since the enactment of the Nuremberg Laws in 1935, and it would be unseemly for SA men to trifle with Jewish women under any circumstances.

To avoid the embarrassment of public investigations and trials, the whole matter was consigned to the secret apparatus of the Nazi Party itself. Several hundred men who had looted Jewish homes and shops were searched out by the Gestapo, but their misdeeds were forgiven and forgotten once they had turned in the loot. Only thirty men were actually put on trial before the so-called Nazi Party High Court under the oversight of Obergruppenführer-SS Walter Buch. The moral dilemma, as summarized by Buch in a secret report to Hermann Göring, was that the party members who committed these "excesses" were under the impression that they had been ordered—or, at the very least, permitted—to punish all of the Jews of Germany and Austria for the deed of one Jew in Paris, and the party could hardly blame them for their ardor, creativity, and diligence in doing so.

Still, the Nazi Party decided not to overlook the worst of their acts. Some of the storm troopers, for example, had committed what the Nazis regarded as the cardinal crime of miscegenation. Rather than taking revenge for the murder of Rath, as they were authorized to do, they had sought to satisfy their "lower instincts" by sexually abusing the Jewish women and girls whose homes they had invaded during Kristallnacht.[37] How many Jewish women were raped or otherwise sexually attacked over two days in a thousand German towns is not recorded, but the Nazi Party High Court put only four men on trial for such crimes.

Two SA men was found to have "sullied the honor of the movement" by forcing a Jewish woman to undress and then molesting her.[38] Another storm trooper was convicted of sexually attacking a thirteen-year-old girl. A fourth man was convicted of theft—the property he had stolen from a Jewish home, as the Nazis saw it, rightfully belonged to the state—as well as sexual assault on the woman whose home he had robbed. The punishment for all four of these men was expulsion from the Nazi Party. Lest they also be charged in the civil courts of the Third Reich by some overzealous state prosecutor, the Führer officially pardoned them. Then the secret files were sealed, and the matter was closed.

The same generous treatment was extended to all thirty men who were tried by the Nazi Party High Court. Significantly, the crime of murder was far less distressing to the judges than the crime of miscegenation. The "vast majority" of the men who were accused of murdering Jews on Kristallnacht were acquitted outright or subjected to disciplinary measures and punishments, and—unlike the rapists—none of them were expelled from the Nazi Party. These loyal Nazis, after all, were only following orders from their superiors, a morally acceptable defense in the Third Reich, and they "had been motivated by an understandable outrage at the murder of Ernst vom Rath."[39]

✦ ✦ ✦

BY WHATEVER NAME IT is called, however, Kristallnacht remains a point of debate among historians. Some scholars argue that it marks "a radical break" in Nazi policy and practice, and others insist that it was merely the next step in the anti-Semitic violence that began when the Nazis first came to power in Germany. Some, like Martin Gilbert, see it as "a violent mass action against the Jews [that] had been in the minds of the Nazi leaders for some time," and others, like Alan E. Steinweis, insist that it was "a massive improvisation."[40]

Yet they all agree that "the magnitude and barbarity of the Kristallnacht were unquestionably without precedent in Nazi Germany," as Steinweis observes in *Kristallnacht 1938*.[41] Indeed, the events of Kristallnacht provided hard evidence of a fearful idea that Herschel Grynszpan had already embraced: the Nazis recognized no bounds to the brutality and cruelty that they were willing to apply in order to rid the Third Reich (and the world) of Jews.

Kristallnacht was therefore merely a turning point and not an end in itself. To be sure, Herschel Grynszpan unwittingly provided the Third Reich with a convenient pretext for the events of November 9 and 10, and the Nazi propaganda machinery put his act of violence in Paris to good use. Beyond the fact that his name appeared in some of the official graffiti, however, Grynszpan cannot be reasonably blamed for Kristallnacht under any circumstance. As Hitler had signaled by the expulsion of 12,000 Polish Jews in October, the Third Reich had come to be dissatisfied with the pace of voluntary emigration, which had so far reduced the Jewish population of Germany by

only 130,000 (out of a total of 525,000). Harsher measures were to
be used to solve the Jewish Problem, especially now that the Jewish
population of the Third Reich had actually increased with the
annexation of Austria.

"The Jew will not be able to survive in Germany," Heinrich
Himmler vowed to a gathering of SS generals in Munich on the day
before Kristallnacht. "We will chase them out with unprecedented
ruthlessness."[42]

The Nazis achieved their tactical goal, and Jewish emigration
spiked after Kristallnacht. Another 118,000 Jews managed to leave
Germany in 1938 and 1939, nearly as many as had escaped over the
preceding five years. "With *Kristallnacht*, the Germans made clearer
than ever two things that everyone could discern: the Jews had no
place in Germany, and the Nazis wanted to spill Jewish blood,"
writes Daniel Jonah Goldhagen in one of the less controversial passages of *Hitler's Willing Executioners*. "As a general 'cleansing' of
Germany of Jewish synagogues, *Kristallnacht* was a proto-geno-
cidal assault."[43]

It is also true, however, that Hitler and his cohorts learned an
essential lesson from Kristallnacht. Order, after all, was a cherished value of Nazism: "Violent mob anti-Semitism must be
avoided," cautioned the 1934 memo that we have already considered. "One does not fight rats with guns but with poison and gas."[44]
Then, too, the Nazis sought every opportunity to rob their Jewish
victims before disposing of them, first by expulsion and later by
murder.

Only a few years after Kristallnacht, both principles would be
applied, quite literally, at Auschwitz, where gold fillings were dug
out of the mouths of Jewish corpses and hair was shaven from their
heads before they were transported from the gas chambers to the
crematoria. And so, on the morning after Kristallnacht, the sight of
shattered window glass and fire-blackened storefronts in the well-

tended streets of Austria and Germany was unsettling to some of the more calculating figures in the Nazi leadership.*

"Are you crazy, Goebbels?" complained Walter Funk, minister of economy. "Night and day I'm trying to conserve the national wealth, and you toss it out the window."[45]

Funk's outrage was shared by Hermann Göring. On Saturday, November 12, 1938, the second-ranking Nazi leader, whose numerous titles included that of plenipotentiary of the Four-Year Plan, convened a meeting of high Nazi officials at the Air Ministry— he was, of course, commander in chief of the Luftwaffe, too—to consider how to clean up the ruination caused by the Brownshirts on Kristallnacht. "I wish you had killed two hundred Jews instead of destroying so many valuables," Göring declared. "In the future, if we consider it necessary for demonstrations to take place, I beg you to see to it that they are directed so as not to wound us."[46]

Still, Göring saw a way to pay for the damage and, at the same time, ratchet up the pressure on the Jews of the Third Reich to emigrate. The idea dated back to the Gustloff assassination in 1936, when a collective fine was formally imposed on the Jewish population of the Third Reich but never actually collected. Now it was decreed that the Jewish community would be punished for the assassination of Rath—and would be required to pay for the damage resulting from the "spontaneous" eruption of anger that it supposedly inspired—with an "atonement payment" of one billion reischs-

---

* The tension between pragmatic bureaucrats and Nazi purists, which begins here, can be observed throughout the Second World War. Although some Jewish inmates were worked to death in German factories, the Nazis sought to exterminate the Jews within their reach rather than exploit them as a labor resource, and trains that were urgently needed to support the war effort were used instead to transport Jews to the death camps until late in the war.

marks that can be seen (and was perhaps intended) as a barbarous parody of the holiest day of the Jewish ritual calendar, Yom Kippur.*[47] "Our darling Jews," cracked Goebbels in yet another display of poisonous sarcasm, "will think twice in future before gunning down German diplomats."[48]

Significantly, the official registration of Jewish assets had been carried out more than six months before Kristallnacht "in wise anticipation of the Grünspan murder and its atonement," according to the wry diary entry by Victor Klemperer, who chronicled his experience of Jewish persecution throughout the Nazi era.[49] His suspicion, of course, is that the pogrom and its consequences were planned long in advance. Klemperer confirms, too, that the goal of Kristallnacht was to make the stresses and terror of life in Germany so odious that the Jews would hasten to depart. "Certainly things were getting manifestly worse and worse in the course of the year," he noted. "First the Austrian triumph. . . . Then in September the frustrated hope of a war that would deliver us. And then the decisive blow. Since the Grünspan affair the inferno."[50]

Additional punitive measures were enacted in the days after Kristallnacht to remind the remaining German Jews—as if they needed a reminder—that life in the Third Reich would be made unbearable. A Jew could no longer attend a concert, a circus, or a cinema. A Jew could not drive an automobile. And, significantly, a Jew could no longer own a weapon. After all, the shooting of Rath appeared to validate an old and familiar theme of Nazi propaganda—the notion that an international Jewish conspiracy was making war on the German people. So it was that Jews across Germany and Austria were now required to report to the local police

* One billion reichsmarks was equal to approximately US $400 million in 1938. Read and Fisher, 133.

stations and turn over their handguns, rifles, and shotguns.* At least one Jew in Fürth mounted a symbolic show of resistance.

"My father, instead of surrendering his Browning pistol to the police," recalls Edgar Rosenberg, "tossed it into the exceedingly dirty Pegnitz River."[51]

The decision to dispose of a now illegal weapon rather than conceal it reveals something crucial and profound about the mind-set of European Jews in general and German Jews in particular. Hundreds and perhaps thousands of Jewish households in Germany possessed weapons—war souvenirs that recalled service in the Great War, sporting and hunting weapons, and handguns that were carried for self-defense. A time would come soon when the ghetto fighters in eastern Europe would risk their lives to add a single battered weapon to their tragically sparse arsenals, and yet the thought did not occur to Rosenberg's father—or any great number of the Jews of the Third Reich—that they might one day need a weapon to defend themselves against the government that sent the Brownshirts into the street on Kristallnacht.

+ + +

WHILE JEWISH BODIES WERE accumulating across Germany, the corpse of the minor German diplomat named Rath was still in France. Soon after his death at the Clinique d'Alma, the remains were moved to a mortuary near the German embassy on the rue de Lille, where his fellow diplomats maintained a vigil throughout the night. The coffin was draped with a commodious Nazi flag and flo-

---

* On November 27, 1938, two policemen showed up at Victor Klemperer's house in Dresden. "Did I have any weapons?—Certainly my saber, perhaps even my bayonet as a war memento, but I wouldn't know where. . . . The saber was found in a suitcase in the attic, the bayonet was not found." See Klemperer, *I Will Bear Witness: A Diary of the Nazi Years, 1933–1941*, trans. Martin Chalmers (New York: Modern Library, 1998), 275.

ral wreaths sent by the governments of France and Italy. On November 12, the body was moved to the German Lutheran Church on the rue Blanche for a religious service that was attended by the foreign minister of France, Georges Bonnet, and emissaries of the French president and prime minister. The German contingent was headed by Ernst von Weizsäcker, state secretary in the Foreign Ministry, who delivered a funeral oration in which he described Rath as "the first martyr to fall for the Third Reich" in diplomatic service.

"Commence the journey to the homeland," cried Weizsäcker with the bombast that was a Nazi habit of mind. "All Germany awaits you!"[52]

Not until the following Tuesday did the coffin, loaded onto a catafalque, commence its solemn journey home. At 10:15 p.m. on November 15, it was placed aboard a special French train at the Gare de l'Est, the bustling railroad terminal that stood not far from the apartment where Herschel Grynszpan had lived and the hotel where he spent his last night before the assassination. Ambassador Welczeck, who had unwittingly encountered Herschel Grynszpan at the embassy on that day, now ceremoniously boarded the train along with the dead man's family and various other official attendants and emissaries.

At dawn on the next day, the train reached the German frontier, and there began the grand spectacle that had been planned for the newly elevated martyr of the Third Reich. Like a funeral cortege for a head of state, the train carried its passengers at the stately pace of twelve miles per hour through the stations, where black bunting had been mounted and the Nazi flags fluttered at half-mast in the breeze. Various units of the Nazi Party, some of whom had bloodied themselves on Kristallnacht, now stood at attention in dress uniforms along the route. The weather provided a suitably grim scrim of heavy fog. When the train reached the historic frontier town of Aachen, the coffin was moved to a German train for the last leg to Düsseldorf, where the coffin was placed on a caisson for the final ride to an arena known as the Rheinhalle, some two miles away. The body lay in state for the rest of the day as the crowds filed by in two orderly lines to pay their respects to the slain young diplomat.

The funeral of Ernst vom Rath inspired a maximum effort by the German propaganda apparatus. The scale of the ceremony would have been suitable for a kaiser's funeral in bygone days, but the iconography was purely Nazi. A vast hall was bedecked with swastika banners, and the flag-draped coffin was displayed on a bier. Four uniformed figures—representing the SA, the SS, the Hitler Youth, and the Wehrmacht—stood at attention at each corner of the coffin. Behind the coffin was an outsized gold eagle with a swastika in its talons, and Rath's party badges and decorations were displayed on a black velvet cushion at the foot of the coffin. Floral wreaths and light standards were placed around the bier, and the whole tableaux was singled out with spotlights in the otherwise darkened hall. Now and then, the scene was bathed in a momentary light from a flashbulb as the photographers captured the scene, not only for the daily newspapers but also for the thousand-year history of the Third Reich.

The spectacle reached the zenith of its cadaverous splendor on Thursday, November 17, when Adolf Hitler arrived at noon to join the fifteen hundred mourners at the state funeral that had been painstakingly organized and was now being broadcast live on radio stations across the Third Reich. The Führer entered the Rheinhalle, paused piously in front of the bier, and then took his seat in the front row next to the parents of the slain man. Perhaps out of respect for their bereavement—or maybe because of the rumored friction between the Rath family and the Nazi regime—the Führer did not speak a word to the grieving mother and father.

The service was accompanied by the strains of the funeral march from Beethoven's *Eroica* symphony, a favorite trope of Nazi dramaturgy to signify moments of solemnity. Hitler himself, however, remained silent. The oration was delivered by a functionary of the Foreign Office, Gruppenführer-SS Ernst Wilhelm Bohle, who now confirmed the place in the Nazi firmament that had been assigned to Rath. Along with Wilhelm Gustloff and a few Nazis who had served in the German expeditionary force during the Spanish Civil War, Ernst vom Rath was embraced as a blood martyr: "The shots fired in Davos, Barcelona, and Paris," averred Bohle, "are aimed at the Third Reich." His implied threat was made explicit by the next speaker, Joachim von Ribbentrop, the former champagne peddler who now served as Nazi foreign minister.

"We understand the challenge," said Ribbentrop, pointedly quoting the very words that Hitler had uttered at the funeral of Gustloff in 1936, "and we accept it."[53]

The funeral service closed with the playing of the familiar strains of the German national anthem: *"Deutschland, Deutschland über alles . . ."* Hitler rose from his front-row seat, muttered a hasty condolence to the Rath family and offered a trademark Roman salute to the crowd. Then he hastened out of the hall. The Führer was long gone by the time the body of Rath was carried to the cemetery on a gun carriage and interred in the family burial plot to the sound of rifle shots fired in salute, a Nazi flag still draped over the coffin.

Hitler, in fact, never wrote or uttered a single word for public consumption about the Grynszpan affair. His public silence notwithstanding, Hitler would have much to say in private about the fate of the seventeen-year-old Jewish boy who put Rath into the grave.

✦   ✦   ✦

AT THE FÜHRER'S BIDDING, Joseph Goebbels carried out an elaborate propaganda campaign whose goal was to convince the German people and perhaps even an international audience that Herschel Grynszpan—the son of a poor Jewish tailor from Hanover, an overwrought adolescent given to anxieties and fantasies and perhaps even paranoid delusions, someone who had never fired or even held a gun until the day he entered the Germany embassy in Paris—was the cunning agent of a vast Jewish conspiracy, like something out of the febrile pages of *The Protocols of the Elders of Zion*.

His mission, the Nazis insisted, had been to provoke a war between France and Germany. The means to achieve his strategic goal was to carry out a sanguinary act of terrorism against Ernst vom Rath. The master he served was the bogeyman who haunted Hitler's imagination, a shadowy villain that he called "World Jewry." So the real target of the shots he had fired on the rue de Lille was not a single diplomat but the German people. The Nazi line was wholly plausible to an increasingly pusillanimous French government: "The impression must not be allowed to grow that the French Jews want war to avenge their luckless brethren in Germany," lectured Foreign Minister Bonnet, a man long and thoroughly cowed by Nazi Germany, to Baron de Rothschild, an iconic figure of the Jewish community in France.[54]

Grynszpan, who proclaimed himself to be a figure of significance in world history, only stoked the anxieties of appeasers like Bonnet. Ironically, if the Jews of Germany had recognized Herschel Grynszpan in the role that he assigned to himself, the Nazi propaganda line might have seemed more credible. After all, thousands of Jewish men in Germany and Austria were combat veterans of World War I. Many of them, like Edgar Rosenberg's father, owned weapons and, quite in contrast to Grynszpan himself, knew how to use them. Virtually without exception, however, Herschel's fellow Jews across the world publicly rejected him and rushed to distance themselves from his act of violent protest against Nazi Germany.

A thousand years of struggle to survive in the Diaspora had taught the Jewish people an entirely different strategy for coping with anti-Semitic violence. Ironically, no one understood the habits of mind of the Jewish population better than the Nazis themselves, and they planned and executed the destruction of the Jewish people with no real anxiety that they would follow Grynszpan's example. After all, Edgar Rosenberg's father back in Fürth did not hide his Browning so that he could use it to defend himself; rather, he threw it into the river in silent and hapless protest against his persecutors. If Herschel Grynszpan meant to strike a spark of resistance among his fellow Jews, his effort produced the opposite result.

"To compensate for lost national autonomy, the religious tradition elevated powerlessness into a positive Jewish value," explains Lucy Dawidowicz in *The War Against the Jews, 1933–1945*. "It fostered submissiveness and cautioned against rash rebellion. 'The Holy Spirit says, I adjure you that if the earthly kingdom decrees persecutions, you shall not rebel in all that it decrees against you, but you shall keep the king's command.'" During the years leading up to Kristallnacht, according to Dawidowicz, and arguably long thereafter, "the general strategy was for Jews to hold on and hold out, while their leaders, through official negotiations, backstairs bargaining, and petition, sought to protect the Emancipation."[55]

One deeply characteristic impulse among the Jews of the Diaspora, in fact, was to inquire anxiously about the Jewish affiliation of anyone whose misdeeds came to public attention, whether it was a child murderer, a financial speculator, or a crooked politician.* If it turned out that the malefactor was *not* Jewish, they would express relief that the Gentiles would be denied yet another excuse for victimizing the Jewish community: "At least he wasn't a Jew!" When it came to Grynszpan, however, the assassin was not only Jewish; he

---

* "'It's a shame for the people' was Nanny's line about any Jewish person who committed a crime, lapsed in behavior, or called attention to themselves," recalled Alice Kaplan about her grandmother, an immigrant from eastern Europe, in *French Lessons: A Memoir* (Chicago: University of Chicago Press, 1993), 11.

had even announced that his motive was to punish Germany for its mistreatment of the Jews.

For that reason, among the Jews themselves in Germany and elsewhere, Herschel Grynszpan's act of revenge was seen mostly as a catastrophe that was sure to bring down even more suffering on the Jewish population of the Third Reich—and Kristallnacht convinced them that they were right. Although some Jewish organizations assisted Herschel Grynszpan and his family in hiring attorneys to defend them in the French courts, Jewish community leaders and Jewish newspapers rushed to disavow his deed.

"We remain faithful to the inalienable integrity of the human person and reject once again all form of violence, regardless of author or victim of such an act," stated the Alliance Israélite Universelle, a leading organization of French Jews. "We condemn the act of homicide which resulted in the loss of a German official and indignantly protest the barbarous treatment inflicted on an entire innocent population which was made the scape-goat for the crime of an individual."[56] In a remarkable example of the apologetic and self-effacing stance that had long been a coping mechanism in the Diaspora, a leading Jewish newspaper in Paris, L'Univers Israélite, published an open letter to Rath's mother in which the editorialist "expressed great sorrow on the death of her son" and implored her that "it was unjust to blame all Jews for her son's death."[57]

Even those who were stirred by Grynszpan's act of resistance to Nazism were quick to condemn it. Writing from his latest place of exile in Mexico, Leon Trotsky—the founder of the Red Army and, not incidentally, a Jew—affirmed his "open moral solidarity" with the young man and conceded, "What is most astonishing is that so far there has been only one Grynszpan." But even Trotsky insisted that his daring act of armed resistance to the Third Reich was, as he delicately put it, "inexpedient." Rather than "convulsive acts of despair and vengeance," he wrote in a New York newspaper, the correct path was collective action against both Stalinism and Hitlerism: "Not the lone avenger," concluded Trotsky, "but only a great revolutionary mass movement can free the oppressed."[58]

Meanwhile, Herschel Grynszpan himself was living behind bars in a section of the prison at Fresnes, a few miles south of Paris, where juvenile offenders were incarcerated. Although his old stomach troubles had flared up again, surely exacerbated by the heightened stress and anxiety, Herschel was regarded by his guards and fellow prisoners as a polite and amiable young man, accomplished at table tennis and chess, but not especially forthcoming about the remarkable circumstances that had landed him there. Indeed, Herschel was fully aware that he had little in common with the boys whose crimes were ordinary acts of delinquency—theft, vandalism, assault, and the like. Alone among them, he was an authentic celebrity, a role that he sought, exploited, and now acted upon, as if he had been preparing for such a spectacular debut on the stage of history all along.

Another fact that set Herschel apart from the other young prisoners at Fresnes was the parade of attorneys and family members who presented themselves at the gate to confer with him in the weeks and months that followed the assassination of Rath. The attention they paid to his case only served to confirm and perhaps even to inflate Herschel's sense of self-importance and to reinforce his delusions of grandeur. "I must protest so that the whole world hears my protest and this I intend to do," he had written to his parents on the day of the assassination. Now he recorded in his prison diary, with not a trace of megalomania, exactly what his callers had told him: "They gave me money so I could procure the special food I wanted, and they told me not to worry at all since the whole world was behind me."[59]

7

HIGHER POWERS

E VERY SUNDAY EVENING AT 9:00 IN THE AUTUMN OF 1938, five million Americans listened to the weekly broadcast of *The General Electric Program* on the NBC Red Network. The show opened with the big-band music of Phil Spitalny and His All-Girl Orchestra, featuring Evelyn and Her Magic Violin, but one of the featured female voices belonged to Dorothy Thompson, the "First Lady of American Journalism," whose news commentaries injected a distinct note of alarm into the otherwise lighthearted banter, comedy, and music.

Thompson had first achieved a measure of success when she managed to secure an opportunity to interview Adolf Hitler and followed up with a best-selling book titled *I Saw Hitler!* in 1932. Her dispatches from "Hitler's Kingdom," as she described Germany, so vexed the Führer that he expelled her in 1934. "Ironically, her expulsion turned her into an international celebrity," writes Thompson biographer Susan Hertog, "a martyr to the anti-Nazi cause."[1] Back in the United States, she started writing a syndicated column, "On the Record," and she was paired with Eleanor Roosevelt as "undoubtedly the most influential women in the U.S.," according to a *Time* magazine cover story in 1939.[2] Indeed, Thompson was such a famous (and acerbic) critic of the Third Reich that *The New Yorker* published a cartoon in which a woman is shown to address a question to her husband as he reads the newspaper: "Has Germany answered Dorothy Thompson yet?"[3]

"It is humiliating and irritating that such idiotic females, whose brains can consist only of straw," sputtered Joseph Goebbels in a diary entry, "have the right to speak at all in public against a historic figure of the greatness of the Führer."[4]

Thompson had her own claims on history. She had started her career as an activist in the suffrage movement, earned her credentials as a foreign correspondent in various trouble spots around Europe during the 1920s, and reported from Berlin on the Nazis' rise to power in the early 1930s. With her bobbed hair and energetic good looks, she fit the role of the hard-edged newspaperwoman, but she was just as commanding in the company of her husband, Nobel Prize–winning novelist Sinclair Lewis, in the literary salons of Paris, London, or New York. Now that she was a broadcaster on a leading radio network, the cutting-edge mass medium of the 1930s, she was an authentic celebrity.

Thompson's commentary on the broadcast of November 14, 1938, focused on the seventeen-year-old Jewish youth whose deed the Nazis blamed for the "spontaneous demonstrations" of Kristallnacht, an event that was still resonating in the headlines that night. She was almost alone among non-Jewish American intellectuals in her support of European Jewry in the 1930s, and now she boldly turned the blame for Kristallnacht back on Nazi Germany and implored the world to look on Herschel Grynszpan—"an anaemic-looking boy with brooding black eyes"—as a victim rather than a perpetrator.

"I want to talk about that boy," said Thompson to her listeners. "I feel as though I knew him, for in the past five years I have met so many whose story is the same—the same except for this unique desperate act. Herschel Grynszpan was one of the hundreds of thousands of refugees whom the terror east of the Rhine has turned loose in the world."[5]

Thompson did not excuse his act of violence in the German embassy, but neither did she apologize for it. "Herschel read the newspapers, and all that he could read filled him with dark anxiety and wild despair," declared Thompson. "But is there not a higher justice in the case of Herschel Grynszpan, seventeen years old? Is there not a higher justice that says that this deed has been expiated with four hundred million dollars and half a million existences, with beatings, and burnings, and deaths, and suicides? Must the nation, whose Zola defended Dreyfus until the world rang with it, cut off the head of one more Jew without giving him an open trial?"[6]

The rhetorical appeal to "higher justice" for an acccused assassin, of course, had been made before and under strikingly similar circumstances. The defenders of Sholom Schwartzbard, who shot the Ukrainian pogromist Simon Petliura on the streets of Paris in 1926, had succeeded in securing an acquittal on the same argument. The defenders of David Frankfurter, who shot the Nazi emissary Wilhelm Gustloff in Davos in 1936, had tried but failed. Now Thompson previewed the theory of defense that she advocated in the Grynszpan case.

"Who is on trial in this case?" insisted Thompson. "I say we are all on trial. I say the Christian world is on trial."

Thompson reminded her radio audience that the survival of the remaining Jewish population of Germany and Austria depended on how the rest of the world approached the Grynszpan case. "No man of his race, anywhere in the world, can defend him," she argued. "The Nazi government has announced that if any Jews, anywhere in the world, protest at anything that is happening, further oppressive measures will be taken. They are holding every Jew in Germany as a hostage." For that reason, she asserted, Christian morality demands

that the Jewish people be relieved of the burden of defending Herschel Gryszpan.

"Therefore, we who are not Jews must speak, speak our sorrow
and indignation and disgust in so many voices that they will be
heard," concluded Thompson. "This boy has become a symbol,
and the responsibility for his deed must be shared by those who
caused it."[7]

So Thomson, the daughter of a Methodist minister, took it upon
herself to champion the cause of Herschel Grynszpan. She devoted
two installments of her newspaper column, "On the Record," to the
Grynszpan case, and she wrote so movingly of his plight that her
readers were inspired to send some three thousand telegrams and
"uncounted" letters in support.[8] Many of them added a small dona-
tion to pay for his legal defense, and Thompson was inspired to
organize the Journalists' Defense Fund to raise additional funds.

She set up an office on Fifth Avenue in New York and recruited
other celebrity journalists to the cause, including fellow columnists
Heywood Broun, Westbrook Pegler, and Alexander Woollcott, the
curmudgeonly Broadway critic who was the inspiration for similar
characters in *The Man Who Came to Dinner* in 1939 and *Laura* in
1944. So the obscure young man who had once written an unanswered letter of appeal to Franklin Delano Roosevelt now enjoyed
the public attention of some famous supporters, among them Alice
Roosevelt Longworth, the daughter of Theodore Roosevelt and a
cousin of the current American president.

Significantly, as she observed during her broadcast on November
14, Thompson's crusade was to be *Judenrein*. She understood the
deeply conspiratorial tendencies of the Nazi mind, and she stressed
that she would refuse to accept contributions from Jews "so the
Nazis can't say this is another Jewish plot."[9] Later, she insisted on
the appointment of a non-Jewish attorney to represent Herschel
Grynszpan, and her choice was Vincent de Moro-Giafferi, a French-

man of Corsican descent. A colorful character with generous jowls, a handlebar mustache, and a monocle, he was something of a celebrity in his own right in France.

Thompson's earnest effort to inoculate the Grynszpan defense against charges of Jewish manipulation, however, came too late to prevent the Nazis from characterizing the assassination of Ernst vom Rath as the latest act of a vast, shadowy, and sinister Jewish conspiracy. No idea was more firmly rooted in the imagination of Hitler and the official ideology of the Nazi Party than the notion that "international Jewry" was the deadly enemy of the German people. The spindly adolescent with the nervous stomach who now occupied a cell in Fresnes prison was, as the Nazis shrilly proclaimed, the chosen and paid agent of a relentless conspiracy whose bloody hand they detected in every era of world history and every aspect of world affairs. Hitler and his servitors resolved to make their own case against "the Jew Grynszpan," as he was invariably called in the diaries of Goebbels and the abundant Nazi propaganda.[10]

Nor were the Nazis the only ones to look on the Grynszpan case as the handiwork of plotters. A great many conspiracy theories would attach themselves to *l'affaire Grynszpan* and turn the shooting into something far stranger than the idée fixe that had impelled the boy's act in the first place.

✦   ✦   ✦

ON THE DAY AFTER the shooting of Rath, Judge Jean Tesnière was appointed to serve as the chief examining magistrate in the Grynszpan matter, thus officially setting in motion the criminal investigation and prosecution of the self-confessed assassin by the government of France. Tesnière, a seasoned and well-regarded jurist who specialized in cases involving juvenile offenders, was responsible for gathering and evaluating the evidence against Grynszpan, determining whether an indictment was justified, and preparing the case for a formal trial where his guilt or innocence would be decided and, if found guilty, a sentence would be imposed.

At the first of many hearings in the case, which took place barely twenty-four hours after the assassination, Herschel appeared in Judge Tesnière's chambers in the company of two attorneys— H. Szwarc and R. de Vésinne-Larue—who had been hastily recruited to represent him. Since Herschel spoke French only haltingly, the services of a Yiddish-speaking lawyer were deemed essential by the Grynszpan family. Herschel's plight had not yet caught the attention of Dorothy Thompson, and so it was up to the relatives in Paris to find someone appropriate. And it was only by accident that these two obscure attorneys had been identified and hired in time to accompany Herschel into the chambers of the examining magistrate.

The task of finding a lawyer for Herschel fell to Uncle Salomon because, immediately after Uncle Abraham and Aunt Chava had been questioned by the police, they, too, were arrested and jailed on charges of illegally harboring an illegal and, even more ominously, on suspicion of their complicity in the assassination—the earliest stirring of a conspiracy theory in the Grynszpan case. When Salomon first learned of the arrests, he hastened to the local courthouse, searching for the only lawyer he knew by name—a man named Isidore Fränkel—but when Fränkel could not be found, Salomon accepted a stranger's suggestion to talk to a fellow called Szwarc. The case was so daunting to Szwarc that he pressed Salomon to hire a second lawyer, and so it was that the two-man defense team was first deployed.

As it happened, Judge Tesnière, a fluent German speaker, required no translators in order to interrogate the accused and even "helped him find the right words."[11] According to an account of the case that appeared in the Paris newspaper *Le Temps*, Grynszpan was able to achieve the same eloquence that characterized all of his public utterances and writings. "It was not with hatred or for vengeance against any particular person that I acted, but because of love for my parents and for my people who were unjustly subjected to outrageous treatment," Grynszpan was quoted as saying. "Nevertheless, this act was distasteful to me and I deeply regret it. However, I had no other means of demonstrating my feelings."[12]

Grynszpan revealed nothing that suggested the existence of a conspiracy, but he readily conceded that he had been afflicted by the fate of his family and his people under Nazi rule.

"It was the constantly gnawing idea of the suffering of my race which obsessed me," Grynszpan continued. "For 28 years my parents resided in Hanover. They had set up a modest business which was destroyed overnight. They were stripped of everything and expelled. It is not, after all, a crime to be Jewish. I am not a dog. I have the right to live. My people have a right to exist on this earth. And yet everywhere they are hunted down like animals."[13]

At this point in the two-hour hearing, Herschel began to subtly revise the account he had given so readily at the scene of the crime. Whether relying on his own acute instincts or prompted by his newly engaged attorneys, he now introduced a few crucial notions that would be helpful in setting up a legal defense—he had not acted with premeditation when he called at the German embassy, he had not intended to take a life, and he fired his gun only after being provoked into a blind rage by his victim, or so he now told Judge Tesnière.

"I did not wish to kill," said Herschel. "When I committed that act, I was obeying a superior and inexplicable force. What's more, vom Rath, the secretary at the embassy, called me a dirty Jew."

"Was that before or after the shooting?' asked the alert and discerning judge.

"I couldn't tell you exactly," demurred the cagey young suspect. "My mind was in a great emotional turmoil."[14]

The only decision that Judge Tesnière was empowered to make at the first hearing was whether or not to keep the accused in custody. The criminal charge was merely attempted murder so long as the wounded Rath was still alive, but the question was never really in doubt. Herschel Grynszpan was sent to Fresnes prison, and the formal investigation by the French authorities continued. And, while the chief examining magistrate pondered the suspicions and contradictions that accumulated in the case files, so did the journalists, politicians, and prominent intellectuals who monitored *l'affaire Grynszpan* in Paris, Berlin, New York, and elsewhere.

✦   ✦   ✦

ONCE ERNST VOM RATH died of his wounds, the case against Herschel Grynszpan was automatically elevated to the high crime of murder, an offense that carried a potential death sentence in France. The Grynszpan family may have consisted of Yiddish-speaking refugees from Poland who were far more at ease behind a sewing machine in Belleville than in a magistrate's office or a French courtroom, but they quickly grasped that the criminal proceedings against their young nephew had taken on new meanings and dimensions, all of them dire.

With Abraham and Chava Grynszpan already in jail on charges of harboring an illegal alien, Salomon Grynszpan convened an informal family council to assist him in making decisions. The other members were in-laws of the Grynszpan family—Abraham Berenbaum, Chava Grynszpan's brother, and Jacques Wikhodz, Chava's brother-in-law. All of them quickly agreed that Szwarc and Vésinne-Larue were the wrong lawyers for Herschel, if only because they lacked the stature and sophistication that the case clearly demanded. They agreed to approach the most famous advocate of progressive causes in France, Vincent de Moro-Giafferi, the same bejowled Corsican attorney whom Thompson favored. Significantly, and crucially, Maître de Moro-Giafferi had seen only a single client go to the guillotine over his long and celebrated career as a criminal defense attorney.

On November 10, Salomon Grynszpan addressed a polite but firm letter to Moro-Giafferi: "I have the honor to request that you assume the defense of my nephew Herschel Grynszpan," he wrote. "I have decided to dispense with the services of the two attorneys, MM. Szwarc and Vésinne-Larue, whom I had engaged initially. At the same time I request that MM. Frankel and Erlich, who speak Yiddish, work with you."[15]

Not until November 14, however, did the members of the family council make their way to Fresnes prison to confer with Herschel himself. By now, Herschel was already settling into the routine of prison life in the "re-education center" where juvenile offenders were confined, and he was keeping a daily journal at the behest of the jailors who managed the lives of the young inmates. The journal keeping was meant to encourage juvenile delinquents to reflect on their lives of crime and thus assist in their rehabilitation—and to provide raw material for inspection by psychiatrists and social workers—but Herschel's entries in his prison diary were far more grandiloquent than those of the thieves and thugs who were his cellmates.

"They greeted me in the name of my family and in the name of World Jewry for whom I had risked my life," he wrote of his conference with the delegation of uncles. "Then they explained why they had come to see me. They told me that my trial would be an important one, and that because of it, I ought to have the best lawyer in France, de Moro-Giafferi."

Herschel said no.

"For reasons of my own, I did not want him," he recorded, although he did not confide his reasons to his diary. "Then I made a proposal, and said, 'If you can arrange to have my dear parents and my sister and brother come to Paris, then I will choose de Moro-Giafferi as my lawyer.' They answered my proposal by swearing on the heads of their children that as soon as I had appointed that lawyer to defend me, my parents would come to Paris in less than two weeks with the assistance of the lawyer, and that my parents would then come visit me at once."[16]

Nothing quite captures the strange and superheated family dynamics of the Grynszpans—and the vaunting self-regard of seventeen-year-old Herschel—as well as the meeting that was conducted in a visitor's room behind the walls of Fresnes prison. Accused of a capital crime, utterly penniless and powerless, vilified by the vast propaganda apparatus of the Third Reich and reviled in almost all Jewish circles for bringing down a catastrophe of nearly biblical magnitude on his fellow Jews in Germany and Austria, Herschel had the chutzpah to turn down the services of a leading French attorney whose skill and celebrity might be able to spare him from the guillotine.

His refusal, of course, was only a thin ploy to extract a promise that neither the Grynszpans nor even the renowned Moro-Giafferi could make or keep. In yet another example of magical thinking, the boy expected his three uncles to interpose themselves between the embattled nations of Germany and Poland at a moment of international crisis, to extract 4 of the 12,000 interned refugees from the chaos of the camp at Zbąszyń, and to bring them across Europe to Paris at a moment when all refugees from Germany—and Jewish refugees above all—were regarded by some French politicians and journalists as both wretched and dangerous.

Yet Uncle Salomon and his brothers-in-law were apparently willing to offer the preposterous promise that their young nephew demanded and to seal it with nothing less than a vow "on the heads of their children." The overwrought phrase reminds us of the guilt-tripping letter that Grandma Gika Grynszpan sent from Radomsk to her sons in Paris: "Believe me, I am crying as I write this letter. Why do you treat me this way? Every day I await an answer from you."[17]

And it allows us to imagine the vows and threats that must have been exchanged in Uncle Abraham's apartment on the night before the assassination—a heated family argument that was now taking on calamitous implications for the fate of Abraham and Chava Grynszpan, who were themselves suspected of playing a role in the assassination.

Once the uncles offered the promise he sought, Herschel finally consented to the engagement of Moro-Giafferi as the lead attorney. A few days later, Dorothy Thompson sent her own emissary—Edgar Ansel Mowrer, Paris bureau chief of the *Chicago Daily News*—to offer Moro-Giafferi the financial support of the Journalists' Defense Fund. But Mowrer, too, had reasons to dissent: "Moro is considered here as being extreme left," he told Thompson, and he charges "prodigious fees." Yet Mowrer agreed to carry out the mission, and he reassured Thompson that her ulterior motive—a defense of Herschel Grynszpan based on an appeal to "higher justice"—would be well served by Moro-Giafferi.

"He is one of the big shots," conceded Mowrer, "and will do a good job and manage to put Hitler in the prisoners' dock."[18]

✦   ✦   ✦

ADOLF HITLER, TOO, DEEMED it necessary to hire an attorney to represent his own interests in the Grynszpan case.

On the day after the shooting, Hitler issued a special decree by which the matter was entrusted to Friedrich Grimm, a German trial attorney and a professor of international law with a command of the French language and an expertise in court cases in which the honor of Nazi Germany was deemed to be at stake. Herr Professor Doktor Grimm had, for example, represented the legal interests of the Third Reich in the Swiss trial of David Frankfurter for the assassination of Wilhelm Gustloff, and now he was called upon to do the same in the Grynszpan case.

A unique feature of European law afforded Nazi Germany a point of entry into the Grynszpan case as it had in the Gustloff case. France and Switzerland both allowed a party with a stake in the outcome of a criminal trial—a so-called *partie civile*—to be represented by counsel in the proceedings. Only the victim of a crime (or, in the case of murder, the victim's family) was entitled to participate as a *partie civile*, however, and so the Rath family was pressed into service as a surrogate for the Third Reich. Although Gustav vom Rath, father of the slain diplomatic subaltern, was the nominal *partie civile*, Grimm's real clients were to be Adolf Hitler and the government of Nazi Germany.

At the same time, a second Nazi functionary was charged with masterminding the German propaganda interests in the prosecution of Herschel Grynszpan in collaboration with Grimm. Wolfgang Diewerge, who held the rank of minister-counselor in the Propaganda Ministry, was a specialist in "anti-Jewish propaganda" and, like Grimm, a seasoned veteran of the Nazi war of words against the Jews. Indeed, the team of Grimm and Diewerge had previously worked together in stage-managing the Frankfurter case in 1936, and now they were assigned to perform exactly the same role in the Grynszpan case.

Both men, for example, had penned propaganda tracts in 1936 to explain and support the Nazi stance toward Frankfurter, the assassin of Gustloff. Grimm's effort was titled *Political Association and Hero Worship* and Diewerge's pamphlet carried a plainer and more provocative title: *A Jew Has Fired*. At the very first strategy meeting on the Grynszpan case, which was conducted in Berlin on November 11, 1938, it was proposed that both tracts be urgently translated into French and published in Paris—the first effort by Nazi Germany to suggest that both incidents were manifestations of an international Jewish conspiracy.

Grimm was responsible for the legal technicalities of the Grynszpan case. Extradition of Herschel Grynszpan for trial in the Third Reich—the ideal approach from the Nazi point of view—was "out of the question under French law" precisely because Grynszpan, ironically, had never been granted German citizenship and because his crime might be characterized by the French as a political offense, both of which grounds ruled out extradition. Grimm aspired to participate directly in the French judicial proceedings, but he was prepared to engage the services of a friendly French trial attorney—and content himself with the role of "technical advisor"—if he was not permitted to do so.[19] His mission was to encourage the French government to put Grynszpan on trial, convict him of a capital crime, and punish him, all as quickly as possible and without allowing the defense to introduce any evidence of the anti-Semitic atrocities that had driven Grynszpan to his deed.

Diewerge's task was to mine the rich lode of propaganda gold that shot through the Grynszpan case. We have already seen an example of his handiwork: the long list of comestibles that were supposedly provided to Jewish deportees at the Hanover train station on the night of their expulsion—and the account of how the SS carried their hand luggage from the train to the Polish frontier—appeared in a report that Diewerge prepared as a rebuttal to the dispatches that had appeared in newspaper around the world. Now he urgently petitioned Joseph Goebbels for an enhanced budget and an expanded office staff to support his own efforts to use the trial of Herschel Grynszpan to validate a single overarching theme: "Exposure of World Jewry as the initiator of vom Rath's murder by which the Fuehrer's peace policy was to be frustrated."[20]

Rather like the state funeral of Rath, where every moment and every detail was meticulously planned and presented to the public eye, the Nazi accounts of the Herschel Grynszpan case were masterminded by Diewerge and his colleagues. A photographer was sent into the hastily abandoned apartment of Zindel and Rivka Grynszpan in Hanover to show that it had not been vandalized—"Today everything is still as it was," was the caption on a Propaganda Ministry pamphlet that was published in 1939—and five thoroughly terrorized members of the Hanover Synagogue were marched into the apartment, where they were made to swear in the presence of a notary that they had found it "in perfect condition."[21]

The legal aspects of the case were given the same exacting attention. The civil court in Hanover formally appointed a man called Max Israel Sternheim—by then, of course, the law required every Jew in the Third Reich to append a Jewish name to his German one—to act as the trustee of the property that the Grynszpan family had left behind on the night of their expulsion. Sternheim was made to address a letter to the Grynszpans in the refugee camp in Zbąszyń, "asking for instructions regarding where to send items such as linens, beds, dishes, clothing, a sewing machine, and other household goods." The trustee received a reply from Zindel's mother, Gika, who reported that "she could not get in touch with her son who was abroad," referring to the same son who had previously refused to respond to her imploring letters.[22]

All of these extraordinary efforts to suggest that the Grynszpans had not been abused were meant to counter the charges of critics like Dorothy Thompson—"an anti-German in 'Christian-humanitarian disguise,'" according to Grimm. [23] At the same time, however, a campaign of defamation was undertaken to depict Herschel Grynszpan and his relations as the kind of *Ostjuden* who were routinely depicted in *Der Stürmer* and other organs of Nazi propaganda—sly and cunning, predatory and parasitical. Gestapo agents were assigned to search out and interrogate Herschel's friends, neighbors, and teachers in Hanover, and to seize and study his medical and school records. Indeed, the Nazi obsession with Grynszpan led to the creation and preservation of a trove of historical evidence that allows contemporary investigators to analyze the case so thoroughly.

At the request of Grimm and Diewerge, for example, Gestapo officers were sent to the Jewish school and day care center in Hanover that Herschel had attended as a young child, and questioned its director, Klara Dessau. According to their account of the interrogation, Fräulein Dessau conceded that Herschel had been "a very difficult child who was repeatedly ejected from the day-care center due to bad behavior" and the only student whom she had ever slapped "when other means failed." She even asserted that Herschel's own mother "often complained about her son." Other sources, according to the Gestapo, described Herschel as "someone who had relationships with other Jews only, but was without comrades," "a fighter who outside of school made use of his fists," and "mean-spirited, ill-tempered, sullen, and taciturn."[24]

A Nazi agent was even sent eastward into Poland, where the scope of the investigation was widened to include the relatives of both Zindel Grynszpan and Rivka (Silberberg) Grynszpan, who still lived in Radomsk. The agent was charged with finding evidence of embarrassing political associations and activities, pending criminal cases or prior criminal convictions, and anything else that could be used to impugn or embarrass Herschel Grynszpan in French court proceedings or in Nazi propaganda. Alas, the report that was finally delivered to the German embassy in Warsaw and forwarded to the Propaganda Ministry included no such findings. The Grynszpans and the Silberbergs who remained in Radomsk were apparently no different from their friends and neighbors—poor, oppressed, and anxious to avoid any entanglements with the authorities.

Nor were the Grynszpans and their in-laws the only targets of investigation by the task force. "Just having the name Grynszpan, or something akin to it," observes Gerald Schwab, "was enough to attract the attention of Nazi authorities." Diewerge compiled a summary of the criminal charges against thirty-two foreigners whose last names even faintly resembled "Grynszpan," including Grünspan, Gruenspann, Grinszpan, Grinspun, and Grünspahn, all of whom were suggested to be possibly (if not probably) related to the Grynszpan family. Their malefactions, which included passport violations, illegal border crossing, export of currency, selling goods without a license, forgery, fraud, embezzlement, disturbing the peace and traffic offenses, were held by Diewerge to be "indicative of the human and racial qualities possessed by the Jewish immigrants to Germany with the name Grynszpan."[25]

No aspect of the Grynszpan case was deemed to be too trivial or too remote to merit close scrutiny. At Diewerge's request, for example, the Foreign Ministry sent a coded message to the Paris embassy with an inquiry "concerning the ancestry of Moro-Giafferi" in the hope that he could be shown to be a Jew. The report that came back stated that his Jewishness was "questionable but not probable," and further inquiries confirmed that he was a Catholic of Corsican descent. Nevertheless, the Nazi agents in Paris, hoping to be helpful, confirmed that Moro-Giafferi "was totally in Jewish hands."[26]

The Nazis apparently tried to frighten Moro-Giafferi into dropping the case, but they soon discovered that the tough old Corsican was not easily intimidated. Moro-Giafferi reported to Dorothy Thompson that "innumerable threatening letters" had begun to arrive at his office, but he responded with a death threat of his own. He "officially warned the German Embassy that, unfortunately, his people, not being as civilized as the Jews, believe in the blood feud, and that if anything happens to him he fears that there will not be one person dead in the Germany Embassy but they will be lucky if there is one alive."[27]

All of the raw data gathered by Nazi agents and bureaucrats was sifted and refined, reduced to writing, and turned over to Grimm and Diewerge, who maintained one office at the Franco-German House in Berlin and another office inside the German embassy in Paris and who traveled back and forth between these two cities in the performance of their duties. The task force under their direction churned out reports, briefs, and tracts that were variously used to influence the French investigators and prosecutors, support the efforts of German diplomacy, indoctrinate the German people, and shape world public opinion. Ironically, the zealous, tireless, and endless work of Grimm and Diewerge and their Nazi comrades can be fairly characterized as a conspiracy in itself.

✦   ✦   ✦

AMONG THE VARIOUS CONSPIRACY theories that were inspired by the known facts of the Grynszpan case, the very first was targeted at Herschel's earnest but luckless uncle and aunt, Abraham and Chava Grynszpan. Their willingness to take the troubled young man into their home had already exposed them to arrest and incarceration for harboring an illegal alien. Under scrutiny by Judge Tesnière and the French police, as well as by the Nazi task force under Grimm and Diewerge, their every act of kindness and concern now seemed to crackle with ulterior motives. What did they know about Herschel's act of violence, wondered their accusers, and when did they know it?

Abraham Grynszpan, for example, was suspected of making arrangements to travel from Paris to the border town of Valenciennes to meet and escort his young nephew to Paris in the summer of 1936. Abraham denied the accusation and insisted that Herschel had made his way to Paris on his own initiative. At worst, he would have been guilty only of smuggling a fifteen-year-old Jewish refugee from Nazi Germany to a place of sanctuary. Once Abraham came under suspicion as a co-conspirator in the shooting of Rath, however, his motives for bringing Herschel into France—and for denying it under interrogation—seemed ever more sinister.

The same suspicions now focused on the conversation that took place in Abraham and Chava Grynszpan's apartment on the night before the assassination. None of the eyewitnesses were willing to reveal exactly what was said, and their discretion only excited the curiosity and imagination of the investigators in both Paris and Berlin. From his first interrogation, Herschel had always insisted, "I did not confide my plans of protest to anyone."[28] Diewerge, however, argued that Herschel had announced his murderous intentions to his family and implied that something other than family loyalty explains why they had done nothing to stop him. Perhaps, the Nazis suggested, Abraham and Chava Grynszpan remained silent because they had aided and abetted Herschel all along as fellow conspirators in an elaborate plot to assassinate a symbolic Nazi victim.

Another point of speculation was the source of the money that Herschel used to buy the murder weapon. Abraham, Chava, and Herschel mentioned during their various interrogations that Zindel Grynszpan had provided a fund of 3,000 francs to support his son in Paris. The weekly allowance that Abraham doled out to Herschel, for example, was supposedly deducted from the fund, and so was the sum of 600 francs that Abraham gave to Herschel to buy an overcoat. Perhaps the 200 francs that Abraham thrust upon Herschel on the night before the shooting—the cash he put on the counter at À la Fine Lame—also came out of the same stash. Whether the money was provided or only promised by Zindel, however, was never quite clear, and Alain Cuénot questions "whether the sum actually existed."[29]

Yet, to some investigators, no other aspect of the Grynszpan case suggested the existence of a plot quite so powerfully as those mysterious 3,000 francs. Indeed, the money has been regarded as crucial evidence by all of the conspiracy theorists, although they disagree about whether the plotters were Jews or Nazis. After all, if the Third Reich restricted the export of Jewish capital to ten reichsmarks, and if Zindel and Rivka Grynszpan were so poor that they were forced to rely on welfare, how could they have come up with the equivalent of 3,000 francs and smuggled it out of Nazi Germany to Paris? Surely, the money itself was the best evidence that Herschel Grynszpan was a paid agent, or so goes the argument, although it was never quite clear whose conspiracy it was.

Grimm and Diewerge argued that the 3,000 francs were self-evidently provided by rich and powerful Jewish interests and passed to Herschel Grynszpan by his handler in Paris. "I am convinced that behind this assassination stand the higher powers of International Jewry and bolshevism," declared Friedrich Grimm.[30] The "higher powers," according to Grimm, included the "Jewish press" and various Jewish organizations, among them a French antifascist alliance called Ligue Internationale contre l'Antisémitisme (International League against Anti-Semitism, or LICA) that extended its support to the Grynszpan defense team.

Non-Jews also attracted the attention and suspicion of the Nazi task force, including Dorothy Thompson and the Journalists' Defense Fund, the Society of Friends, the Jehovah's Witnesses, and even Fiorello La Guardia, the mayor of New York, whose mother happened to be Jewish and who was an honorary member of LICA. Yet the highly aggressive and sophisticated investigative apparatus of Nazi Germany was never able to come up with any real evidence to support the existence of what Gerald Schwab terms "the undefined and utterly mysterious factor called 'World Jewry.'"[31]

Ultimately, the Nazis were forced to rely on the Kafkaesque proposition that the best evidence of conspiracy was the absence of evidence. Shortly after the shooting of Rath, for example, an official of the LICA hastened to announce that Grynszpan was not a member. Grimm seized on the announcement to argue that "he who excuses himself, accuses himself," and suggested that "it was easy for the LICA to remove such evidence because, in violation of French laws, it did not maintain a permanent register but a collection of membership cards which could be easily removed."[32]

What intrigued the Nazis most of all was the fact that *two* young Jewish men had carried out assassinations of Nazi officials within a

few years of each other. Grimm and Diewerge had already participated in the proceedings against Frankfurter, the assassin of Gustloff, and now they portrayed Grynszpan and Frankfurter as fellow
operatives in the same relentless conspiracy. Some unremarkable
points of comparison between the two cases took on sinister implications in the search for evidence of that conspiracy. "One could
be led to believe that the Frankfurter affair perhaps could have
influenced Grynszpan, even if only unconsciously," allows Cuénot.
Grimm and Diewerge, however, were convinced that the "curious
analogies," as Cuénot puts it, amounted to evidence rather than
coincidence.[33]

Both of these young Jewish assassins armed themselves with handguns. Both stayed in a hotel and went to a movie on the night before
their crimes. Both carried unmailed postcards whose contents suggested premeditation. Both claimed that their victims addressed them
as "Dirty Jew." Both submitted to arrest by the police after the shoot-
ings and readily admitted their guilt. "Frankfurter declared, like
Grynszpan a few years later, 'I could not act in any other manner,'"
Cuénot points out.[34] For the conspiracy hunters in Berlin, nothing
more was needed to confirm that both Frankfurter and Grynszpan
had acted in service of "the hate-filled power of our Jewish foe,"
according to the words that Hitler uttered at Gustloff's funeral.[35]

"My conviction that Grynszpan's act is not that of a single individual finally is based on the recognition of the similarity of the
Frankfurter and Grynszpan cases," insisted Grimm. "The similarity
of the assassination and the conduct of the assassin after the act is so
striking that it can only be explained if one supposes that one and
the same 'manager' is behind both and has instructed the culprits in
all the details before the assassination."[36]

No opportunity to make the case for conspiracy was afforded to
Grimm and Diewerge in the trial of Abraham and Chava Grynszpan, which took place in the Seventeenth Correctional Chamber of

the Department of the Seine on November 29, 1938, less than three weeks after the shooting of Rath. The allegation that they had played a role in the assassination of Rath was omitted from the case, and they were tried only for harboring their seventeen-year-old nephew even though they knew he did not possess a *permis de séjour.* Moro-Giafferi acted as their attorney, and he pleaded for mercy.

"When Herschel came to our home, he was in such a state of depression that it was pitiful," testified Abraham Grynszpan, who corrected his previous testimony and now admitted that he knew that Herschel had remained in Paris in defiance of an expulsion order. "He was ill and suffering greatly from stomach trouble. Could we have thrown him out?"[37]

An agent of the Propaganda Ministry sat through the proceedings, and his report was forwarded by Diewerge to Goebbels in Berlin along with a German translation of the court transcript. Moro-Giafferi, the Nazi agent noted, adopted "his well-known tactic," that is, "to wear down the court, if need be, with his exceptional knowledge of the specific provisions of the law in order to unleash at the appropriate moment—towards the end—his tremendous oratory." But the agent also suspected that a deal had been struck in advance of the trial since the prosecution recommended against "an excessively long sentence."[38]

The Grynszpans were found guilty, and the judge imposed a fine of one hundred francs and a jail sentence of four months on each defendant. The court of appeals later adjusted the sentence, reducing Chava's jail time to three months and increasing Abraham's to six months, but they were both quietly released on bail after only a month behind bars. The charge that they had aided and abetted their nephew in the assassination of Rath was formally dropped, and a separate expulsion order that had been issued against them was suspended pending the trial of Herschel Grynszpan.

One opportunity to prove the existence of a Jewish plot to kill

Rath had passed, and two of the suspected co-conspirators were now at liberty. The Nazi task force would have to wait until Herschel Grynszpan sat in the dock to make the case for conspiracy, and it only escalated its efforts to do so.

✦ ✦ ✦

THE NAZIS, HOWEVER, WERE hardly the only ones who claimed to detect the fingerprints of invisible but nefarious plotters in the Grynszpan case. A mirror image of the Nazi conspiracy theory was bruited in some Jewish and antifascist circles. Perhaps, they suggested, Herschel was only the innocent dupe in an elaborate Nazi plot to assassinate Rath in order to provide a pretext for Kristallnacht, or to do away with a man whom they regarded as an enemy of the Third Reich, or both at once.

To explain why Rath—an SA member and *Alter Kämpfer*—was selected as a target for assassination, it was necessary to reimagine him as a "a very tepid Nazi" who "had a Jewish girlfriend while in college."[39] His aristocratic family, according to the advocates of a counterconspiracy, looked on the Nazis with distaste, and that is why Hitler appeared to treat Rath's grieving mother and father so coldly at the state funeral for the slain diplomat.

The notion that Grynszpan was actually a cat's-paw for the Nazis was first proposed in print shortly after the shooting of Rath in an article titled "The Truth behind the Assassination," which appeared in a magazine published by the LICA, *Droit de Vivre* (Right to Live). The elusive 3,000 francs figured here, too. Since Nazi Germany forbade its Jewish population from sending or taking money out of the country, the magazine speculated, the otherwise inexplicable ability of the Grynszpan family to transfer the cash from Hanover to Paris was itself evidence of Nazi complicity. And if Grynszpan managed to carry a loaded revolver into the tightly guarded German embassy, it was "undoubtedly because he was known there."[40]

Perhaps the single most extraordinary version of the mirror-image conspiracy was proposed by Hannah Arendt, the revered German-Jewish intellectual whose face later ended up on a postage stamp in postwar Germany in honor of "Women in German History." She was still only a young philosophy student, pretty but also cerebral, when Hitler came to power; her mentor and lover, Martin Heidegger, promptly joined the Nazi Party, but Arendt understood the threat of Nazism and managed to escape to Paris.* Later, she was among the hundreds of artists and writers who were able to find refuge in America with the assistance of American journalist Varian Fry. By coincidence, she had been born in Herschel's hometown of Hanover, and she was living in Paris at the time of the shooting of Rath.

Arendt reprised *l'affaire Grynszpan* in a brief but inexplicably toxic passage in her famous account of the trial of Adolf Eichmann in 1961, *Eichmann in Jerusalem.* "The motives for Grynszpan's act have never been cleared up," wrote Arendt, who acknowledged Herschel's stated motive of avenging the 12,000 Polish Jews who were expelled from Nazi Germany but then asserted that "it is generally known that this explanation is unlikely." A more likely explanation, according to Arendt, is that Grynszpan—whom she dismissed as "a psychopath, unable to finish school, who for years had knocked about Paris and Brussels, being expelled from both places"—was recruited and paid by the Nazis to kill Rath, "who had been shadowed by the Gestapo because of his openly anti-Nazi views and his sympathy for Jews."[41]

Alas, no more evidence exists for Arendt's account than for the

---

* Arendt later came to the defense of her former lover in a broadcast on West German radio on the occasion of Heidegger's eightieth birthday in 1969. "Heidegger's Nazism, she explained, was an 'escapade,' a mistake, which happened only because the thinker naïvely 'succumbed to the temptation . . . to "intervene" in the world of human affairs.'" Adam Kirsch, "The Jewish Question: Martin Heidegger," *New York Times*, May 7, 2010.

one offered by Grimm and Diewerge, both of which are equally implausible, and she cited no sources for her own version.[42] None of the three French psychiatrists who examined Herschel Grynszpan—and submitted an 82-page report to Judge Tesnière—concluded that he was mentally unstable, much less psychotic, before, during, or after his crime. He was never actually expelled from Paris or Brussels. To accuse him of serving as an agent of the Gestapo is nothing less than a historical slander, and to credit his victim with "openly anti-Nazi views" and "sympathy for the Jews" is a fantasy. Yet Arendt, who displayed so little compassion for any of the victims of the Holocaust in *Eichmann in Jerusalem*, was hardly the only Jewish observer who found nothing praiseworthy or even sympathetic in the boy and his deed.

One reason why the Grynszpan case has attracted so much speculation about the existence of a conspiracy is that Herschel was clearly susceptible to flights of fancy and gestures of grandiosity, and he unwittingly encouraged the conspiracy theorists when he conjured up new and ever more astonishing versions of his own exploits. His habit of confabulation, in fact, may explain why Arendt convinced herself that Grynszpan was psychotic. After all, Herschel was repeatedly interrogated by detectives, magistrates, psychiatrists, physicians, and social workers over his months of confinement—and he dispatched countless letters about the case to family, friends, and complete strangers—but he was never capable of sticking to a story.

Sometimes Herschel declared that he had decided to "kill a member of the German Embassy" as an act of "protest and vengeance"—"The person himself," he said, "was of slight importance"—and sometimes he denied any intention to take his victim's life: "I did not wish to kill him but only to wound him," he wrote to Uncle Isaac.[43] Sometimes he claimed that he had acted in a trance state from the moment he purchased the revolver to the moment that he fired it at Rath—another notion that the French forensic psychiatrists flatly rejected. Sometimes he insisted that he had intended to kill no one but himself and claimed that he planned to commit suicide while standing in front of an official portrait of Adolf Hitler at the embassy or, in a variant of the same story, to fire a symbolic shot at the portrait.

On one point, however, Grynszpan was clear and consistent throughout the investigation. He was the sole author of the mission he had undertaken, he had acted alone, and he had told no one about what he intended to do. *L'affaire Grynszpan*, he always maintained, was a conspiracy of one.

✦   ✦   ✦

MAÎTRE VINCENT DE MORO-GIAFFERI was such a commanding figure in French legal circles that younger and lesser lawyers flocked to the little hearing room where Abraham and Chava Grynszpan were on trial in November 1938, in order to see the famous advocate at work. Born to a Corsican father and a French mother, he had been wounded in combat at Verdun and he received a battlefield promotion to the rank of lieutenant. After the war, he served in the Chamber of Deputies as a deputy for Corsica and later as a cabinet secretary in the French government. But he achieved his greatest celebrity in the courtroom.

Just as Edgar Mowrer had warned Dorothy Thompson, Moro-Giafferi's politics were famously and solidly antifascist, and his appearance in the case was itself a provocation to Nazi Germany. They recalled, for example, the role he played in a mock trial that was held after the Reichstag fire, an incident in which a fire of suspicious origins broke out in the Reichstag building, the seat of Germany's democratically elected legislature, shortly after Hitler came to power. Here, too, the Nazis claimed to detect the workings of a conspiracy, and they staged a show trial at which the crime was blamed on a cabal of Communist agents, but the trial failed to erase the suspicion in Germany and abroad that the real conspirators were the Nazis themselves. At the mock trial that was held in 1933, Moro-Giafferi appeared for the prosecution and argued persuasively that Hitler and Göring were culpable for the crime.

Moro-Giafferi, however, was not an ideologue when it came to defending his private clients, and he understood that the French attitude toward "higher justice" had changed since Sholom Schwartzbard had been acquitted for the assassination of Simon Petliura in the heady days after World War I. By 1938, mindful of the terrible price that had been paid in lives, treasure, and property for that victory, the politicians who governed France were terrified of provoking Germany into war yet again. As the Third Reich had pushed its borders outward—first by remilitarizing the Rhineland and reabsorbing the Saar in 1935, then through the *Anschluss* with Austria in March 1938, and finally by dismembering Czechoslovakia in September 1938—France joined Great Britain in adopting an abject policy of diplomatic appeasement.

For that reason alone, Grynszpan's act of violence in the Nazi German embassy was regarded as a worst-case scenario of the French version of the Jewish Problem. The number of Jews in France had increased from 90,000 at the turn of the twentieth century to some 300,000 by the late 1930s, mostly because of the influx of immigrants, who now occupied the same teeming neighborhoods in Paris where the Grynszpans lived and worked. According to *Nazi Germany and the Jews* by Saul Friedländer, the distinguished historian who arrived in Paris with his parents in 1939 as Jewish refugees from Prague, two-thirds of the Jewish population lived in Paris, and half of the Jews in Paris were foreigners. Of the foreign Jews in Paris, 80 percent were *Ostjuden* and—again like the Grynszpans—fully one-half were from Poland. These foreign-born Jews were characterized by politicians, the press, and even some native-born French Jews as an alien and awkward presence in the French body politic.[44]

Some elements of French public opinion, in fact, embraced the

Nazi argument that Herschel Grynszpan meant to provoke a war between France and Germany, "less in order to defend France's direct interests than to destroy the Hitler regime in Germany," as the French politician Gaston Bergery wrote in *La Flèche* in 1938, "that is, the death of millions of Frenchmen and [other] Europeans to avenge a few dead Jews and a few hundred thousand unfortunate Jews."[45]

To put Hitler in the dock, as Mowrer had described the trial strategy that he expected Moro-Giafferi to adopt, or to allow Herschel Grynszpan to speechify about the sufferings of the Jewish people, was not likely to inspire much compassion in a French courtroom, or so Moro-Giafferi himself concluded. And the only case in which he lost a client to the guillotine had taught him how important it was to evoke some measure of sympathy for the defendant. Henri Landru, dubbed in Paris newspapers as "Bluebeard," was convicted of murdering ten elderly widows whom he met, seduced, and swindled after placing lonely-hearts ads that held out the promise of marriage. Even putting aside the homicides—and no bodies were ever found by the police—Landru's caddish behavior was itself an affront to French notions of chivalry.

Then, too, Dorothy Thompson herself and the various Jewish organizations that were also contributing to the defense of Herschel Grynszpan had come to realize that putting Hitler on trial in the Grynszpan case was unacceptably dangerous. "After the Kristallnacht," explains Lucy Dawidowicz, "the Jews in Germany became little more than hostages."[46] So Moro-Giafferi saw that he had to find a way to keep politics and propaganda out of the courtroom and to portray "the child" or "the little one," as he called his client, as a victim rather than a criminal.[47]

Once the rotund and round-faced Moro-Giafferi had sized up Herschel Grynszpan—a short, slender, slightly-built youth who spoke with a lisp, a sharp dresser with "black brooding eyes" and exotic good looks—the astute and worldly attorney was inspired to suggest a scenario that may or may not have been wholly invented but promised to transform Grynszpan's act of violence from a political assassination to a *crime passionelle*. Whether the idea that occurred to Moro-Giafferi was rooted in fact or only a clever legal ploy, it was one that might well keep Herschel Grynszpan from losing his head.

The precise words that Moro-Giafferi spoke to Grynszpan in the visitor's room at Fresnes prison are not recorded, but the aging attorney, a few years before his death in 1956, confirmed that the conversation had taken place. He was attempting to elicit from *l'enfant* the testimony that he preferred to present in court without committing the crime of suborning perjury. As an experienced criminal trial lawyer, however, Moro-Giafferi was surely adept at planting suggestions through leading or wholly hypothetical questions, and he must have been confident that his highly inventive client would understand what the attorney wanted him to say.

Moro-Giafferi's version of *l'affaire Grynszpan* began with the notion that Ernst vom Rath and Herschel Grynszpan had already encountered each other—and knew each other intimately—long before the day of the shooting. He speculated that they first met somewhere on the streets of Paris, perhaps on the sidewalk in front of the Tout Va Bien, where Herschel sometimes waited for someone to treat him to a beverage or a snack. The elegant and affluent diplomat was attracted to the penniless young man, or so Moro-Giafferi suggested, and Rath invited Herschel to accompany him to a hotel for a furtive sexual encounter, perhaps the Hôtel de Suez or one of the other convenient little hotels around the Gare de l'Est. Once he had lured the boy into a homosexual love affair, however, he then refused to pay what he had promised.

Embroidering the scenario that cast Rath as a sexual predator who preyed upon adolescent boys, Moro-Giafferi proposed another and even more sympathetic story line. Perhaps Rath seduced the innocent young boy by holding out the promise that the diplomat would use his good offices to obtain exit visas for the Grynszpans and bring them safely out of Nazi Germany— and then did nothing when the boy's parents and siblings were rounded up in Hanover and forced into no-man's-land on the Polish frontier.

Either of these versions of the events leading up to the shooting of Rath would allow Moro-Giafferi to reframe the case against his client and turn it from a political assassination into an affair of the heart. If only Herschel would agree to embrace the startling new theory of the case—and Moro-Giafferi was confident that his articulate and imaginative client could find a way to flesh it out with color and detail—then the attorney could argue in court that "the child" had taken his own private revenge against a sexual predator.

Herschel himself would not be the only beneficiary of sexualizing and personalizing the case. Moro-Giafferi was an earnest anti-Nazi, and he shared Dorothy Thompson's well-founded fear that the repercussions of the murder of Rath had not ended with Kristallnacht. By stripping away the political baggage, he hoped to reduce the risks to the Jews who remained in captivity in Nazi Germany. To be sure, the depiction of Rath as a homosexual predator would be an embarrassment to the Third Reich—"a gain for the cause," according to Cuénot—but the anti-Semitic excesses of the Third Reich need not be mentioned at all.[48] In fact, the only atrocity that Moro-Giafferi would present in court was the scandalous sexual abuse of a seventeen-year-old boy. Even if Herschel were convicted, he calculated, his tender age and the extenuating circumstances of his crime of passion would spare him from the guillotine or even a long prison sentence.

Despite Moro-Giafferi's entreaties, however, Herschel said no.

If the scenario was nothing more than the invention of an artful attorney, of course, Herschel would have been outraged by the mere suggestion that he renounce his role as the righteous avenger of the Jewish people and instead announce that he was a *faygeleh*.* "Avid for glory," writes Cuénot, "the only thing of importance was the universal interest that his act would excite and reflect in the public opinion."[49] And if the story of seduction and prostitution contained even the slightest grain of truth, then the shame would have been all the greater. Indeed, Herschel must have been appalled at the thought of how his God-fearing and fault-finding family would react if he stood up in open court and declared that he was both a homosexual and a prostitute, regardless of whether the declaration was true or false. Death by guillotine would have seemed a far kinder fate.

As Herschel waited for a trial date in Fresnes prison, Moro-Giafferi deployed his famous powers of persuasion against his own client. He appealed to the conscience of Grynszpan by pointing out that Herschel's act of violence against Rath, rather than serving the Jewish people, had only "made Jewish blood flow" by providing the Nazis with a pretext for Kristallnacht. "If only he would deny the political motives of his crime and assert that he only had personal vengeance in mind, vengeance as a victim of homosexuality," argued Moro-Giafferi, "the Nazis would lose their best pretext for exercising their reprisals against the German Jews who are victims of his fit of madness and now, of his obstinacy."[50]

The mere mention of homosexuality only aggravated what was already a tense relationship between the celebrated attorney and his now famous client. Grynszpan and Moro-Giafferi had never been comfortable with each other—"Both of them were bad-tempered and shared an equal lack of flexibility," asserts Cuénot—and some of his uncles had long suspected that Moro-Giafferi, an activist in the antifascist movement, was less interested in defending Herschel

*The Yiddish colloquialism for a male homosexual (literally "little bird") is derived from the German word for "bird" and is unrelated to the English word "fag."

Herschel Grynszpan's grade school classroom, c. 1930. (*Mémorial de la Shoah*, CDJC)

Rue du Faubourg Saint-Denis in the Tenth Arrondissement, the neighborhood where Herschel Grynszpan and other members of the Grynszpan family lived and worked in 1938. (*Mémorial de la Shoah*, CDJC)

Apartment at 8 rue Martel, former home of Abraham and Chava Grynszpan and hiding place of Herschel Grynszpan. *(Photograph by author)*

Polish army barracks at Zbąszyń, where Jews deported from Germany on October 31, 1938—Herschel Grynszpan's parents and siblings among them—were interned. *(Yad Vashem)*

The shop where Grynszpan purchased a small revolver and a box of shells on the morning of his attack at the German embassy. *(Mémorial de la Shoah, CDJC)*

Ernst vom Rath
(Yad Vashem)

The office of Ernst vom Rath, a low-ranking diplomat on the staff of the German embassy in Paris, where Grynszpan was invited to seat himself after announcing that he wanted to share "important documents." *(Yad Vashem)*

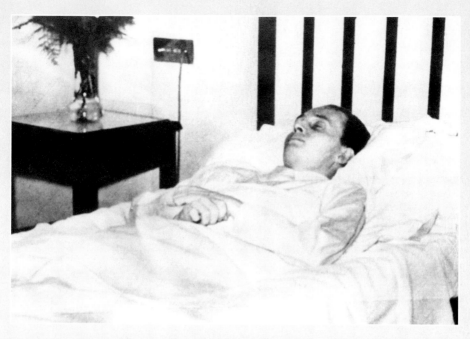

Rath on his deathbed in a Paris hospital. *(akg-images / The Image Works)*

Funeral service for Ernst vom Rath in Duesseldorf. *(akg-images / The Image Works)*

Grynszpan in custody of the French police immediately after the shooting on November 7, 1938. *(Yad Vashem)*

Herschel Grynszpan was conveyed by French detectives to police headquarters for interrogation on the day of his arrest in Paris. *(Mémorial de la Shoah, CDJC)*

Among the officially designated targets for arson on Kristallnacht were Jewish synagogues across Nazi Germany. Here, a synagogue in Wiesbaden is set afire on the night of November 9–10, 1938. (*Yad Vashem*)

The broken window glass that littered the streets of Magdeburg and other German cities and towns on the morning after Kristallnacht inspired the lighthearted designation of the official pogrom as "Crystal Night." (*Yad Vashem*)

At a court session on March 1, 1939, during the trial of Abraham and Chava Grynszpan for harboring their nephew, the couple was represented by Herschel's attorney, Vincent de Moro-Giafferi, who is visible to the left of Abraham. *(Yad Vashem)*

Millions of French residents, including Herschel Grynszpan, fled southward ahead of the German army after the invasion of France in June 1940, a phenomenon known as *l'exode*—the exodus. *(LAPI / Roger-Viollett / The Image Works)*

Zindel Grynszpan, Herschel's father, survived World War II and
testified at the trial of Adolf Eichmann in Jerusalem on April 25,
1961. Eichmann, as the Third Reich's "competent specialist" in
Jewish affairs, was assigned to interrogate Herschel Grynszpan
while he was awaiting trial in Berlin after the fall of France.
(*Mémorial de la Shoah, CDJC*)

in a French court than in defending the Jews in Germany against further persecution.[51] Herschel now regretted his reluctant decision to accept the man as his counsel, and he shrilly ruled out the homosexuality defense. So angry and frustrated was Moro-Giafferi at Herschel's decision that he unburdened himself to an acquaintance whom he encountered on the boulevard Saint-Michel, a Communist activist and newspaper editor from Germany named Erich Wollenberg who had found refuge in Paris.

"That young man is a fool, infatuated with himself," Moro-Giafferi confided to Wollenberg. "He refuses to give a non-political character to his act by saying for example that he assassinated vom Rath because he had had money quarrels with him following homosexual relations. Yet, such an attitude in regard to the murder of vom Rath is necessary, in order to save the Jews of the Third Reich, whose lives are becoming more and more precarious in regard to their property, their health, their future."[52]

"Did Grynszpan really have relations with vom Rath?" the man asked.

"Absolutely not!" answered Moro-Giafferi.

"But as defender of Grynszpan," the man persisted, "shouldn't you protect not only the interests of your client, but his honor as well?"

"Honor! Honor! What is the honor of that absurd little Jew in the face of the criminal action of Hitler? What does the honor of Grynszpan weigh in the face of hundreds of thousands of Jews?" sputtered Moro-Giafferi, who frankly confessed that his trial strategy was an artifice: "Whether vom Rath might be a homosexual or not, I don't know and, besides, it doesn't interest me."[53]

The account of a confessional sidewalk conversation between Moro-Giafferi and Wollenberg surfaced only in 1964 and only under the most curious circumstances. Back in 1938, however, the homosexuality defense was abandoned by Moro-Giafferi, and no hint of a *crime passionelle* entered the considerable record of the French criminal investigation of the Grynszpan case. As Herschel waited for the day of his trial—nursing his nervous stomach, conferring with his family and his attorneys, playing table tennis with his fellow prisoners, making copious entries in his journal, and writing countless letters—his defense remained purely political, if sometimes also phantasmagorical.

"We talked about the letter that I would write to all the leading personalities of Europe and America," Herschel penned into his prison journal after a working session with Maître Szwarc, whose only remaining role was apparently to bring a bit of Yiddishkeit into Herschel's prison cell. "We began to write the letter to Hitler. I wrote that the best answer to my letter would be a humanitarian act. I stated that I meant that he should re-establish things as they had been in the past, that he re-build what had been destroyed, and that he return to us those things which had been taken. If he did this, we would be ready to pardon him immediately. I will show the letter to the Rabbi before mailing it. Meanwhile I went off to eat and my lawyers left after the meal."[54]

Herschel Grynszpan may have denied and rejected the sensational story of seduction and betrayal that Moro-Giafferi proposed, but it seemed to take on a life of its own. Indeed, a whole new set of conspiracy theories have been inspired by the notion that Grynszpan and Rath were sexual partners in one way or another. And, at the single most dangerous moment in the fraught and abbreviated life of Herschel Grynszpan, the story would be reprised in shocking and salacious detail in the most unlikely place and from a startling source—the boy himself.

8

PHONY WAR

FOR THOSE INTREPID AMERICANS WHO STILL SOUGHT THE high life in the City of Light in 1939, the political horizon—already clouded by the atrocities of the Spanish Civil War, the Italian adventures in Ethiopia, and Hitler's escalating threats and demands—was darkening all across Europe. American expatriates Gertrude Stein and Alice B. Toklas, both Jewish by birth but wholly detached from their origins, retreated from Paris to their country house in Bilignin and took their storied collection of art and books with them. Gossip columnist Elsa Maxwell, famous for the parties that she hosted at the Ritz Hotel in Paris, replaced RSVP with the playful acronym ICNW on her much sought-after invitations: "In Case No War."[1]

The abject surrender of the Western democracies at Munich in the fall of 1938 succeeded in dismembering Czechoslovakia but failed to appease Hitler. Indeed, the supine diplomacy of France and England only seemed to incite the Führer. On March 15, 1939, the Wehrmacht marched into Prague, followed shortly by Hitler himself, and what remained of Czechoslovakia was absorbed into the Third Reich. The next target of German expansion was Poland, whose sovereignty France and Britain finally felt obliged to guarantee. Then, in a volte-face that resulted from Stalin's conviction that the West was hoping to turn German aggression in his direction, Nazi Germany and Soviet Russia entered into a nonaggression pact in August. War now seemed inevitable.

"Ed Murrow as gloomy as I am," American journalist William L. (Bill) Shirer recorded in his diary. "We agree on these things: that war is now more probable than ever, that it is likely to come after the next harvest, that Poland is obviously next on Hitler's list."[2]

The Grynszpan case, which had seemed so sensational and consequential in 1938, was overshadowed by the events of 1939. The predicament of his parents and siblings—who managed to leave the refugee camp at Zbąszyń and return to Radomsk in August 1939—and the 12,000 other Polish Jews who had been driven into no-man's-land on the German–Polish frontier seemed trivial now that three million Jews in Poland faced the imminent threat of invasion and conquest by Nazi Germany. The half-million Jews who remained in Germany and Austria were seized with dread as the meager opportunities for escape finally evaporated. The last contingent of German-Jewish children to escape the Third Reich aboard the so-called *Kindertransport*, for example, crossed the border on the very day that World War II began.

Yet the preparation of the official case against Herschel Grynszpan had continued in the early months of 1939, and so had the shadow investigation conducted by Grimm and Diewerge, but *l'affaire Grynszpan* was overshadowed by the diplomatic maneuvers that now dominated the headlines and radio broadcasts. By June 1939, the defendant and all of the witnesses had been interrogated—many of them repeatedly—and the final reports of the detectives and the various physicians, psychiatrists, and other forensic experts had been submitted. Judge Tesnière ended his work as chief examining magistrate, and the act of indictment for murder was forwarded for scheduling on the calendar of the Criminal Court for the Department of Seine.

The timing of the trial was a matter of much concern to both the Grynszpan defense team and the Nazi task force. In January 1939, for example, Grimm had reported to Berlin that he hoped to secure a trial date in March even though he suspected that Moro-Giafferi preferred to postpone the trial. By mid-March, however, Grimm pointed out that, as a result of the German invasion of Czechoslovakia and Hitler's triumphal entry into Prague, "it is in our interest not to expedite the trial." Indeed, he predicted that "if the trial were held tomorrow, the assassin would go free."[3]

In June 1939, both sides of the Grynszpan case, each acting independently of the other, were now urging the judge to set a trial as soon as possible. Grimm and Diewerge were eager to use the trial to blame the growing tension between France and Germany on a Jewish conspiracy, and Grynszpan was just as eager to denounce the anti-Semitic excesses of Nazi Germany. By the end of summer, all of the interested parties sought to put the case back into the headlines and believed that the trial itself would be a venue where its political subtext could be writ large.

Grimm, for example, personally called on Judge Tesnière in June and conveyed the urging of his government that the Grynszpan trial commence no later than the following month. Grimm's audacious demand demonstrated the low regard in which Nazi Germany held the sovereignty of France, but the fact that Judge Tesnière granted a private audience to a Nazi emissary can be seen as yet another act of appeasement.

The magistrate regretfully informed the Nazi emissary that such an early date was impossible but held out the hope that the trial might begin as early as September 1939.

✦   ✦   ✦

HERSCHEL GRYNSZPAN WAS NO longer the lonely and brooding adolescent who was arrested on the day of the shooting. The signs of his self-regard were noted by all who encountered him. When he entered an examination room at Fresnes prison to be interviewed by forensic experts, for example, he displayed a certain swagger and insisted on formally shaking hands around the room. His letters were still scrawled in an adolescent script, but the signature that he affixed to them was bold, confident, and adorned with flourishes.

Such grandiosity may suggest that Herschel was merely delusional, and yet, thanks to Dorothy Thompson and other journalists who monitored his plight and kept his name in print, Herschel was an authentic celebrity. He received so much admiring and even adoring correspondence from around the world—including ardent love letters and generous offers of cash—that the prison authorities passed along only a few of them "because of his already marked tendency to think of himself as the center of the universe."[4] One letter that reached him, for instance, was sent by a physician in San Francisco named George Herzog and included a check.

"Many, many thanks for the money which you sent, but I cannot take it as I have done nothing to deserve it," wrote Herschel in reply. "If you want to do something which I want very much, I ask you to take the money and give it to the [12,000] innocent Jews robbed, exiled and suffering on the Polish border."[5] Herschel's sense of his own significance was only encouraged by his family and his attorneys, all of whom flattered and pampered him. Maître Szwarc "told me that he would teach me Esperanto," Herschel wrote in his prison journal, "and I told him that I would like to study it if it would give him pleasure." Maître Weill-Goudchaux "told me that never in his life did he think there existed a young man of 17 years who would have the courage to carry out an act as I had."[6] To his parents and siblings, he boasted, "I have the best lawyers in France."[7]

The prison authorities may have recognized and tried to contain the prisoner's narcissism by censoring his mail, but the attention and care that he received in Fresnes only reinforced his sense of self-importance. "I would like you to know, my dear ones, that here in prison I am well and have everything I need," he wrote to his family. "You do not have to be concerned for me. I am in very good hands here. What is not available here in the prison, I buy outside. Uncle Schlome [Salomon] sends me a little money every week to buy food. Even unknown people from America send me money, which I do not wish to accept."[8]

The defense team had grown as large and contentious as the Grynszpan family. Although Salomon Grynszpan had announced his intention to dismiss the first two lawyers on the case, Szwarc and Vésinne-Larue, they protested against their removal in a newspaper interview and even threatened to file a formal complaint with the Paris bar against "all machinations which are designed to exclude us from the case."[9] Moro-Giafferi finally consented to their participation, but they remained on the periphery, and the Yiddish-speaking Szwarc seems to have spent much of his time assisting Herschel in composing the imploring letters that were mailed off to various public officials.

Meanwhile, Moro-Giafferi had associated with another Jewish attorney, Serge Weill-Goudchaux, and he also hired the same lawyer whom Salomon had originally tried but failed to find at the courthouse on the day of the shooting, Isidore Fränkel. To his various Jewish colleagues, Moro-Giafferi entrusted the task of "hand-holding" while *le Grand Patron* (the Big Boss), as his associates wryly dubbed him, reserved to himself the role of strategist and advocate in the upcoming trial.[10]

Significantly, one of the Jewish attorneys whom Moro-Giafferi consulted was Henri Torrès, an old lion of the Paris bar who had successfully defended Sholom Schwartzbard on the charge of having assassinated Simon Petliura. The record of the Schwartzbard trial in 1927 suggested the script that Moro-Giafferi was preparing for his own client: Torrès had put the dead victim in the dock in place of the defendant, calling some eighty witnesses to attest to the atrocities that had been committed in Ukraine by the army under Petliura's command, and even reciting some of Shylock's lines from *The Merchant of Venice*: "Hath not a Jew hands, organs, dimensions, senses, affections, passions? If you prick us, do we not bleed? If you poison us, do we not die? And if you wrong us, shall we not revenge?"[11] Torrès's courtroom theatrics had won the acquittal of Schwartzbard, and Moro-Giafferi hoped he could do the same for Grynszpan. Since Grynszpan had ruled out a defense based on Rath's supposed sexual predations, of course, *le Patron* had no other choice.

Theatrics continued to roil the Grynszpan family, too. Once Abraham and Chava Grynszpan were released from jail, Uncle Abraham reasserted his right to act in loco parentis, but Herschel's three other uncles in Paris continued to express their dissenting opinions about trial tactics and the selection of attorneys. Abraham and Salomon, for example, had been mostly estranged from each other prior to the shooting, and now these two Grynszpan brothers were at odds over new and more consequential matters. "As perhaps you already know, discord reigns in my family once again," Herschel wrote to Moro-Giafferi in January 1939. "I am so tormented, to speak frankly, I think I'll go mad if it continues."[12]

Moro-Giafferi, admired and feared in legal circles, quickly realized that he was powerless to impose order on the fractious Grynszpan family. Soon after Herschel's arrest, for instance, Uncle Abraham Berenbaum, Chava Grynszpan's brother, had traveled across Europe to the refugee camp in Zbąszyń to consult with Herschel's father, and Berenbaum returned to Paris with a letter of authority bestowed upon him by the paterfamilias. "You must confer with M. Berenbaum about everything and you must do what he tells you," wrote

Zindel Grynszpan to his son. "With God's help, everything will turn out right once again."[13]

Ironically, Zindel reassured his son that the family in Zbąszyń was not suffering the kind of hardship that apparently drove the boy to his act of vengeance in the first place: "You must not allow yourself, dear Hermann, to have gloomy thoughts in regard to us," wrote Zindel Grynszpan. "Things are not so bad. We have enough to eat and drink and otherwise we lack for practically nothing. We are, thank the good Lord, all in good health." Then Zindel closed his reassuring letter "with hopes that we will soon all be happily together once more" and "many good wishes and kisses." If it occurred to Herschel that a letter like this one might have dissuaded him from his deed if it had arrived a bit earlier, however, he made no mention of it.[14]

Dorothy Thompson had been among the first journalists to call attention to the Grynzspan case, and she continued to raise and spend money to defend Herschel in the French courts, although she always sought to balance the welfare of the young defendant against the best interests of the endangered Jews in Germany. The legal defense fund that she had organized in the days after the shooting monitored the case from its Fifth Avenue offices in New York and doled out funds from the $40,203 that had been raised from some 25,000 contributors. The paymaster for the Journalists' Defense Fund in Paris was a man named Elias Sofer, the proprietor of a manicure shop and treasurer of an antifascist organization called the Union contre la Persécution Hitlerienne.

In place of his customary fees, Moro-Giafferi agreed to accept such sums as the Journalists' Defense Fund was able to provide. Even more modest amounts were paid to Szwarc and Vésinne-Larue for their work on Abraham and Chava Grynszpan's trial and the marginal role they were allowed to play in Herschel's defense. A total of 300,000 francs—about $30,000—was paid to the various attorneys, and a few francs were allotted to Herschel to pay for food and stamps from the prison canteen, thus putting Dorothy Thompson in the role that Uncle Abraham had once played.

The Journalists' Defense Fund also paid the expenses that were incurred in an effort to bring Herschel's parents and siblings out of Poland. The plan of action was proposed by an enterprising British newspaperman named A. R. Pirie, who boldly called on Herschel at Fresnes prison. In exchange for exclusive publishing rights to Herschel's prison diary, which eventually bulked up to two dense volumes, Pirie offered to travel to Poland and fetch the Grynszpan family. He returned to Paris without them, however, and it was Herschel himself who played a key role in making sure that Pirie's mission would fail. Although Herschel had earlier demanded that his family be reunited in Paris—and even though he was perfectly willing to write open letters to Roosevelt, Hitler, and various government ministers and newspaper editors—he resented Pirie's request for permission to publish the private musings that appeared in his diary.

"I do not wish to give it since I am against its publication," Herschel wrote to his parents in March 1939. "For this reason, I request of you that, in case you are asked to sign anything whereby you might promise to give them my 'journal,' you refuse. I hope you will do as I ask."[15]

The Grynszpans had not seen Herschel—or Hermann, as they continued to call him—since he left Hanover at the age of fifteen nearly three years earlier. When they had seen him off at the train station in Hanover, Herschel gave the impression of being only a child. Now they could tell, as much from the tone of his prison letters as from the photographs in the Polish newspapers, that he was a child no longer and, in fact, a veritable stranger to his family.

✦   ✦   ✦

QUITE A DIFFERENT FAMILY melodrama can be discerned on the German side of the Grynszpan case. Rumors had circulated from the

outset that Ernst vom Rath was, at best, "a very tepid" Nazi or perhaps even an enemy of the government that he served.[16] Much was
made of the fact, for example, that only a single photograph of Rath
in his SA uniform was circulated to the press, which suggested to
some observers that few such photographs existed. The same surmise was applied to the young diplomat's father, Gustav vom Rath,
who had retired to run the family business after long service as a
government counselor (*Regierungsrat*) and who had never joined the
Nazi Party. Perhaps Rath—not unlike Reck-Malleczewen, the Prussian artistocrat who fantasized about shooting Hitler—was among
the Prussian aristocrats who disdained the thuggish Nazis and the
former corporal who was their Führer.

The apparent coolness that Hitler displayed toward the mother
and father of Rath at his state funeral was also noted by reporters
who covered the event. According to one overheated report, Gustav
vom Rath and one of his other sons, Günter, had been arrested and
confined in a concentration camp because of their refusal to cooperate with the Nazi authorities. No real evidence was available to validate any of these tales, but Grimm and Diewerge felt it was necessary
to address the rumor and speculation.

Early on, the Rath family—Gustav, his wife, and their two other
sons—had been asked to put themselves in service to the Nazi cause.
At a meeting with the high officials assigned to the Grynszpan case,
which was held at the Breitenbacher Hof in Düsseldorf when all of
them were present for the state funeral of the victim, the elder Rath
was "urged" to enter the Grynszpan case as the *partie civile* and to
delegate the management of the legal proceedings to Grimm and his
handpicked French lawyer, Maurice Garçon.

Gustav vom Rath "indicated that he would have preferred to bear
his grief silently and in private," according to Gerald Schwab, but he
complied with the demand. Putting his name on a pleading, of
course, was nothing more than a legal fiction because the real party

in interest was the Third Reich. Indeed, the Führer was not satisfied with a mere legal ploy. He suspected that any aristocratic German with a "von" or a "vom" in his last name was not wholly trustworthy, and he demanded a more visible and enthusiastic display of personal loyalty from the Rath family. So Gustav vom Rath dutifully returned to Paris to offer his testimony to Judge Tesnière on January 7, 1939.[17]

The scene inside the chambers of the examining magistrate reveals the fearful and deferential stance of the French authorities toward Nazi Germany. The session, which had been arranged at the special request of Grimm and Diewerge, was conducted in private and without the participation of the defense attorneys. Rath entered the room with only his French attorney of record, Maître Garçon, and one of Garçon's associates, but it was soon noticed and pointed out that the official translator was a Jew. "This gave us the opportunity to bring Professor Grimm as translator," Diewerge would later report to the Ministry of Propaganda in Berlin. Judge Tesnière, no less an appeaser than Daladier, obligingly dismissed the Jewish translator and summoned Grimm from the anteroom to join the proceedings. Only then did Rath finally discharge his duty to the Führer by giving voice to the Nazi party line.[18]

"In order to reestablish the truth, in light of certain press campaigns, and in order to prevent any false legends from arising, I consider it of importance to confirm that my son was a member of the National Socialist movement," he declared in a statement that was later circulated to the press. "He was in complete accord with his government and was fully devoted to the cause of National Socialism." As for himself, the old man affirmed, "I am fully in accord with my son's politics."

Remarkably, and pointedly, the elder Rath acknowledged and repudiated even the most damaging rumors. "It is very painful for me to read in certain newspapers that I had difficulties with my government, and that on the occasion of my son's funeral, I even am supposed to have had differences with the Führer. I declare that these are all lies," he stated. As for the report that he and one of his sons had been sent to a concentration camp, Rath observed, "I trust that my presence in this courtroom, together with my second son, Guenter, is sufficient refutation of this new lie."[19]

With his scripted testimony now in the official record, Gustav vom Rath returned to Germany and played no further role in the case. Diewerge, however, was not quite done with him. A hasty propaganda tract titled *Affair Grynszpan* was published in Berlin in 1939 under the byline of Gustav vom Rath, although Grynszpan scholar Ronald Roizen insists that "more likely, his name was merely appropriated to it by the Nazis in order to enhance the book's propagandistic value."[20] Aside from the pseudonymous book, almost surely the product of Diewerge's propaganda mill, Rath himself had nothing more to say about the assassination of his son.

Gustav vom Rath's service to the Third Reich, however, was not over yet. He was later elevated to a high rank in the Berlin police department, where he was assigned special responsibility for "Jewish affairs." To make the capital of the thousand-year Reich *Judenfrei* was a point of honor for Joseph Goebbels, *Gauleiter* of Berlin, and for the Führer himself. A certain wishful rumor credits Rath with efforts "to be of some help to victims of Nazi policies and actions."[21] Like so much of the lore that has come to be attached to the Grynszpan case, however, no hard evidence exists for his good deeds.

✦   ✦   ✦

ON THE NIGHT OF August 31, 1939, a squad of soldiers wearing Polish uniforms and carrying Polish weapons attacked a German radio station in the town of Gleiwitz on the German–Polish frontier. One of the soldiers seized the microphone in the broadcast studio and announced in Polish that "the time had come for conflict between Germans and Poles."[22] When the soldiers broke off the attack, they left behind the bodies of their comrades who had fallen in the exchange of gunfire with German defenders. Or so it was made to appear.

The incident at Gleiwitz, however, was strictly a sham. The attackers were SS men whose Polish equipment had been acquired by German army intelligence at Hitler's personal command. The corpses were those of concentration camp inmates who had been murdered by injections of poison, then supplied with purely cosmetic gunshot wounds, and left behind at the radio station to suggest that a firefight had taken place. The man at the microphone had been a Polish-speaking German soldier with a script that had been provided to him by the SS. The masterminds of the phony battle, code-named Operation Himmler, were the same men who had orchestrated the "spontaneous" events of Kristallnacht—Obergruppenführer-SS Reinhard Heydrich, second-in-command to Himmler and one of the key executors of the Holocaust, and Gestapo chief Heinrich Müller.

Just as Hitler had used the shooting of Rath as a pretext for Kristallnacht, the Führer now resorted to a staged attack on the Gleiwitz radio station to provide a *cause de guerre* for his long-planned invasion of Poland. At dawn on the next morning—September 1—the troops and tanks of the Wehrmacht crossed the frontier in force. Two days later, after years of appeasement and at a moment when the Polish cause was already lost, Britain and France finally honored their treaty obligations to Poland by declaring that a state of war existed with Germany. The fate of Herschel Grynszpan changed overnight.

On the day that war was declared, British composer Michael Tippett—an openly gay conscientious objector who was later sentenced to prison for his principled refusal to fight—set to work on an oratorio in honor of Herschel Grynszpan titled *A Child of Our Time*. On the far shore of the English Channel, however, France was suddenly confronted with an existential threat that wholly eclipsed the Grynszpan case. Judge Tesnière was called up to serve in the French army, and so was Maître Weill-Goudchaux. Grimm, Diewerge, and the German diplomatic mission in Paris in its entirety were evacuated to Berlin, and the embassy at 78 rue de Lille was locked and shuttered. The dossier for the Grynszpan case was assigned to a new examining magistrate, a judge named Glorian, but he conducted only a single hearing. The Grynszpan file was shelved and forgotten.

The state of war between France and Germany was a curious one. Poland fought alone and fell to the Third Reich before the end of September. The only substantial show of arms on the ground by France and Britain in the early months of World War II was a skirmish that took place in Denmark, where an expeditionary force was put ashore and promptly defeated by the Wehrmacht. Along the Maginot Line, the string of fortifications on the Franco–German frontier, French troops sat inside their bunkers and watched the enemy through the gunports without firing a shot. The western front was so proverbially quiet after the outbreak of the Second World War that it came to be called the *drôle de guerre*—the phony war.

Indeed, a certain lightheartedness manifested itself in the preparations for war that were undertaken in Paris. At the Place Vendôme, encircled by the fashionable and expensive shops that were the glory of peacetime Paris, sandbags were stacked around the victory column that Napoleon had erected to celebrate his victory over Austria and Russia at the Battle of Austerlitz in 1805 to protect it from German bombardment if the Wehrmacht managed to come within artillery range of the French capital. These earnest precautions were parodied by the window dressers who put gas masks on the mannequins in the stylish shop fronts, and the same theme was taken up by one chocolatier on the avenue de l'Opéra who offered boxes of bonbons that were fashioned to resemble gas masks.

As it happened, Paris remained unmolested as the Third Reich turned its attention to absorbing and exploiting its newly conquered Polish territory. Along with more than three million other Jewish citizens of Poland, Herschel's parents and siblings were now cut off from any possibility of escape to the west, although the Grynszpans were among the fortunate Polish Jews who scrambled to reach the Russian-occupied portion of Poland, which was allocated to the Soviet Union in a secret addendum to the nonaggression pact between Hitler and Stalin. Then Hitler turned his attention to Scandinavia, where he conquered and occupied Norway and Denmark in early 1940. France was in his crosshairs, to be sure, but not a single German bullet had yet been fired on French soil.

All the while, Herschel Grynszpan was confined to a cell at Fresnes prison, where his anxieties and ambitions were at war with each other. Several of his attorneys were now in uniform, the exchange of letters with his family in Poland was cut off, and the world press had largely forgotten about him, all of which was deeply unsettling. A single idea now obsessed him: the trial must be held, and the long wait for a verdict must come to an end at last. At Herschel's urging, Moro-Giafferi succeeded in obtaining a hearing before Judge Glorian on December 23, 1939.

Herschel demanded, yet again, to be put on trial or set free. As an inducement, he reprised an idea that he had used without success in a letter to the minister of justice in the summer of 1939. "Mr. Minister, I know that France is passing through a tragic period," Herschel had written. "I therefore request you to allow me to enlist in the French Army. I wish to redeem the act which I committed with my blood, and thus repair the troubles which I have caused the country which accorded me its hospitality."[23]

The young man went on to suggest to Judge Glorian, audaciously if also desperately, that a trial would surely end in acquittal and thus enable him to enlist in the army and serve on the fighting front against Nazi Germany. Judge Glorian, like the minister of justice, was unmoved by Herschel's plea—surely no battle with the seemingly invincible Wehrmacht would turn on the presence or absence of the scrawny defendant—and so Herschel was sent back to Fresnes with no trial date on the calendar. Herschel therefore came up with an entirely new and even more outlandish notion. On January 11, 1940, he unveiled his new idea in a remarkable letter to the public prosecutor.

"I have written you several letters in which I have asked you when my trial would take place," Herschel argued. "Up to now, you have not answered. I ask once more when you plan to hold the trial. If I don't have an answer by March 1, I will be obliged to go on a hunger strike for 24 hours as a warning. And if the trial is not held by March 31, I will find it necessary to go on a hunger strike until my strength fails."[24]

The miscalculation of the young prisoner, frantic and perhaps even delusional, is astounding. Convinced of his own place in history, Herschel assumed that the public prosecutor would be forced to submit to his demand rather than risk the scandal of his death by starvation behind a locked cell door. The reality was that Herschel's slow suicide probably appealed to the French authorities as a neat solution to an awkward problem. In any event, his latest letter, like all of his earlier ones, went unacknowledged and unanswered. No one in the government of France had time or reason to concern himself with Herschel Grynszpan while the tanks and troops of the Third Reich were deployed on the far side of the Maginot Line.

As the deadline for Herschel's hunger strike approached, Moro-Giafferi finally bestirred himself to write a letter of his own to the prosecutor. "I have repeatedly had the opportunity to express to you the wish that the case of Grynszpan come to trial," he reminded the prosecutor. "Today I can no longer wait to express to you my opinion." The mighty advocate seemed to acknowledge that he was being pressured by his own client—"he has such a strong character, this seemingly weak child"—but he also expressed his solidarity.

"My client requests his judgment—or freedom," wrote Moro-Giafferi. "There is no valid reason which empowers you to reject the request which is in keeping with law and justice. Shall we stand aside and view this drama of a youth who, faced with the passivity of the responsible powers, decides to die because of the postponement for many months of a trial whose preparations have long been completed?" The Corsican ended his plea with a phrase first uttered by Hillel, a revered rabbi of antiquity, and often invoked in Zionist circles: "If not now, when?"[25]

Not surprisingly, Moro-Giafferi's impassioned letter, too, was ignored. The deadline for the hunger strike passed and no trial date had been calendared, but Herschel did not carry out his threat, which is hardly surprising in light of his exalted sense of himself. Now a letter arrived from the French army base where Maître Weill-Goudchaux was then stationed. "I am sure that this will be a short war," wrote Weill-Goudchaux. "As soon as I am demobilized, after our victory, I will do my best to prepare your case, to take care of you, and march toward the glorious acquittal that you are waiting for."[26]

Meanwhile, after nearly two years of captivity, Herschel sat alone in his cell, nursed his nervous stomach, and fretted over his fate. If the promise of his doting Jewish attorney could be credited, he might one day appear in a French courtroom in the role of defendant. But if Weill-Goudchaux's cheerful prediction of a quick Allied victory over Nazi Germany turned out to be accurate, would his case still be the focus of international attention? After all, not unlike Martin Heidegger as described by Hannah Arendt, Herschel Grynszpan had "succumbed to the temptation . . . to 'intervene' in the world of human affairs," and what the boy must have feared most of all was to be forgotten.[27]

✦   ✦   ✦

THE PHONY WAR, WHICH had previously inspired in frivolous Parisian window dressers a sense of mischievous gaiety, turned into an authentic one on May 10, 1940, when the Wehrmacht finally moved against the armies of France and Britain along the western front. The Maginot Line was revealed to be an utter folly as Germany, adopting the same stratagem that had been successful in the First World War, attacked through neutral Belgium, Holland, and Luxembourg, and thus outflanked the fortified stretches of the Franco–German border.

On May 15, after a mere five days of fighting, the leadership of France was reduced to despair. "We have been defeated!" said the French premier, Paul Reynaud, in a panicky telephone call to his counterpart in London. "Impossible!" answered Winston Churchill.[28] But Reynaud was right. By the next morning, French officials were already burning official archives at the Quai d'Orsay, and government offices in their entirety were being trucked out of Paris in the direction of southern France, where the ministers and bureaucrats sought a place of refuge, first in Orléans, then in Bordeaux, and later in Vichy. The transmitters of the French state radio were shut down, and the populace of Paris was left to save itself.

"The panic in Paris was indescribable," Bill Shirer noted in his diary on his arrival in Paris. "Everyone lost his head. The government gave no lead. People were told to scoot, and at least three million out of the five million in the city ran, without baggage, literally ran on their feet toward the south."[29]

The same panic, in fact, swept over all of Belgium, Holland, and northern France in a vast human tsunami that came to be called *l'exode*—"an exodus without a leader," according to Victor Brombert, "and without miracles."[30] Some eight to ten million newly made refugees took to the roads in the days and weeks after the launch of the German invasion, if possible by train, truck, automobile, bicycle, or horse cart, or, if no other means of conveyance were available, on foot. Among them were political, artistic, and literary luminaries, both Jewish and non-Jewish—Henri Bergson, Colette, and Charles de Gaulle among them—but the vast majority consisted of ordinary French citizens.

"If a neighbor or the baker or, still worse, the local mayor was seen piling belongings into his car, it was hard not to follow his example," explains Alan Riding. "Most found themselves hungry and homeless, refugees in their own country."[31]

All the while, the French army continued to fall back under the punishing blows of the German blitzkrieg while the British Expeditionary Force—and 120,000 fleeing French troops along with them—executed a desperate evacuation from the beaches of Dunkirk between May 26 and June 4. On June 10, lest Fascist Italy be denied its small role in the defeat of the Western democracies, Mussolini belatedly declared war on France: "The hand that held the dagger," observed President Roosevelt, "has plunged it into the back of its neighbor."[32] The road to Paris was now open to the tanks and infantry of the Wehrmacht, and Paris itself was wholly undefended. To spare the French capital the devastation that had been visited upon Guernica, Rotterdam, and Warsaw, among other cities that had been targets of the Luftwaffe over the last several years, Paris was officially declared an open city on June 12.

"Everything was cracking up all around us," recalled the famous aviator and beloved author Antoine Saint-Exupéry, who was serving in the French air corps during the invasion. "The collapse was so entire and death itself seemed to us absurd."[33]

Paris surrendered on June 14, and the Wehrmacht marched en masse down the Champs-Elysées as the swastika flag flew from the Eiffel Tower. "Paris was a city of frivolity and corruption, of democracy and capitalism, where Jews had entry to the court, and niggers to the salons," declared a front-page editorial in the *Völkischer Beobachter*. "That Paris will never rise again."[34] Yet the bars and the brothels of Paris, which had been closed for the duration, promptly reopened, some of them offering German-language menus and signage for the convenience of their new patrons.

✦   ✦   ✦

THE FIRST WORLD WAR had lasted more than four years and cost some 1.4 million French lives, but the German flag had never fluttered over Paris. By contrast, the victorious German campaign on the western front in 1940 took only five weeks. France suffered some 100,000 casualties, killed and wounded, civilians and soldiers, a tiny fraction of the French body count in some of the bigger battles of World War I. From the first day of the German occupation of Paris, where the very best hotels—the Crillon, the Meurice, the Lutetia— were promptly repurposed as offices and dwelling places for the Nazi high command, the soldiers in field gray were all too often received not as conquerors but as new customers, perhaps overly aggressive but with money to spend. Looking back on the two decades of appeasement and defeatism by Britain and France that had followed the victory of 1918, the fall of France in 1940 seemed to take on a certain inevitability.

"I am completely indifferent to the defeat," wrote the conservative critic Paul Léautaud in his literary journal, "as indifferent as I was when I first saw a German soldier the other morning."[35]

Adolf Hitler, rarely one to forgo the opportunity for pomp and with his sure sense of showmanship, insisted on a richly symbolic ceremony for the signing of the armistice between France and Germany. The Wehrmacht sent a squad of field engineers to the museum where the French displayed the railroad car in which German emissaries had—ignominiously, as they saw it—signed the instrument of surrender that ended the First World War. An exterior wall was demolished, the wagon-lit was hauled out, and the car was set up on the very spot in the forest of Compiègne where it had stood in 1918. On June 21, 1940, Hitler personally received the French emissaries who now surrendered to Germany.

"I observed his face," wrote Bill Shirer. "It was grave, solemn, yet brimming with revenge. There was something else, a sort of scornful, inner joy at being present at this great reversal of fate—a reversal he himself had wrought."[36]

Revenge was more than a ceremonial act, however, when it came to Hitler's plans for the conquest and occupation of France. Indeed, the events of 1940 had been meticulously planned. Long in advance of the invasion, Himmler's staff had been charged with the responsibility of composing arrest lists that would be carried into France by the army of occupation. Some of the names on those lists belonged to politicians, public intellectuals, and other *Prominenten*. Some were activists, agents, and operatives of governments and organizations that the Nazis regarded as the enemies of the Third Reich. High on the list was the name of Herschel Grynszpan.

Grynszpan, in fact, was regarded as nothing less than a prize of war. From the day of the shooting of Rath, Nazi Germany had sought a way to extradite the boy from French custody and put him on trial in Berlin, where they could orchestrate the proceedings to maximum propaganda effect and then take off his head, quite literally, in a political auto-da-fé. The model was the notorious 1933 trial of a Dutch anarchist named Marinus van der Lubbe, who was convicted and beheaded for setting the fire in the Reichstag building that was the pretext for the Nazi seizure of power in Germany. The so-called Reichstag fire trial was badly bungled, but Goebbels had learned a lesson on how to run a show trial and knew that he would do a much better job with Grynszpan in the dock. French law may have protected Grynszpan from extradition until now, but such legal niceties no longer concerned Grimm and Diewerge now that France was under the German boot.

The efforts to arrest Herschel Grynszpan and seize his official dossier began on the very first day of the German occupation. The man in charge of the mission was one of the "peculiar intellectual gangsters," in Shirer's phrase, who could be found here and there in the Nazi ranks—a thirty-year-old Gestapo officer with a doctorate of philosophy named Helmut Knochen. (His name means "bones" in his native German.)[37] On June 14, Knochen and his men set up operations in the Hôtel de Louvre, and the next day he dispatched SS-Sturmbannführer Karl Bömelburg to the prefecture of police to recover the Grynszpan case files. Bömelburg, however, was told by the French police officials that, *hélas*, the boy and his papers were no longer in Paris.

Herschel, as it turned out, was the beneficiary of a few modest gestures of Gallic self-assertion that were undertaken by the government of France. During the last days of the war, some of the more sensitive files of the Ministry of Justice—and Grynszpan himself, along with other high-profile prisoners of the French Republic—were sent to southern France, which was distant from the fighting front and outside the zone of occupation that was soon imposed on France. To the consternation of Hitler and the Grynszpan task force, Herschel Grynszpan had slipped out of their grasp at the very moment of triumph, and his whereabouts were unknown.

✦   ✦   ✦

THE FATE OF THE French dossier for the Grynszpan case provides a rare instance of historical burlesque amid so much atrocity.[38] On the day of the German entry into Paris, a judge named Thevenin hastened to the Justice Ministry offices on the Place Vendôme to see whether he could be of service at the moment of crisis. The staff had already fled, however, and the place was empty. To his astonishment, he saw on one of the tables a small collection of objects that he recognized as the official state seals of the Republic of France, the very symbol of French sovereignty, which had been abandoned in the hasty flight. Judge Thevenin dutifully took the seals into his custody and reported the incident to the attorney general, a man named Cavarroc.

At that moment, as it happened, the attorney general was attending to another urgent matter of state. The official files of the most politically sensitive prisoners in French custody, the Grynszpan dossier among them, were being assembled and prepared for conveyance to the offices of the Justice Ministry in Orléans in southern France. Amid the chaos that prevailed in Paris, the rescue of the files was a matter of pure improvisation. Cavarroc entrusted the papers to a court official named Menegaud, who packed them in his own valise, put the luggage in the trunk of his car, and prepared to drive himself and his cargo on the crowded road in the direction of Angers, where the headquarters of the French court system was to be reestablished.

In a scene out of a Marx Brothers comedy—movies that had been popular in French cinemas in the 1930s but could no longer be exhibited under German occupation—Menegaud's departure was delayed when Cavarroc asked him whether he had room in the valise for one more item. The extra cargo, Cavarroc revealed, represented an item of consequence in the governance of *la Patrie*—the state seals of France. Menegaud rearranged the papers, nestled the seals among them, and struggled to close the valise again. With the valise back in his car, he headed south along a highway that was choked with retreating troops and panicked refugees. Now and then, German fighters appeared overhead on strafing missions, sometimes picking out official vehicles and sometimes contenting themselves with firing on private automobiles and their civilian passengers. Menegaud managed to reach Orléans before he was caught in a German air raid and his car was damaged beyond repair.

The resourceful and dutiful civil servant extracted the valise from his car and lugged it to the branch office of the Ministry of Justice in Orléans. Here, too, the government building had been abandoned and stood empty. The only person who remained at his post was the doughty concierge, who agreed to take custody of the valise and its valuable contents without knowing exactly what was inside. Having placed the files and seals in safekeeping with the concierge, Menegaud ventured back into the streets of Orléans and set out to find his way back to Paris.

Grynszpan's dossier—and the seals—were out of reach of the Gestapo, if only momentarily, and yet Herschel himself was embarked on an even more perilous journey.

✦   ✦   ✦

ON JUNE 1, 1940, the government of France reached the decision to remove the inmates from the prisons around Paris and secure them in various lockups around southern France. Herschel Grynszpan was among a contingent of ninety-six prisoners who were transferred from Fresnes to the prison at Orléans, some one hundred kilometers south of the capital. Under the threat of the accelerating German invasion, however, the prisoners were sent still deeper into southern France aboard a convoy of buses and trucks headed for the town of Bourges.

The convoy attracted the attention of a flight of German dive-bombers on combat patrol. The buses and trucks turned off the road, and both the prisoners and their guards scattered into woods and gullies for shelter against the falling bombs and the machine-gun fire. Most of the prisoners, and a few of the guards, took the opportunity to keep on going. Amid the chaos of the German invasion, they decided that the best way to save their own lives was to run. A few of the inmates, however, lingered submissively at the stopping point and waited for the remaining prison guards to tell them what to do.

Grynszpan dutifully stayed behind.

The boy had been capable of carrying out a single daring act on his own initiative, but he had spent the last twenty months inside a cell, where his daily needs and his security were provided by the government of France. Outside the prison walls were the armies and police agencies of Nazi Germany, which wished him only ill. As he reflected on his chances of survival on the run in the countryside—a friendless and penniless lad who spoke French only haltingly and with a thick foreign accent—the prospects of finding a safe refuge in France or finding a way across the far-off and well-guarded frontiers of Spain or Switzerland seemed remote. If the French villagers did not turn him away or turn him in, or so he must have concluded, then a German patrol would shoot him on sight or hand him over to the Gestapo.

So Grynszpan, with no fretful uncles or solicitous lawyers to help him, decided to stay with the convoy and to place his trust in the French guards to protect him. When the German planes broke off the attack, he presented himself to the sergeant in charge of the convoy and pleaded for safe passage to the prison at Bourges. The sergeant took custody of Herschel and a handful of other prisoners who had stayed behind, six in all, and the pitiful little band resumed its trek southward. On Sunday, June 17—the same day that the government of France petitioned Nazi Germany for an armistice—they rolled into Bourges, a quaint provincial town dominated by its soaring Gothic cathedral.

The prison warden at Bourges was both shocked and distressed to discover that Herschel Grynszpan—the single most notorious inmate in France—was among the ever-growing number of ordinary prisoners who were being dumped on him for safekeeping. He understood that the assassin of a Nazi diplomat was a high-value prisoner who would surely attract the attention of the invading German army. On the advice of the public prosecutor in Bourges, Paul Ribeyre, the warden simply left Grynszpan's name off the register of newly arriving prisoners and sought a way to pass him along to the prison at Châteauroux.

Perhaps because the warden tampered with the prison rolls, a report that later reached the watchful agents of the Ministry of Propaganda in Berlin held that "Grynszpan was not among the remaining six prisoners who arrived in Bourges" and that the prison officials "reported that they did not know Grynszpan."[39] Rather, the young man supposedly straggled into Bourges on foot and presented himself at the prison. By whatever means he succeeded in reaching Bourges, Herschel did not stay there long. The warden alerted the boy to the imminent arrival of the Germans and urged him to set out for Châteauroux, another sixty-five kilometers farther south.

Grynszpan must have followed the cars, trucks, and carts that were rolling through Bourges, day and night, as yet another manifestation of *l'exode*. Perhaps one of the drivers offered him a place inside a crowded sedan or a perch on an overloaded truck bed; more likely, Herschel, like countless other refugees, simply walked out of town and through the farmland that lay between Bourges and Châteauroux. The road passed through a forest reserve and followed the banks of the Indre River, but no one was pausing to admire the scenery on that day. If Grynszpan looked at anything except the harried man or woman walking ahead of him, it would have been an anxious skyward glance to see whether another Luftwaffe fighter was approaching for a strafing run.

The faintly Chaplinesque caravan eventually delivered Grynszpan at Châteauroux, and he somehow found his way to the gates of the provincial prison, whose warden was no happier to see Grynszpan than his colleague at Bourges had been. From there, Herschel was supposedly forwarded another three hundred kilometers southward to Toulouse. According to one of the various conflicting accounts, Herschel made his own way to Toulouse, where he arrived alone, fatigued and famished, penniless and panic-stricken. He pounded on the prison gate and tearfully begged to be taken into custody, more like a child in need of rescue than the avenger he once fancied himself to be. By now, Grynszpan had exhausted whatever resources of courage and endurance that he still possessed, and he sought only to place himself in the custody of any official caretaker who was not wearing a German uniform. At last, he found a French prison officer who was willing to perform an act of mercy by locking him up in a cell.

"Grynszpan's trip across France, knocking on prison doors in search of officials to accept his surrender," the *New York Times* reported on September 8, 1940, "will probably remain unique in prison annals."[40]

A variant of the same saga was reported by an unlikely hero of the Second World War, a thirty-two-year-old journalist with a Harvard degree named Varian Fry. Under Article 19 of the Franco-German armistice, France was obliged to "surrender on demand" any refugee from the Third Reich who was now in France—a category that included a vast number of escapees from both Germany and Austria and various conquered nations of Europe. Fry had been dispatched to France by the newly organized Emergency Rescue Committee in the summer of 1940 with the mandate to bring out as many of these refugees as he could find and liberate. He carried with him the names of two hundred likely candidates for rescue and $3,000 in currency, all concealed beneath his clothing.

For the next thirteen months, Fry managed to secure exit visas and safe passage for some of the most prominent refugees in France, including artists, writers, musicians, intellectuals, and politicians. Artist Marc Chagall, musician Wanda Landowska, sculptors Max Ernst and Jacques Lipchitz, and author Franz Werfel and his wife, Alma Mahler-Werfel—whose baggage contained the musical compositions of her late husband, Gustav Mahler—were among the beneficiaries of his efforts, and so was a then obscure German-Jewish refugee named Hannah Arendt. By contrast, Herschel Grynszpan, whose only claim to fame was the assassination of Rath, was not a person of interest to Fry even though the young prisoner was a priority target for extradition under Article 19.

Still, Fry was privy to the rumors that circulated among the refugees, and he picked up one tale about the fate of Herschel Grynszpan. According to Fry's version, the boy was sent by train from Orléans to Limoges, escaped when the train was attacked by German fighters, then walked to Limoges and surrendered to the public prosecutor, who sent him on to Toulouse in the company of two guards. When they arrived in Toulouse on a Sunday, they found no one at the prefecture of police who would accept the prisoner. So the guards released him, told him to find a place to spend the night, and invited him to report back to them the next morning. Grynszpan obliged and ended up in the only safe refuge that was available to the friendless young man—a French cell.

"Grynszpan's case is typical of the attitude of the French authorities," wrote Fry; "they would give a man a chance to escape before they arrested him, but if he didn't take it, they would arrest him and turn him over, in obedient fulfillment of the terms of the armistice."[41]

Whether he traveled via Châteauroux or Limoges, alone or in the company of French guards, Herschel ended up in Toulouse, and he concluded that no one was prepared to assist him other than the officials of the local prison. His relatives, his attorneys, and all of the various activists and sympathizers who had supported his cause were far away in Paris under German occupation, or so he thought. Ironically, he was wrong.

As it happens, Uncle Abraham, Aunt Chava, and Chava's brother were all swept up in *l'exode*, and all of them managed to reach Toulouse. So did Maître Fränkel, and *le Grand Patron*, Vincent de Moro-Giafferi, was only 130 kilometers away in the little town of

Aiguillon on the road to Bordeaux. The Grynszpans even ran into Fränkel on the hectic streets of Toulouse, and they shared their regrets and anxieties over the fate of their nephew. Amid the chaos and congestion, none of them had any ready way of knowing that Herschel, too, was close at hand.

Fränkel, however, was eventually alerted to the fact that Herschel was now being held in Toulouse, and he hastened to the prison to apply for permission to visit his client. Perhaps Fränkel would be able to secure his release and find him a hiding place, and in the meantime, he could provide a food parcel, some pocket money, a letter from his uncle Abraham and aunt Chava. A familiar face and a few words of Yiddish would have been a comfort in themselves. By the time the prison officials processed the request, however, Herschel Grynszpan had vanished yet again.

PART III

PARIS TO
BERLIN

9

IN THE BELLY
OF THE BEAST

THE INMATE IN CELL 50 OF THE CHERCHE-MIDI MILITARY
prison in Paris was marched to the interrogation room yet
again on July 11, 1940. Alfred Dreyfus had once been held at Cherche-Midi, but the old lockup had been put to use by the German
army of occupation for the confinement of political prisoners. The
jack-booted interrogator in field gray with a pistol on his belt was a
familiar figure to the man under questioning, but the session under-
way on that day was different from the preceding ones. The German
intelligence officer put his gun on the table, invited the prisoner to
write a final letter to his family, and ordered him to turn his face to
the wall. The prisoner was told that it was the last day of his life.

The prisoner was Paul Ribeyre, the public prosecutor of Bourges.
The Nazi investigators were convinced that he knew more than he
was willing to reveal about the maddening disappearance of "the
Jew Grynszpan." They had confirmed Grynszpan's departure from
Fresnes in the direction of Orléans, but they could not pick up his
trail after the prisoners scattered when their convoy was strafed by
the Luftwaffe. The French sergeant who had escorted the remaining
six prisoners to Bourges after the air attack testified that Grynszpan

had been among them, but the prison warden at Bourges insisted that "no one by that name had been interned there."[1] With refugees scattering in every direction, the Nazis fretted that Grynszpan might have found a secure hiding place in France or escaped to a safe refuge in another country.

No one in the Nazi security apparatus relished the prospect of reporting these facts to Hitler, who took a special interest in the Grynszpan case, and so the investigation continued. Attorney General Cavarroc, for example, had been questioned repeatedly in his office at the Ministry of Justice in Paris, but he insisted that he knew nothing about the whereabouts of the missing prisoner. A decision was made to put the attorney general to yet another round of questioning under threat of formal arrest. Surely one or another of these recalcitrant French officials would crack under the brutal techniques of Nazi interrogators and tell the Germans where to find Grynszpan.

One vexing mystery, in fact, had been solved during the latest round of questioning of the attorney general. While the interrogation was in progress, an exhausted figure appeared at the door of Cavarroc's office in the Justice Ministry; it was Menegaud, the man who had been entrusted with Grynszpan's dossier and the state seals of France. He confirmed what Cavarroc had told the Gestapo about his humble but all-important valise and readily disclosed where he had stashed it. A squad of Nazi officers was dispatched to the lodging place of the concierge in Orléans. So the Grynszpan dossier, if not Grynszpan himself, was in German hands at last.

Paul Ribeyre, too, had been questioned several times by the Gestapo before his arrest on June 30, and then he was conveyed from Bourges to Paris to be examined under more harrowing circumstances. The death sentence that the German officer imposed on Ribeyre on July 11 was merely a bluff, one of the various tools available to the expert interrogators of the Nazi security services. The

Germans wanted to break the will of the suspect and extract a confession, and they finally succeeded in doing so.

Under the threat of death by *Genickschuss*, Ribeyre finally admitted that he had received Grynszpan in Bourges and then sent him on his way ahead of the approaching German army. He defended the release of the prisoner as a rightful exercise of his authority and gallantly insisted that it had been his decision alone, thus attempting to spare the local prison warden from culpability. With Ribeyre's confession in hand at last, the Nazi interrogator sent him back to Cell 50. Now that Ribeyre had broken down and revealed what he knew regarding the whereabouts of Grynszpan, the public prosecutor was released from Cherche-Midi two days later and sent home to Bourges.

The Germans, as it turned out, had already found the prisoner they wanted, but the arrest of the Jew Grynszpan had been the result of old-fashioned diplomacy rather than questioning under torture.

✦   ✦   ✦

BY EARLY JULY, UNOCCUPIED France—the southeastern portion of the country along a line of demarcation meandering from the Swiss border to the Spanish border—was under the nominal authority of the collaborationist regime, whose seat of government was located in Vichy, a town formerly known only as a salubrious spa resort where one could take the waters. To symbolize the new state, the national motto that had originated during the French Revolution—*Liberté, égalité, fraternité* (Liberty, equality, fraternity)—was replaced on the official coinage of Vichy France with *Travail, famille, patrie* (Work, family, fatherland), a credo that echoed the propaganda line of its Nazi overlords.

"Our defeat was a result of our laxity," scolded Marshal Philippe Pétain, the aging hero of the Battle of Verdun who was now the premier of the Vichy government, in a radio broadcast. "The spirit of enjoyment destroyed what the spirit of sacrifice had built."[2]

Since a compliant regime was in place in the unoccupied zone of France, a diplomatic note was dispatched from Berlin to Vichy with a query regarding the whereabouts of Herschel Grynszpan. The French officials at Vichy were considerably more forthcoming than their colleagues at the Ministry of Justice in Paris, and they hastened to assist the German authorities. A few days later, they reported that the missing prisoner had finally been found among the inmates in the prison at Toulouse.

The good news was passed along to Friedrich Grimm, the Foreign Ministry legal expert who had arrived in Paris on the heels of the Wehrmacht to resume the operations of the Grynszpan task force. Two years earlier, Grimm himself had warned his superiors that French law would not permit extradition of Herschel Grynszpan to the Third Reich. Given the convenient circumstances of the occupation, Grimm now prepared and sent a request for extradition under the terms of Article 19 of the armistice agreement, which obliged France to surrender persons of interest to the Third Reich. The Vichy regime, unlike the French Republic, was perfectly willing to overlook the letter of French law and comply with the Nazi demand.

"In so doing," observes Dr. Alain Cuénot, Vichy France sought "to demonstrate its good will towards the 'New Order,'" the phrase that Hitler used to describe the thousand-year era of Nazi rule that had now begun.[3] The surrender of "the Jew Grynszpan" would be only the first such demonstration of good will at the expense of the Jewish population of France, but it came as especially welcome news to the Führer. Grimm and his boss, Foreign Minister Joachim von Ribbentrop, took pride in pointing out that the arrest had resulted from their exercise of diplomacy rather than the more brutal measures of the Gestapo.

Strictly speaking, and ironically, the extradition was illegal even under the terms of the armistice agreement, which obliged the French government "to surrender upon demand all Germans named by the

German Government in France."[4] But Herschel, even though born in Hanover, had never been granted German citizenship. "Everyone seemed to agree," Gerald Schwab dryly notes, "that Herschel Grynszpan was a Pole."[5] Indeed, that was the rationale for the expulsion of 12,000 Jews with Polish passports that had provoked Grynszpan to pick up a gun in the first place. Such technicalities did not go unnoticed by Herschel himself. For now, however, he would be reminded that the Third Reich simply dispensed with legal formalities whenever they interfered with Hitler's will.

Still, it was a legalism that explains why the Third Reich devoted so much time and trouble to the search for the missing Grynszpan. If the assassin of Rath were merely to be punished for his crime, he could have been given "special handling," the standard Nazi euphemism for summary execution. Grynszpan, however, had already been selected to appear as the principal player in a Nazi passion play—a show trial that was intended to demonstrate why every Jewish man, woman, and child in the world was a deadly enemy of the Third Reich.

✦   ✦   ✦

ALL OF THESE INTRIGUES were unknown to Herschel Grynszpan as he sat in his cell at the Toulouse prison in the early days of July 1940. The noise and clamor around him must have been unfamiliar and unsettling; Fresnes, after all, had been a model facility for the rehabilitation of juvenile offenders, but now he was in an old-fashioned prison that was a dumping ground for the criminal population of occupied France. He may have still hoped for rescue or, at least, the safety of a cell in the portion of France that was not yet under German occupation. Even if he had badly misjudged the significance and consequence of his deed, he surely continued to believe that his role in history was not yet over. Grynszpan may have been delusional, but on that point he was right.

His confinement in Toulouse ended on July 5. Herschel heard footfalls in the corridor outside his cell and then the sound of a heavy iron key being inserted and turned in the door lock. He had been called out of confinement a hundred times before at Fresnes, but it had always been a sign that one of his relatives or his Yiddish-speaking lawyers was waiting for him in the visitor's room with a food parcel, a letter from his parents or siblings, perhaps a legal document to sign. The men who called for him now, however, were grim-faced French prison guards with a very different duty to perform.

Grynszpan, now nineteen years old, still slender but less boyish in appearance than on the day of his arrest, was taken in shackles from Toulouse to Vichy, where he was held by the French authorities while the paperwork for his extradition to Germany was finalized. He must have been startled at how quickly the machinery of French justice turned now that the Nazis were in charge. On July 18, he was driven in a police vehicle to the demarcation line between Vichy France and the zone of German occupation.

Awaiting him on the other side of the line was an elite deputation of German officers under the command of SS-Sturmbannführer Karl Bömelburg. No matter how stern the French guards at Toulouse may have seemed to Herschel, he was now braced by agents of the dreaded Gestapo. Bömelburg later complained that "the French government gave every indication that it would have preferred the prisoner to escape," but the little ceremony of surrender on the demarcation line was brisk and orderly.[6] The prisoner was escorted under close guard to the crossing point, German hands replaced the French hands that braced his upper arms, and he took the last step that delivered him into the belly of the beast.

Now that Grynszpan was finally in the hands of the Gestapo, the German officers ferried him out of France without further delay. Not even Grimm, who had spent the last two years in pursuit of Grynszpan, was permitted to glimpse the prisoner during his brief layover in Paris. Grynszpan was promptly put aboard a night flight to Berlin—his very first journey by airplane—and then hustled from the airport to the headquarters of the Reich Main Security Bureau at Prinz-Albrecht-Strasse 8, the notorious address that served as ground zero of the vast terror apparatus of Nazi Germany. On the morning of July 20, Herschel Grynszpan awakened from a fitful night to find himself in a Gestapo cell.*

Grynszpan had seen the interior of lockups in police stations, jails, and prisons across a broad swath of France—Paris, Fresnes, Bourges, Châteauroux, Toulouse—but now he was confined in a place that was universally known and feared as the site of unimaginable terror. Yet it is possible that he comforted himself even now with the kind of fanciful notions that were his habit of mind. After all, he had once penned a letter to Hitler that dared to suggest "a humanitarian act" on the part of the Führer as a condition for Herschel's forgiveness.[7] Perhaps he wondered whether the Gestapo would kindly provide him with the special foods that settled his nervous stomach.

Only one thing we know with certainty. Until now, Herschel had been able to rely on the attention and assistance of intimates and admirers in profusion. Maître Szwarc had aided him in composing the letter to Hitler, and Herschel had proudly shown it to the prison rabbi. The prison psychiatrists and social workers at Fresnes had

---

* On the same day four years later, a titled officer of the Wehrmacht, Count von Stauffenberg, attempted to do what his fellow aristocrat Friedrich Percyval Reck-Malleczewen had only fantasized about: Stauffenberg smuggled a bomb into the conference room where Hitler was presiding over a meeting of the Nazi high command. Hitler, of course, survived the explosion, and Stauffenberg was arrested and put to death by a firing squad on the same day. Unlike Grynszpan, Stauffenberg was, in fact, the agent of a conspiracy. His co-conspirators, many of whom were rounded up and executed, were German officers who imagined that they could strike a favorable deal with the western Allies if they replaced Hitler with a more agreeable leader.

pored over his journal entries and invited him to tell heart-tugging stories about his childhood. No less celebrated a figure than Dorothy Thompson had sent him pocket money. The *mishpocheh* had brought him food parcels, and the little army of lawyers had soothed him with stirring promises: "I will do my best to prepare your case, to take care of you, and march toward the glorious acquittal that you are waiting for."[8]

Now Herschel was alone in a Gestapo prison in Berlin. No family, no attorneys, no social workers, and no prison rabbis were available to succor him. If he were to survive at all, he could rely only upon himself. He must have wondered—and we are entitled to wonder, too—what he would be able to summon up from within himself, a scrawny, sparsely educated Jewish boy who was, as Grynszpan undoubtedly believed, confronting Hitler, Goebbels, Himmler, and the countless others who sought to humiliate him in court and then cut off his head.

✦   ✦   ✦

PERHAPS THE SINGLE BEST measure of where the Jew Grynszpan, stateless and friendless, ranked among the enemies of the Third Reich is found in the fact that SS-Obersturmbannführer Adolf Eichmann was called upon to personally interrogate him. Eichmann described himself as "the specialist for Jewish questions at the Reich Security Headquarters" and was regarded as such by his superiors, Himmler and Heydrich.[9] That is why he was placed in charge of the Central Office for Jewish Emigration, the apparatus that would soon be charged with the responsibility of transporting Jews by the millions to the death camps in Poland. So it fell upon Eichmann to question Grynszpan about his role in the international Jewish conspiracy, whose paid agent he was supposed to be and whose embodiment he became.

Eichmann's credentials as a so-called Jewish specialist were actually quite thin. He spoke a smattering of Hebrew, owned a copy of the *Encyclopedia Judaica* and subscribed to *Haint* (Today), a Yiddish publication with the same title as the newspaper that Herschel Grynszpan read so ardently in Paris. He had even managed to set foot in Palestine in 1937, although the British authorities allowed him to remain for only twenty-four hours. Still, Eichmann was invited to participate in some of the meetings for the planning of the show trial of Herschel Grynszpan, and he received special orders regarding the key assertion of the case—the Jewish conspiracy that had supposedly recruited Grynszpan to kill Ernst vom Rath.

"In the line of my duty I received an order that Grynszpan was in custody in Prinz-Albrecht-Strasse 8, he had had to be further examined concerning who was likely to have been behind the scenes," Eichmann told Captain Avner W. Less, the Israeli police officer who questioned him in preparation for his trial in Jerusalem in 1961.* "I still remember exactly, for I was curious to see what Grynszpan looked like."[10]

Indeed, it was his simple curiosity about the boy assassin that Eichmann recalled best; after all, a Jew who fought back against Nazi Germany was a rarity so early in the war. "He was very brief and brusque," recalled Eichmann about Grynszpan. "[H]e was indifferent and gave short replies to all the questions." Above all, it was

---

* Less was born in Berlin and, like Grynszpan, was a penniless and paperless adolescent when he sought refuge in Paris in 1933. He was thrown out of the hotel where he was staying because he could not pay the bill, and the hotelier kept his belongings. "I was wearing sneakers—not the most adequate footwear for winter in Paris," recalled Less. "But when you are young, you know how to bend under pressure and somehow you manage to get by." Less joined a Zionist youth movement in Paris and obtained an immigration permit for Palestine in August 1938, barely two months before the shooting of Rath. Jochen von Lang, ed., in collaboration with Claus Sibyll, *Eichmann Interrogated: Transcripts from the Archives of the Israeli Police*, trans. Ralph Manheim (New York: Da Capo Press, 1999), xxiv.

Herschel's boyish looks that remained in his memory: "On the whole, he looked well," Eichmann said. "He was a smallish lad, he was such a little man."[11]

Significantly, Eichmann confirmed that Grynszpan was the rare prisoner of the Gestapo who was not tortured. Precisely because he was to be put on trial with the world press in attendance, the prisoner could not be bruised, much less disfigured, and Eichmann's orders on this point had apparently been clearly communicated. "He was not examined in a particularly severe way," Eichmann later confirmed to his own interrogator in Jerusalem. "In any event, we would have had to have authorization."[12] When it came to Grynszpan, as with millions of other Jews whose deaths he facilitated, Eichmann insisted that he was only following orders.

Eichmann, however, failed in his mission to find evidence of a conspiracy to kill Rath. After all, he shrugged, the case had been under investigation since the day of the shooting several years earlier, and nothing had turned up yet. "If they had not found this out during all those years, then this examination would be pointless, this would be useless, but an order was an order," he recalled. Still, Eichmann dutifully completed his interrogation of "the little man" and submitted a report to the Gestapo: "It was a short report, because nothing came of it."[13]

Adolf Eichmann was only one of a parade of German officials who put Herschel Grynszpan under close examination. Herschel was prodded and probed by German physicians, psychiatrists, and other forensic experts, all of whom supplemented the copious notes that had been taken by their counterparts in France. He was deposed by German attorneys and magistrates. He was questioned repeatedly by the expert interrogators who were the pride of the Gestapo. What Herschel revealed to them was capable of shocking even Hitler himself.

✦   ✦   ✦

EICHMANN FOUND NO EVIDENCE of Jewish conspiracy in the assassination of Rath, but lack of evidence was never an impediment to the Third Reich. If some pretext were needed to justify an act of violence or aggression, for instance, it could easily be forged or staged. The counterfeit attack on the radio station at Gleiwitz in 1939 is one example, and the propaganda tract about the Grynszpan case that was published under the expropriated byline of Gustav vom Rath is another. What is striking is that such "evidence" mattered at all to brutal and ruthless men who were plainly willing to commit any crime, great or small, in service of their will to power.

Yet the trial of Hershel Grynszpan was a matter of utmost priority as far as Hitler was concerned, and it was always meant to serve the propaganda interests of the Third Reich, whether the trial was held in Paris or in Berlin. The guilt of the defendant on the charge of shooting Rath was self-evident and, indeed, self-confessed. Since Grynszpan was now in German custody, he could have been dispatched with a bullet to the back of the neck like thousands of other, less celebrated enemies of the Third Reich. Hitler, however, insisted on a show trial in order to put a face and a name on the international Jewish conspiracy that had always figured so importantly in his writings and rantings.

Yet it is also true that the propaganda function of the Grynszpan case changed significantly over time. In 1938, the point of the Grynszpan trial, as the Nazis saw it, was to deter France from going to war against the Third Reich by characterizing any opposition to German aggression as the result of Jewish manipulation and provocation. In 1940, the point was to blame Jewish influence for manipulating the government of France into declaring war on Germany after the invasion of Poland. By 1941, when Germany had invaded the Soviet Union and the mass murder of Jews was in progress, the Grynszpan trial took on a new and portentous meaning: the impulsive attack by a distraught Jewish boy on a German diplomat would be portrayed as an act of war by "world Jewry" against the Third Reich and would be made to justify the extermination of every Jewish man, woman, child, and baby within its reach.

"On November 7, 1938," Grimm would say in the speech he had prepared for the Grynszpan trial, "there fell in Paris in the modest office of Ernst vom Rath the first shot of the Jewish War."[14]

✦　✦　✦

WITH GRYNSZPAN AT THEIR disposal, propagandist Wolfgang Diewerge and attorney Friedrich Grimm set to work on scripting and stage-managing the upcoming trial, which was regarded by Goebbels as "less a judicial than a political matter," as he recorded in his diary. Indeed, Goebbels was obsessed with making sure that "things will be dealt with and arranged psychologically correctly." The trial must "attribute the war guilt primarily to the Jews," he instructed, "so that we can expect from it a great boost for our war effort."[15] Although the "steering committee" for the Grynszpan trial was staffed by Grimm and Diewerge—and included high-ranking representatives of the Justice Ministry and the Foreign Ministry— Goebbels was the mastermind. The Grynszpan trial was to be, above all, an extravaganza of Nazi propaganda.

Still, the men who were in charge of these elaborate preparations were always mindful that a show trial could backfire. The Nazis had stumbled badly in 1933 when they staged a trial of Marinus van der Lubbe, commonly described by historians as "a half-witted Dutch Communist with a passion for arson," on the charge of setting fire to the Reichstag building on the night of February 27, 1933.[16] Göring had rushed to the scene of the fire and declared on the spot, as if Bolshevik arson produced a distinctive odor, that it had been the work of a Communist conspiracy. The Communists, who were still sitting as parliamentary delegates in the Reichstag, accused the Nazis of setting the fire as a pretext to seize absolute power in Germany, which is exactly what they did on the day after the incident. "The idea for the fire," argues William Shirer, who served as an American foreign correspondent in Nazi Germany during the 1930s, "almost surely originated with Goebbels and Goering."[17]

To support their accusation of conspiracy against their political adversaries, and to acquit themselves of the same accusation, the Nazis charged four Communists—including Georgi Dimitrov, a Bulgarian who served as general secretary of the Communist International—as co-conspirators and put them on trial along with van der Lubbe.* Dimitrov acted as his own attorney and bested Göring in an expert cross-examination that prompted the Nazi leader to threaten the defendant from the witness stand. "Are you afraid of my questions?" taunted Dimitrov. "You wait until we get you outside this court, you scoundrel!" raged Göring.[18] Remarkably, all of the defendants except van der Lubbe were acquitted. Van der Lubbe was convicted and beheaded, the executioner who operated the guillotine dressing for the occasion in "tails, top hat and white gloves."[19]

Yet the Reichstag fire trial, for all of its flaws in execution, was the prototype of a certain kind of Nazi theatricality that was repeated on Kristallnacht and on the eve of the invasion of Poland, among many other occasions when the Third Reich displayed "the same deliberate and conspiratorial cunning which had been first shown on 27 February 1933," according to historian A. J. P. Taylor.[20] The Nazi regime, however, was even more experienced in 1940 than it had been in 1933 when it came to the staging of events that were meant mostly or only for their propaganda value. None of the mistakes that had been made in the Reichstag fire trial would be repeated in the Grynszpan trial, or so vowed Grimm and Diewerge.

* A mock trial was staged by anti-Nazi activists in London in 1933 to counter the Nazi allegations in the Reichstag fire trial. Vincent de Moro-Giafferi traveled to London to play the role of prosecutor and argued that Hitler and Göring were culpable as co-conspirators.

The trial would take place in the *Volksgerichtshof* (People's Court), an arm of the Nazi Party designed as a "revolutionary tribunal to purify the nation," rather than in the official courts of Germany.[21] The largest available courtroom, with a capacity of 250 seats, was to be used in order to accommodate the reporters from the various occupied, allied, and neutral countries who would be invited to cover the trial. A public address system was to be installed, along with phone lines and phone booths for use by the press, and interpreters would be recruited to translate the proceedings into various foreign languages. Still, the planners vowed that every effort was to be made to avoid "the circus atmosphere of the Reichstag trial" and to conduct the trial "in a solemn and effective manner."[22]

Thus the judge, the prosecutors, and even the defense attorney—a compliant fellow named Weimann who was to be "instructed by [People's Court President] Thierack in the appropriate manner regarding his duties in the course of the trial"—were handpicked by the planners and approved by Hitler.[23] Since German courts lacked jurisdiction over the assassination of a diplomat that had taken place abroad, Grynszpan would be charged not with murder but with high treason, a crime that was so vaguely defined under German law that the jurisdiction of the Nazi court arguably reached all the way to Paris. The trial would last exactly seven days, and a long list of witnesses and a detailed description of their testimony were composed. Even the verdict—guilty on all counts—and the death sentence were all specified in advance in the master plan for the Grynszpan trial.

On one crucial point, the trial planners were confident. The defendants in the Reichstag fire trial had managed to call the attention of the world to their protestations of innocence and their accusations against the Nazi regime, and Dimitrov was even allowed to put Göring under cross-examination. No such gestures of defiance were to be permitted in the Grynszpan trial, and no word of testimony would be unscripted. Indeed, Grimm told the steering committee, the defendant had already announced that he did not desire to take the witness stand and intended to remain silent throughout the trial.

Or so Grynszpan said during the early interrogations on German soil in 1940. Still, he had told more than one version of his story to his French examiners, and he would do so again now that he was in the custody of the Gestapo.

✦   ✦   ✦

ONLY AFTER THE END of World War II did the preparations for the Nazi show trial of Herschel Grynszpan come to light. Gerald Schwab, an American then serving as a German translator for the International Military Tribunal at Nuremberg, happened to uncover the Grynszpan documents while reviewing the files of the Ministry of Justice for possible use in the trials of Nazi war criminals.* The German clerk who retrieved the papers and delivered them to Schwab turned out to be none other than Nagorka, the receptionist at the German embassy in Paris who had shown Grynszpan to Rath's office on the day of the shooting in 1938. Nagorka's name showed up on one of those documents as a principal witness for the prosecution in the Grynszpan trial.

The files that had been assembled in Berlin in 1940 by Grimm and Diewerge reflected the extraordinary reach of the Nazi security apparatus. The official dossiers of the police, the examining magistrate, the public prosecutor, and various prisons around France had been seized. The law offices of Moro-Giafferi and Grynszpan's other attorneys had been ransacked within twenty-four hours after the

---

* Gerald Schwab was born to a Jewish family in Freiburg in 1925. Shortly after Kristallnacht, his parents secured a place for him aboard a Kindertransport, and the family was reunited in the United States in 1940. Schwab served as a corporal in the U.S. Army during World War II, and he was recruited to serve as a translator for the prosecution at the Nuremberg trials in 1946. He subsequently had a long career in the State Department.

German army entered Paris. Even the headquarters of the LICA (Ligue Internationale contre L'antisémitisme) had been scoured for evidence of the elusive international Jewish conspiracy. All of the Grynszpan files had been transferred to the trial planners in Berlin, along with the interviews of Herschel's childhood friends and teachers by Gestapo agents, his medical and school records, photographs of the family apartment in Hanover, and even the precise amounts that had been received by his father in welfare payments and paid by his uncle for rent in Paris.

Every scrap of paper was studied and evaluated by Grimm and Diewerge in preparation for the show trial, which was initially scheduled to take place as early as 1941. Grynszpan was to be the featured player in the show trial, and they measured his strengths and weaknesses in intimate detail. The Nazis knew, for example, that Herschel was once diagnosed with infantile rickets, a condition that was known in German as "the English sickness."[24] They knew that he carried a scar on his right thigh as the result of an accident when he was thirteen years old. They detected in his "crenated" teeth a sign that he suffered from something they called "hereditary syphilis." Herschel's nervous stomach "could have stemmed from either neuropathological causes or from an ulcer."[25]

The goal of the show trial was to depict Grynszpan as fully capable of—and culpable for—the crime of assassination. Van der Lubbe had been described by critics of the Reichstag fire trial as a mental defective who must have been manipulated by the Nazis themselves, for example, but the comments of Grynszpan's grade school teachers could be put into evidence to prove that he was a "quick study and of above-average intelligence." To rebut the allegation that his studies suffered from anti-Semitic discrimination in the classroom, they examined his report cards and perversely concluded that his grades actually improved after Hitler came to power. At the same time, the testimony of his teachers would be used to characterize

Herschel as someone who "possessed a violent nature," "a fighter who made use of his fists," a boy who was "mean-spirited, ill-tempered, sullen, and taciturn."[26]

Above all, Herschel Grynszpan was to be presented to the world as an incarnation of "the Eternal Jew," stereotypically crafty and degenerate, and a plausible agent of the Jewish conspiracy that afflicted the imagination of the Nazis. The boy would be made to match the demonic figure that had been featured in the propaganda of the Nazi Party from its outset: "the [tool] of a gruesome international power," as Hitler had put it at the funeral of Gustloff, and the willing operative of "the higher powers of International Jewry and bolshevism," as Grimm was prepared to say in his testimony at the Grynszpan trial.

Yet the single most remarkable assertion in the Grynszpan case, as it turns out, was not detected by the German trial planners until the defendant himself revealed it to a Gestapo agent while under interrogation in a Gestapo cell in the fall of 1941, more than a year after his return to the Third Reich.

✦　✦　✦

ON JANUARY 18, 1941, Herschel Grynszpan was transferred from a Gestapo cell at Prinz-Albrecht-Strasse to Sachsenhausen, some thirty-five kilometers north of Berlin, one of the first of the *Konzentrationslager* that came to serve as iconic fixtures of the Nazi regime, to await the day of his trial. He was confined in an area of the concentration camp known casually as the bunker, a place where other high-value prisoners were held. These *Prominenten*, including military officers, church leaders, and foreign diplomats, were all deemed to be enemies of the Third Reich for one reason or another and yet important enough to be kept alive in case they could be profitably exchanged for German prisoners in Allied custody or, in Grynszpan's case, for a show trial.

Grynszpan was unique among the millions of Jewish "subjects" of the Third Reich. The camp guards were under strict orders, originating with the Führer himself, to keep the boy alive, well, and presentable. Unlike other inmates, his head was not shaved, and he was allowed to wear civilian clothes, or so reports Harry Naujoks, a German political prisoner whose memoir describes his encounters with Grynszpan at Sachsenhausen. Grynszpan was allowed to eat the same meals that were served to his guards, and he was given a job as an orderly, which spared him from the hard labor that was a form of torture and even murder throughout the camp system. They called him *Bubi* (Baby), perhaps as a taunt, a homosexual innuendo, or maybe because a few of them found the boyish prisoner to be somehow endearing.

Like Adolf Eichmann, the officers and guards at Sachsenhausen understood that the prisoner was being held for a show trial and must not be treated with the kind of casual cruelty that was permitted and even encouraged toward most other inmates. After all, the propaganda effect of a show trial would be ruined if the reporters in the gallery were able to discern that the defendant had been starved or tortured. And the trial of Herschel Grynszpan could not take place at all if the defendant died in custody. Indeed, Grynszpan, whose slightness made him appear to be especially fragile, was treated with even greater care and delicacy in Nazi Germany than he had been in France.

After more than a year in the custody of the Gestapo, the Nazi investigation was nearing completion, although Grimm and Diewerge were still tweaking the script for the seven-day trial under the watchful eye of Joseph Goebbels. No firm date had yet been set for the trial, but the prisoner was periodically reexamined to make sure that he was in a suitable condition for public display and that there were no surprises in the open court. That was why, in fact, a Gestapo agent named Jagusch was assigned to question Grynszpan yet again in the fall of 1941.

Herschel Grynszpan had been the object of continuous investigation over the preceding three years by journalists, attorneys, psychiatrists, social workers, police detectives, and security agents in two countries. Jagusch could not have expected to extract anything from the prisoner that was not already in the dossier of the Grynszpan case. Yet the Gestapo man discovered that Grynszpan had one more secret to reveal.

10

PARAGRAPH ONE HUNDRED SEVENTY-FIVE

THE STORY THAT HERSCHEL BEGAN TO REVEAL TO HIS latest Gestapo interrogator harked back to a rainy Saturday afternoon in Paris in the summer of 1938.

According to his account, Herschel was idling on the sidewalk at the Place de la République, a public square on the edge of the Tenth Arrondissement and the Marais, not far from Uncle Abraham's apartment-workshop. He was approached by a man in his late twenties, attired in a light-colored overcoat, a confident, handsome, and well-attired fellow who struck up a conversation with him. The exchange of words, tentative and oblique at first, soon turned into a frank proposition; the older man invited the boy to accompany him to a hotel for a sexual encounter. The man, according to Herschel, was Ernst vom Rath.

Herschel agreed to the arrangement and rode with the stranger in a taxicab to the Montmartre district, where Rath escorted him into a hotel that conveniently offered rooms by the hour for the use of couples of various sexual orientations and combinations. Behind the closed doors of the hotel room, Rath and Grynszpan engaged in a brief tryst, and then Rath handed the boy a wad of currency. To judge from Herschel's version, both Grynszpan and Rath were practiced at such encounters, and circumstances that Herschel described certainly conjure up a mercantile encounter between two willing participants in the ancient trade of prostitution.

As Grynszpan conjured up the scene, in a Gestapo interrogation room, Rath was enchanted by—and perhaps even obsessed with—the slender boy with brooding brown eyes. He implored Herschel to meet him again, and a date was set for their second encounter. Now, however, Herschel's account subtly changed in tone and direction. After his second afternoon in bed with Rath, the boy decided that the experience was "distasteful" and resolved to "end the affair."[1] Rath, however, was not easily persuaded to break off the dalliance. Indeed, he began to stalk the boy he had seduced in a desperate effort to lure him back into bed.

The diplomat lurked in a doorway across the street from the apartment house on the rue des Petites Écuries, and when Herschel stepped out of the building, Rath approached and pleaded for another rendezvous. Herschel refused, and the man turned suddenly resentful and threatening. Now Herschel was panicked: Was the man so agitated that he would ring the bell of Maison Albert and reveal the details of their unspeakable relationship to Uncle Abraham and Aunt Chava? The fact that the man was a Nazi diplomat would make the whole affair seem even more shameful. Herschel's fretful nature would not allow him to contain these new anxieties, and he convinced himself that a shattering scandal was about to be visited upon the Grynszpan household.

Herschel resolved to confront Rath again and make another and even forceful effort to break it off. He, too, could play on the fear of scandal by showing up at the German embassy and making threats of his own against the diplomat. The setting itself, with Hitler's official portrait hanging on the wall and his colleagues all around him, would remind Rath of the peril that he faced if Herschel revealed their affair. So the boy invented a tale about secret papers in order to conceal the more intimate purpose of his visit, and once his presence was announced to Rath, the diplomat would have no choice but to receive him.

On November 7, 1938, Herschel presented himself at 78 rue de Lille and managed to enter the German embassy with his story about secret papers. Once ushered into Rath's office, he confronted the man who had seduced him into a homosexual liaison and now refused to leave him alone. They exchanged bitter accusations and recriminations, each one growing more agitated and distraught. At the most heated moment of the argument, Herschel drew his revolver and fired at Rath. Once in police custody, he concealed the real motive for the murder by dressing it up in the guise of a political assassination.

Or so ended the story that Herschel presented to his Gestapo interrogator boldly and even courageously, a new and even more scandalous variant of the one he had told so many times before.

✦   ✦   ✦

THE SCENARIO, OF COURSE, is the same one that had been suggested to him in Paris two years earlier by his own attorney Moro-Giafferi. At the time, it was presented as a ploy to persuade a French jury that the whole affair had been a *crime passionelle* rather than a political assassination. Herschel had rejected it outright, and no mention of a homosexual encounter between Grynszpan and Rath ever entered the French records. Now, utterly alone and acting on his own initiative, and emboldened by the fact that his supposed suitor was not available to rebut his testimony, Herschel resurrected the story, dressed it up with colorful but also plausible details, and offered it to the Gestapo interrogator.

The young man was thoroughly practiced at self-delusion, and it seems likely that he had convinced himself that he enjoyed some kind of immunity even in the custody of the Gestapo. Surely he suspected that his best chance of survival was to allow the Nazis to believe that he would cooperate in the show trial and to hope that the trial itself would continue to be delayed as Hitler attended to more-urgent matters of politics, diplomacy, and war. He may have even allowed himself to believe that if the trial were delayed long enough, the war would be over and he would be set free by the Allies.

Yet Herschel apparently intuited that he possessed the power to frustrate the Nazi plan to use him as a caricature of the Eternal Jew in the show trial whose real target was the Jewish people. He seemed to recognize that the Nazis—and Hitler himself—regarded homosexuality with fear and loathing. He must have also known that any sexual contact between "Aryans" and Jews had been criminalized under the Nuremberg Laws. So Herschel understood that any suggestion that an official emissary of the Third Reich was a sexual predator with a taste for Jewish boys would be an embarrassing and even explosive matter. He had entertained the idea of challenging the legality of his extradition to Germany—or so the trial planners had discussed in one of their private deliberations—but now he had raised a far more effective threat to the success of the show trial.

Grynszpan seems to have concocted two alternate versions of his homosexual exploits. To the Gestapo interrogator, he depicted himself as a novice prostitute and Rath as a customer, perhaps his very first one. When a pair of German psychiatrists were later assigned to assess his mental condition in advance of the trial, he elevated his relationship with Rath from a commercial transaction into a love affair. Rath had courted him and then seduced him, Herschel now told the psychiatrists, all the while whispering promises that he would use his influence as a German diplomat to spare Herschel's parents and siblings from expulsion. Rath, however, did nothing to shelter them on the night of the arrest, shrugged off Herschel's desperate pleas for rescue from Zbąszyń, and spurned his inconvenient young lover. Herschel's motive for shooting Rath, according to the latest version of the story, was a breach of promise.[2]

The allegations of homosexual seduction and betrayal that Herschel had injected into the case provoked the excitable Goebbels into a frenzy. "Once again it can be demonstrated with what perfidious infamy the Jews give one the slip when one wishes to seize them by the scruff of the neck," he raged in his diary.[3] The Grynszpan trial was his pet project, and it was essential to put on a persuasive show. To be sure, Grynszpan could have been physically prevented from telling his scandalous story in open court, but Goebbels recognized that gagging the defendant would ruin the propaganda value of the trial.

Goebbels was now forced to report Grynszpan's threat to Hitler himself. Goebbels understood that Hitler might cancel the trial outright, and he struggled to find a way to persuade the Führer that he would be able to prevent Grynszpan from entering the witness box and testifying that Rath was a sexual predator who preyed on Jewish boys, which constituted not only an embarrassment to the Third Reich but a crime twice over under the Nuremberg Laws. "I will see with the experts in charge whether the trial should be continued under the present conditions," wrote Goebbels, "and if so, what means must be taken to avoid any possibility of such an outcome."[4]

✦   ✦   ✦

THE NAZIS, OF COURSE, directed their rage toward a long list of enemies, some real and some imaginary: Communists, socialists, Freemasons, and Jehovah's Witnesses, among many others. Still, they reserved a special contempt for homosexuals, whom they insisted on associating with the archenemy of the Third Reich, the Jews. "Among the many evil instincts that characterize the Jewish race, one that is especially pernicious has to do with sexual relationships," warned a Nazi newspaper in a 1929 article. "The Jews are forever trying to propagandize sexual relations between siblings, men and animals, and men and men. We National Socialists will soon unmask and condemn them by law." Indeed, the Nazis promised to punish these "vulgar, perverted crimes" with "banishment or hanging."[5]

The label of "homosexual pig" was freely applied by the Nazis to political rivals of various kinds.[6] Marinus van der Lubbe, the man accused of setting the Reichstag fire in 1933, was denounced as a homosexual, and so was Werner von Fritsch, a high-ranking general in the Wehrmacht who was falsely accused of homosexuality by Heinrich Himmler. On the so-called Night of Long Knives in 1934, Hitler moved against the radical left-wing faction of the Nazi Party by arresting Ernst Röhm, chief of the Sturmabteilung, and his inner circle of SA leaders. Until then, Röhm's sexual orientation and his easygoing attitude toward homosexuality in the ranks of the SA had been overlooked by the Führer—"It is the SA's task not to keep watch on the attire, complexion, and chastity of others," Röhm had declared, "but to haul Germany to its feet by dint of their free and revolutionary fighting spirit"—and yet his homosexuality was suddenly invoked as a pretext for his summary execution.[7]

Because he was an *Alter Kämpfer* who had marched at Hitler's side in the front rank of the Beer Hall Putsch—Röhm may have been a homosexual, but he enjoyed the privilege of addressing the Führer by first name or the familiar pronoun *du*—he was offered a pistol and an opportunity to take his own life. When the officer in charge of the execution returned to Röhm's cell, he found the condemned man alive and defiant. "Let Adolf do it himself," Röhm replied.[8] The fatal gunshots were administered by men in the uniform of the SS, the elite armed force of the Nazi Party whose men faced the death penalty if they engaged in homosexual conduct.

Once in authority, the Nazis acted quickly to abolish the tolerant attitude toward sexual orientation that had prevailed under the Weimar democracy. Bars and restaurants where gay men gathered were raided and closed down, and organizations that advocated the decriminalization of homosexuality were declared to be illegal. Men who were arrested for criminal sexual conduct—a mere glance at another man was enough if it was deemed to be "lewd"—were sent to a concentration camp after they had served their prison sentences, and they were identified by armbands bearing a patch in the shape of a pink triangle.[9]

The law that criminalized homosexuality in Germany was Paragraph 175 of the criminal code, a clause that dated back to 1871 and applied to "a male who indulges in criminally indecent activities with another male or who allows himself to participate in such activities."[10] For that reason, homosexual men were sometimes referred to as "One-Hundred-and-Seventy-Fivers."[11] By contrast, sexual relations between women were never a crime, although a few lesbian women were persecuted on an ad hoc basis in the Third Reich.

Himmler, the grand inquisitor of Nazi Germany and a zealous crusader against what he called the "plagues" and "abominations" of abortion and homosexuality, fortified the legal apparatus by ordering the Gestapo to establish a "Reich Center for the Combating of Abortion and Homosexuality" and securing from Hitler a "Purification Decree" that imposed the death penalty on homosexuals in the SS and the police.[12] Still, it was Paragraph 175 that remained the fundamental basis for the criminal prosecution of homosexuality in the Third Reich.

Once Grynszpan had disavowed his original high-minded motive for shooting Rath—and instead claimed that it resulted from his sordid sexual relations with the Nazi diplomat—the dutiful and literal-minded bureaucrats in the Justice Ministry promptly added a reference to the crime of sodomy under Paragraph 175 to his indictment on October 16, 1941, noting that the defendant now claimed that "he had been used by [Rath] several times for homosexual purposes."[13] The decision struck Goebbels as an act of idiocy, if not outright sabotage: "Grynszpan has until now always claimed, and rightly so, that he had not even known the counselor of legation whom he shot," he wrote. "The Ministry of Justice, however, did not hesitate to incorporate this claim in the indictment and to send the indictment to the defendant," thus "supply[ing] the Jew Grynszpan with the argument of Paragraph 175."[14]

Goebbels struggled to find a solution to the vexing problem that Grynszpan had created for the trial planners. If the defendant insisted on testifying about seduction or prostitution on the stand, Goebbels resolved, the judge could be instructed to clear the courtroom and conduct the examination of the defendant in closed session. Or the charge could be repudiated in open court as a groundless Jewish slander. Yet the master propagandist realized that such heavy-handed tactics threatened to turn the proceedings into a reprise of the Reichstag fire trial. He knew that he needed to find new and more inventive ways of showing the world that Grynszpan was a liar and that Rath preferred women over boys.

✦   ✦   ✦

THE GRYNSZPAN TRIAL WAS intended by Friedrich Grimm and Wolfgang Diewerge to be an orderly and exhaustive course in the malefactions of "World Jewry," seven full days in length. Grynszpan's act of violence against Rath was to be the centerpiece, and they had hoped to put Grynszpan on the stand on the first day, along with the key witnesses whose testimony related to the actual crime that Grynszpan committed at the German embassy in Paris.

Nagorka and other embassy staff members who had encountered Grynszpan face-to-face on the day of the shooting would be called to the stand. Paris police officer Autret, the owners of À la Fine Lame, and even a chambermaid from the Hôtel de Suez were all to be brought to Berlin from Paris. Judge Tesnière offered to appear as a witness in an effort to secure his release from the prisoner-of-war camp where he had been interned since the fall of France. Gustav vom Rath would be called to the stand, but only "if he is prepared [to testify],” according to a telling aside in the official trial schedule that seems to confirm the rumors of tension between the Rath family and the Nazi regime.[15] By the end of the first day of trial, the case against Herschel Grynszpan as the assassin of Ernst vom Rath would have been made in full detail.

The trial was also to feature a series of lectures by professors, diplomats, and other government officials, including the former foreign minister of France, Georges Bonnet, and both Grimm and Diewerge, all of whom were supposed to put the assassination of Rath into a suitable historical and political context. The greatest risk that the steering committee faced, at least until Herschel told his scandalous story of pederasty and prostitution, was sheer tedium as one putative expert after another took the stand and delivered his scripted testimony.

The trial planners, in fact, felt obliged to present every item of evidence, real or imagined, that they had accumulated over the years of investigation and speculation. Day five of the trial, for example, was scheduled to feature “confiscated documents, articles and newspapers which prove the intellectual origin of the shooting in World Jewry.”[16] Grimm and Diewerge were so enthused by the paper conspiracy they had concocted that they arranged to publish the collection in German under the title *Denkschrift* (Memoir) and later in French as *L’Affaire Grynspan: Un Attentant contre la France!* (The Grynszpan Case: An Assassination against France!).* According to Grimm, the assassination “was not an isolated act, explained by personal motive, but rather a prepared, premeditated political crime,” and he linked Grynszpan to “the Jew Schwartzbard,” who had assas-

---

* Grimm was credited as the author of *Denkschrift*. He used a pseudonym (Pierre Dumoulin) for the French edition in order to conceal its German authorship. Grimm is also the author of a book published in German under the title *Der Grünspan Prozess* (The Grynszpan Trial) and in French under the title *Affaire Grynszpan*. The French edition was published under the byline of Gustav vom Rath, the victim’s father.

sinated Petliura in Paris in 1926, and "the Jew Frankfurter," who had assassinated Gustloff in Davos in 1936.[17]

"The international Jewish circles, so quick to exploit the case, were not strangers to the attack. [T]hey were accomplices," wrote Grimm. "[A] thorough study of Grynspan's trial, of its intention, of its motifs, of its political framework, leads us to understand it is necessary to start the possible beginning of the actual war from the Grynspan attack. The first shots of the Jewish war were fired in Paris on November 7, 1938 . . . an infernal date, a fateful day. It is a kind of war declaration from international Judaism and its city, New York, against Germany."[18]

With his sordid new version of the incident at 78 rue de Lille, however, Herschel succeeded in shattering the case that Grimm and Diewerge had prepared so meticulously, and each shard reflected a different and ever more bizarre variant of the conspiracy theories that were already attached to *l'affaire Grynszpan*. Herschel had provided new and unsavory motives to the various players in the melodrama that he had described, and he opened the way to ever more outlandish speculation about the items of evidence that had been collected over the preceding three years. Indeed, he even provoked Goebbels, an expert and fearless artificer, into forging evidence where none existed.

The simple question of what words Grynszpan uttered in order to gain entry to the German embassy in Paris, for example, suddenly took on crucial implications. Did he ask to see "a gentleman from the embassy," as one witness said, or did he name a particular member of the embassy staff? If so, did he ask for "His Excellency, the Ambassador," as Ambassador Welczeck later claimed in a report to the Foreign Ministry?[19]

One witness said that Grynszpan asked for "one of the embassy secretaries," a phrase that might plausibly apply to Rath but also raised the risk that he would be ushered into the office of someone other than his intended victim.[20] Perhaps Grynszpan knew that Rath was the only one of the three legation secretaries on duty on the morning of the assassination and thus could ask for his intended victim by rank rather than name. Or maybe the story he told on the day of his arrest in Paris was true: Grynszpan fired at the target that chance had provided and did not even know the name of the man he murdered.

Evidence that was already in the German files took on new meanings. An unsigned note in the German language had been retrieved from the office of Moro-Giafferi by Nazi agents in Paris. The anonymous correspondent likened the assassination of Rath to "a second Reichstag fire," and insisted that it had been contrived by the Nazis themselves, not only to provide a pretext for Kristallnacht but also to liquidate an enemy of the regime. Grynszpan had been "encouraged by agents of Goebbels" to assassinate Rath because "[he] was anti-Nazi, a friend of the Jews, and the Nazis detested him."[21] What must have struck Moro-Giafferi as the rantings of a crank was now regarded with a measure of credulity.

"He knew too much and had to be done away with, one way or another," wrote the anonymous source. "The object of the Nazis was to kill two birds with one stone, to get rid of vom Rath and the Jews with their money."[22]

Goebbels, too, referred to "some sort of anonymous letter by a Jewish refugee" in one of his diary entries, but the letter that was known to Goebbels "hints at the likelihood of homosexual intercourse between Grynzpan and vom Rath." Although Goebbels dismissed the contents of the letter as "an absurd, typically Jewish claim," he was sufficiently unsettled by the charge of homosexuality to manufacture evidence to suggest that Rath's sexual appetite focused on lusty French women rather than skinny Jewish boys, or so one writer has argued.[23] Goebbels supposedly ordered the German postal censors to seize and forward any love letters from women in France to their boyfriends or husbands who were held in Germany as prisoners of war, especially if the letters contained explicitly erotic passages. The letters were to be altered by Gestapo forgers so that they appeared to be addressed to Rath "and would thus furnish proof of his 'normal' comportment in regard to women."[24]

These two versions of the case were later fused into a single all-encompassing scenario by Hannah Arendt in *Eichmann in Jerusalem*. She proposed that Herschel "acted as an unwitting tool of Gestapo agents in Paris," as we have already noted, and she credits the Gestapo for slandering Rath as a pederast: "[Rath] had been shadowed by the Gestapo because of his openly anti-Nazi views and his sympathy for Jews," she argued. "[T]he story of his homosexuality was probably fabricated by the Gestapo." Having embraced the argument, however, she blamed the Nazis for failing to realize "they could not have it both ways, that is, could not slander vom Rath as a homosexual having illicit relations with Jewish boys and also make of him a martyr and a victim of 'world Jewry.'"[25]

The bizarre notion that Grynszpan was a Gestapo agent has been cited by some researchers and commentators to explain why the boy did not take advantage of the opportunity to run and hide during the German invasion of France. If promises had been made to Grynszpan by a Gestapo handler, as one East German journalist later suggested, the boy might have insisted on putting himself back in a French cell in the confident expectation that he would be "liberated" by the Wehrmacht: "Perhaps Herschel was a Nazi *agent provocateur* who felt that he would be safe in the hands of German authorities."*[26]

---

* A simpler and more plausible explanation, however, is provided by the desperate circumstances that prevailed across France during *l'exode*. "Since my father could of course no longer drive and since in addition there was no gas to be had, we were on foot like so many others," recalls Gerard Caspary about his family's escape from Paris, in his unpublished memoir "From the Edge of the Holocaust." "The roads were so crowded—I remember on one occasion we had to proceed East for a few miles because the crowds pushed us in what was clearly the wrong direction—that it took us five full days to cover these 75 kilometres. The Wehrmacht overtook us just

Yet another item that entered the German dossier in the Grynszpan case is a so-called *Führerinformation*—that is, an official memo prepared for and directed to Hitler—regarding the plausibility of Grynszpan's accusations against Rath. An official of the Justice Ministry reminded Hitler that Grynszpan had accused Rath of being an active homosexual with multiple partners. "In this connection it is of interest that a brother of the murdered vom Rath, First Lieutenant and chief of a cavalry squadron, was sentenced to one year's imprisonment and loss of rank for sexual offenses with men by the Field Court Martial of Division 428, Special Mission."[27]

The Gestapo and other agents of the Nazi security apparatus monitored every aspect of German life, including the gossip and jokes that were passed among the citizenry. Among the items that came to the attention of the authorities was the rumor that Grynszpan had been "vom Rath's male whore and procurer for some time in 1938," the allegation that Rath was an habitué of various places where gay men met in Paris—although the Tout Va Bien was not mentioned—and the report that the young diplomat had acquired the nicknames "the ambassadress" and "Notre Dame de Paris."[28]

Even the diseases that Rath supposedly contracted while serving in the German consulate in Calcutta in 1936 came under new scrutiny. The official explanation, as we have noted, is that he received treatment for dysentery and tuberculosis at the Institute of Radiology in Berlin while on medical leave from the foreign service. Yet the Grynszpan files seized in Paris, according to a memorandum from Grimm, included a letter from a former Berlin radiologist, then living in Tel Aviv, who claimed that Rath had actually been treated for

---

a few kilometres before Chartres." Given the chaos that prevailed outside the prison walls, and lacking money, contacts, and even a ready command of the French language, Grynszpan may have despaired of finding food and shelter if he traveled on his own and preferred the apparent security provided by his French warders.

rectal gonorrhea, a disease that he had supposedly contracted "as a result of homosexual relations."[29]

Grynszpan himself, of course, was the source of more than one version of his own story. Harry Naujoks, an antifascist activist whose recollections about Kristallnacht we have already noted, encountered Grynszpan in the Sachsenhausen concentration camp, where he heard an entirely new and different theory of the case. Grynszpan told his fellow inmates that Rath had been actively engaged in smuggling money and property out of Nazi Germany on behalf of various Jewish refugees, including the Grynszpans, but the diplomat was less forthcoming when it came to turning over the loot after it arrived in Paris. Here, then, was an explanation for how the Grynszpans managed to send the mysterious 3,000 marks out of Germany—and yet another motive for Herschel's attack on Rath—even if neither one was supported by any hard evidence.

Rath's appearance as the ideal Nazi diplomat seemed to crack under the scrutiny of the various investigators, each with their own ulterior motives. Yet, just like the allegations of conspiracy, the latest theories of the Grynszpan case were conjured up out of gossip and supposition. Herschel himself—eerily handsome and androgynously thin, with a faint lisp and a taste for fashionable attire—may have realized that his stories of homosexual seduction and prostitution would be plausible enough in the eyes of some observers. And he seemed to intuit that Nazi homophobia bestowed upon him a weapon. Whether or not he was actually gay, he was clearly willing to set and spring a trap for his Nazi captors. Indeed, the story he told in a Gestapo interrogation cell may have been an invention, but it was also his single greatest act of courage.

✦   ✦   ✦

THE SKEIN OF RUMOR and conjecture, no matter how far-fetched, was considered quite seriously at the highest levels of decision-making in the Third Reich. Even if Grynszpan were to be denounced as a liar—and even if he was, in fact, a liar—the Nazi leadership realized that the frail young man had succeeded in raising an issue so ugly and so embarrassing that it might ruin the propaganda value of the show trial that had been so meticulously planned. Much as they might have wanted to solve the Grynszpan problem in the same way they were now solving the Jewish Problem—that is, by a *Genickschuss*—the decision-makers in Berlin realized that greater delicacy and ingenuity was now required.

An informer was placed in Grynszpan's cell—the operation was code-named *Grüne Hefte* (Green Books)—and his reports were conveyed to the chief prosecutor in charge of the case, who was repeatedly asked to share the findings with the Foreign Ministry but refused to do so out of concern for confidentiality. The prosecution was more forthcoming about a wholly remarkable document that supposedly had been hidden under the prisoner's clothing and seized after a routine search—a confession that was dictated by Grynszpan, who was chained and could not write it himself, to a fellow prisoner on April 24 and 25, 1942. The message was reduced to a cipher that utilized Hebrew characters, and much effort was required for the Nazi code breakers to crack it.

According to the translation that was preserved in the German records, Grynszpan confirmed that the "deposition" he had given to the Gestapo about a homosexual affair with Rath was untrue. "When France extradited me to Germany I thought that there would be no trial in that the Gestapo would murder me," Grynszpan declared. "This was naturally more to my liking than a grand propaganda trial whose results would be a death sentence and which undoubtedly would have resulted in bloody pogroms."

When Grynszpan saw that he was being treated "exceptionally very well" by the Gestapo, he deduced that he was being kept alive so he could be used "as a tool of German propaganda," and he resolved to do what he could to prevent a show trial by "utiliz[ing] a touchy phase out of the life of Mr. vom Rath with which my attorney Godcheaux [sic] acquainted me." For that reason, Grynszpan confessed, he had "made up false testimony to the Gestapo" in the hope that "they would murder me so that no outsider would get wind thereof."[30]

The circumstances surrounding the creation and discovery of the encrypted confession, at least according to the German sources, are so extraordinary—and so implausible—that yet another Nazi forgery must be suspected. One clue is provided in the pointed reference to Maître Weill-Goudchaux as the attorney who inspired the scenario of homosexual seduction. Moro-Giafferi, as we have seen, was the man who first suggested it to Herschel, but if the document was fabricated by the Nazis, it is significant that they sought to blame one of Herschel's Jewish attorneys. "Now, it is him who holds all the strings to this somber drama in his hands," wrote Grimm in *L'Affaire Grynspan*, "it is him who puts it all together, it is him who, we will see, organizes everything in secret. Oh, the good Jew!"[31]

Yet the contents of the confession ring true in light of what we know about Herschel Grynszpan's conduct in French custody, when he wrote letters to Hitler and threatened to kill himself by going on a hunger strike. Once in German custody, Grynszpan claimed that he "wrote a letter to the Gestapo in which I protested against my illegal extradition" and announced that "from now on [I] will not testify during interrogations or the trial." When he was transferred from Sachsenhausen to the interrogation unit at the Moabit prison in Berlin, he feared that a trial was imminent and "in order to prevent this I turned to the last available means which remained for me to suicide." Only because of "the vigilance of Guard Hollmurg" was his suicide attempt foiled, but "I have not given up hope that I will still succeed." If the Germans managed to keep him alive and put him on trial, "I will not defend myself at trial and refuse the judge all answers."[32]

The purpose of his secret confession, he revealed, was to send a message to the world about his motives and, not incidentally, to acquit himself of the sexual adventures he had described, a gesture that was entirely consistent with Grynszpan's vision of himself as a heroic and historic avenger of the Jewish people. "I have entrusted this admission to three persons," he stated, "in case they should someday wish to publish it."[33] He had devised a way to avoid the show trial that his Nazi captors had planned so meticulously, and he sought to preserve at least one item of evidence that would prove what he had managed to achieve from the confines of a Gestapo cell, alone and unabetted by attorneys, aunts and uncles, or crusading journalists.

When he first came to public attention in 1938, Herschel Grynszpan was a temperamental adolescent with a delusional notion of his own role in history. He was given to outlandish flights of fancy, ludicrous gestures of grandiosity, and moments of outright prevarication. At the same time, however, he was also intelligent, resourceful, cunning, and courageous. In 1942, at the age of twenty-one, he was facing the likelihood of an imminent and violent death at the hands of his Nazi captors. Yet he was capable of deploying the only weapon within his grasp that would prevent Adolf Hitler from using him as the straw man in a show trial that was meant to vilify the Jewish people and provide a pretext for mass murder.

✦   ✦   ✦

THE TRIAL OF HERSCHEL Grynszpan had been scheduled and postponed even before the startling and troublesome allegations of homosexuality, and the latest trial date was May 11, 1942. Surely the decoded confession, whether authentic or counterfeit, would have been marked as Exhibit 1 by the Nazis, who would have used it to defuse the charge that Grynszpan had laid against Rath. The opportunity never arose, as it turned out, and the confession was locked away in the archives along with the vast storehouse of documents that the Nazis had assembled. Grynszpan himself was secretly transferred out of Moabit prison and disappeared into the labyrinth of prisons and camps where other enemies of the Third Reich were confined while Hitler decided what to do with them.

Some members of the steering committee were still eager to put Grynszpan on trial after years of intensive preparation, but the risk of scandal remained so great that the decision was referred to Hitler himself. An informal query was made to Martin Bormann, the party secretary who served as gatekeeper to the Führer, and he passed back a reply that "there is no question of dropping the Grynszpan case, but only of postponing it."[34] Such an informal and oblique communication was regarded as insufficient by these self-protective survivors of the power struggles inside the Nazi regime, and a *Führerinformation* was prepared and submitted on April 17, 1942, under the plainspoken title "Murder Trial Grynszpan: Information for the Fuehrer concerning the Possibility That the Murderer Will Allege Homosexual Relations with the Victim."

The document pointedly asked whether the Führer was aware of the possibility of embarrassing testimony by Grynszpan about homosexuality and, if so, "should the trial materials remain unused in view of this Jewish lie?" Among the anxious trial watchers in the Foreign Ministry, it was openly acknowledged that "written authorization by the Fuehrer" was required "since trial preparations cannot be continued until then."[35]

On May 13, 1942, Hitler's answer was recorded in a memorandum composed by the head of the legal section of the Foreign Ministry and a member of the steering committee for the Grynszpan case, a man named Ewald Krümmer. The memo offers an intriguing glimpse into the Byzantine decision-making process that took place in the inner circles of the Nazi regime and, not incidentally, Hitler's caginess when it came to committing himself in writing to a decision.

Hitler had queried Ribbentrop "whether he thought the time was right to undertake the Grynszpan trial." Ribbentrop delayed in replying until he had consulted with Goebbels and then reported to the Führer that "the present time is not advantageous." Ribbentrop cited a number of reasons for his recommendation. First, "the people would not understand why such a large trial was being planned because of a single murder while, at the same time, hundreds of Germans were dying on the front." Second, precisely because the war news on the eastern front at that moment in 1942 was so dramatic and consequential, "world interest in the trial is not sufficiently great." Goebbels candidly added a third reason: "[H]e welcomed a postponement in view of Grynszpan's apparent plan to call attention to his illicit relationship with the victim."[36]

That was apparently all Hitler needed to hear. On the same day, a second memorandum was written by Roland Freisler, soon to be named president of the People's Court but then still serving in the Foreign Ministry, to the chief prosecutor in the Grynszpan case: the Führer had ordered the trial to be postponed but "personally reserved the right to determine a suitable future date."[37] On the next day, Goebbels corroborated Freisler's memo with a diary entry for May 14, 1942: "By agreement with Ribbentrop," he wrote, "the Grynszpan trial has been postponed until next autumn."[38]

So it was that Case No. 8-J-393/41-g of the People's Court—the case against Herschel Grynszpan—was shelved on orders from the Führer and abandoned by the cluster of Nazi officials whose mission had been to put him on trial. Grynszpan was discreetly removed from the Moabit prison in Berlin, where he would have been held during the show trial, and sent first to his former place of confinement at Sachsenhausen and finally, around September 26, 1942, to the prison at Magdeburg. No official document of the Third Reich discloses his fate.

11

GRYNSZPAN'S GHOST

THE LAST WORD THAT ZINDEL AND RIVKA GRYNSZPAN received from their son was an International Red Cross postcard that reached them in Poland in March or perhaps April 1940. Instead of the ardent and hyperbolic sentiments that he was capable of putting to paper, the postcard contained only a set of preprinted messages. Like similar forms in use during World War II, a Red Cross postcard afforded an opportunity to a prisoner of war or a refugee to fill in the blanks and underline the phrases that applied to him:

1. I am interned at _____.
2. My health is excellent; good; fair; poor.
3. I am—uninjured; sick in hospital; under treatment; not under treatment.
4. I am improving; not improving; better; well.[1]

Only the signature, clear and bold, had been applied to the postcard by Herschel's own hand.

On the day that Herschel's last postcard arrived, the fragile calculus by the combatants that had resulted in the phony war on the western front still held, although just barely. Strictly speaking, World War II had already commenced with the invasion of Poland, which had been promptly divided up into German and Soviet zones of occupation, but the French army had not yet bistirred itself.

Herschel's parents had fled eastward ahead of the German invasion of Poland, first to Radomsk and then to Swizlocz, a shtetl near Bialystok, and they were now temporarily safe in the portion of Poland had been allocated to the Soviet Union under the Nazi-Soviet nonaggression pact. Ironically, Herschel's anxiety over the fate of his parents and siblings—the motive he gave to the French authorities for the assassination of Ernst vom Rath—turned out to be misplaced.

Like hundreds of thousands of other Jews, Herschel's brother, Mordecai, joined the Red Army, and served on the fighting front against Nazi Germany throughout World War II. His mother and father were evacuated to Astrakhan, on the Volga River, where they remained during the war, and they were reunited with Mordecai in Palestine shortly before the declaration of Jewish statehood in 1948. Only Esther Grynszpan was overtaken by the German invasion of eastern Poland and the Soviet Union in June 1941, when Jewish men, women, and children were marched at gunpoint to open pits, forced to undress, and then shot to death by German soldiers and police officers.

So Herschel Grynszpan found himself in German custody as Prisoner No. 35181 even as the rest of his immediate family, excluding his beloved sister, succeeded in saving their own lives, one way or another. The very last reference to Grynszpan in the German archives was a memo dated December 7, 1942, when Foreign Minister Ribbentrop instructed the German ambassador in Paris to proceed with the publication of *L'Affaire Grynspan* in France in order to prove "the Jewish wire pulling behind the assassination aimed at the peace of Europe."[2] Significantly, the order issued to the Paris embassy noted that the Grynszpan documents should be circulated as widely as possible in France "even though, for the time being, the trial does not take place."[3]

The key phrase, of course, was "for the time being." Hitler had not yet decided what to do with the Jewish boy whose defiant assertions of homosexual seduction and betrayal had caused the Third Reich so much trouble, and the men around him understood that the Führer might order the trial to go forward whenever the impulse seized him. Indeed, the fact that Grynszpan's show trial was postponed rather than canceled may explain why German records do not reveal whether, when, or how he died. The trial planners, as we have seen, were so fearful of a misstep when it came to the Grynszpan case that they sought a written order from the Führer on whether or not to proceed. So long as any possibility remained that Hitler might change his mind and call for a trial, no prison warden or concentration camp commandant in Nazi Germany would have condemned such a high-value prisoner to death without a warrant to do so.

Indeed, any Nazi warder would have felt obliged to keep the prisoner alive and well. If Grynszpan contracted a disease or suffered an injury in an Allied air raid, if he took a beating from an ill-disciplined SS guard or finally made an earnest attempt to take his own life, every effort would have been made to restore him to good health rather than risk the displeasure of the Führer. If the prisoner died in spite of such efforts, the death might have been concealed from higher authorities, especially since Hitler was no longer quite so obsessed with "the Jew Grynszpan."

✦   ✦   ✦

BY THE FALL OF 1942, of course, Hitler had far more vexing problems than the fate of a single Jew, even if he was something of an international celebrity. After three years of war, the high-water mark of German success in combat had passed, and the Nazi leadership was forced to ponder the prospect of defeat. The first American troops landed in North Africa in November 1942, and the Red Army began to turn back the German siege of Stalingrad, a momentous battle that represented the first major Soviet victory over the Nazi invaders. Among all the Nazi officers and officials who clamored for the Führer's attention at his field headquarters in East Prussia, the Grynszpan trial planners found that they no longer enjoyed a strong claim on his attention.

Then, too, the machinery of mass murder that composed the Final Solution was in full operation in 1942, and the Jewish death toll was already mounting into the millions. Even as the Third Reich was beginning to suffer defeat in battle against Allied armies, the war against the Jews was steadily escalating. Quite aside from any concerns over Grynszpan's unsavory allegations about Rath, the notion of putting a single Jewish boy on trial in Berlin at a time when the Jewish Problem was being solved, secretly and efficiently, behind the electrified fences of Auschwitz-Birkenau and other death camps, must have seemed irrelevant if not downright ludicrous.

Even Joseph Goebbels, who had once promoted the Grynszpan trial as a propaganda tool for justifying the war against the Jews, now found other ways to deliver the same message. "When Germany began to lose the war in Stalingrad, the propaganda machine sought to make up in sheer volume of endless repetition for the 'proof' it had failed to obtain in the ill-fated Grynzpan trial," explains historian Raul Hilberg in *The Destruction of the European Jews*. On February 5, 1943, according to an example cited by Hilberg, the Propaganda Ministry issued a stern directive to the German press: "Stress: If we lose this war, we do not fall into the hands of some other states but will all be annihilated by world Jewry."[4]

Yet another irony in the Grynszpan case is that Herschel, who was viewed as an alarmist and an extremist by many Jews in 1938, did not know—and could not have known—the full extent of the atrocities that Nazi Germany was willing and able to perpetrate against the Jewish people. The 12,000 Polish Jews who were expelled from Germany in October 1938 rode in passenger cars, and the SS guards obligingly carried their hand luggage to the Polish border (or so claimed Diewerge). By 1942, the rolling stock consisted of freight cars and cattle cars, and the infernal destinations were Auschwitz and the other death camps in Poland, where the killing capacity of the gas chambers exceeded 12,000 Jews per day.

Indeed, the story of Herschel Grynszpan was eclipsed by the sheer scale of German mass murder. How could the life or death of one Jewish boy, no matter how famous, have mattered anymore? Or so Hitler and his inner circle must have concluded when they canceled the Grynszpan trial in 1942. And the circumstances of their decision-making are significant. Two days before the trial planners gathered in Berlin to discuss the impact of Grynszpan's revelations of homosexuality on the show trial, another meeting took place in the nearby district of Wannsee.

The infamous Wannsee Conference of January 20—convened by Himmler, conducted by Heydrich, and attended by Eichmann, among others—concerned itself with the planning of a much more ambitious and decisive project: the Final Solution of the Jewish Problem. Heydrich explained to the men around the conference table that the policy of the Third Reich had evolved "from 'emigration' to 'evacuation,'" according to Lucy Dawidowicz, "in view of 'the possibilities in the East.'"[5] If we decode the string of Nazi euphemisms used by Heydrich and his co-conspirators, the real purpose of the Wannsee Conference was the implementation of the unambiguous threat that Hitler had famously issued three years before.

"Today I will be a prophet again," ranted Hitler in an address to the Reichstag on January 30, 1939. "If international finance Jewry within Europe and abroad should succeed once more in plunging the peoples into a world war, then the consequence will be not the Bolshevization of the world and therewith a victory of Jewry, but on the contrary, the destruction of the Jewish race in Europe."[6]

As if to confirm the linkage between these two meetings in Berlin, one leading Nazi bureaucrat was present at both meetings. Roland Freisler, then serving as state secretary in the Justice Ministry, participated in the Wannsee Conference, where his role was to provide a thin veil of Nazi legality behind which the extermination of Jews could be conducted. Two days later, on January 22, 1942, at a meeting of the Grynszpan trial planners, Freisler revealed that Grynszpan was now asserting a homosexual affair as his motive for the shooting of Rath.

Still later, Freisler replaced Thierack as president of the People's Court, which suggests that he might have presided over the Grynszpan trial if it had been allowed to go forward. As it happened, it was also Freisler who later pronounced the death penalty on various real and alleged participants in Count von Stauffenberg's elaborate but abortive conspiracy to assassinate Hitler in 1944. Surely Freisler would have reveled in the opportunity to impose the same sentence on Herschel Grynszpan, whose assassination of Rath had been crudely prepared but wholly successful.

✦ ✦ ✦

SO WE ARE LEFT yet more rumor and speculation on how and when the young life of Herschel Grynszpan actually ended. One story, offered by Maître Weill-Goudchaux, a member of the Grynszpan defense team, in the French periodical *L'Arche* after the end of the war, proposes that the boy was marched out of his cell in Toulouse and summarily beheaded. The attorney suggested that the execution took place shortly after Grynszpan's arrest by the Gestapo in 1940, which is patently wrong because the documentary evidence proves that the trial was still being debated in the highest circles of power in Nazi Germany in the spring of 1942.

An account offered after the war by Harry Naujoks, always alert to the rumors passing among the inmates of the camp where he was held as a political prisoner, puts the death of Grynszpan in August or September 1942, when the young man was removed from the bunker at Sachsenhausen and put in a car for transportation to some unknown destination, perhaps the so-called Industriehof, a structure within the camp where summary executions were carried out. When he was called out of his cell, Grynszpan himself concluded that his death was imminent: "The time has come," he supposedly told a fellow inmate on that night. "They want to kill me."[7] A more plausible explanation of the incident is that the Gestapo was merely moving Grynszpan to the penitentiary at Magdeburg, where he arrived around September 26.

A variant of the Grynszpan death rumor focuses on an enigmatic inmate whose name was recorded as Otto Schneider. His last name is the German word for "tailor," the family trade of the Grynszpans, and the prisoner himself was, in fact, described as a tailor in German records. Intriguingly, Schneider's date of birth is the same as Herschel Grynszpan's: March 28, 1921. The prisoner called Schneider—or could it have been Grynszpan?—was moved from Sonnenburg to Brandenburg on the night of January 28, 1945. On that night, some 686 political prisoners were shot by an SS death squad inside the prison at Brandenburg, and so Herschel Grynszpan might have been among these victims.

Perhaps the most authoritative source is an official of the Nazi Foreign Ministry, one Fritz Dahms, who participated in some of the planning sessions for the Grynszpan trial in 1942. Dahms confirms only that the prisoner died in German custody during the war, possibly by gunshot but, more likely, as the result of illness or accidental injury: "The death of Grynszpan occurred shortly before the end of the war, but I am no longer able to say if he died of natural causes or if he lost his life by violence," Dahms wrote to German historian

Helmut Heiber in 1957, a time when interest in the Grynszpan case had been reignited by an inflammatory West German magazine article and the libel trial that it provoked. "At the time, the Foreign Affairs Ministry received no precise details on the manner in which he died."[8]

The Grynszpan case was never formally closed by the Nazi authorities, according to Dahms, and, in fact, "was regularly resubmitted for review until the end of the war," an exercise that would have been utterly meaningless unless the defendant was still alive. Dahms knew of no order from Hitler or other higher authorities to submit Herschel Grynszpan to "special handling," and surely any such directive "would have had to be initiated from the top, by Hitler himself or someone close to him."[9]

An intriguing clue to the demise of Herschel Grynszpan is provided by the recorded facts about the fate of other important Nazi prisoners. For example, Ernst Thälmann, the leader of the German Communist Party, was arrested immediately after the Nazis came to power in 1933 but was not killed until eleven years later, and only then because he was caught up in the frenzy of executions that followed the failed attempt to assassinate Hitler on July 20, 1944. Since Thälmann had spent the whole period in solitary confinement, he plainly had nothing to do with Count von Stauffenberg's conspiracy, but it was abruptly decided, surely by Hitler himself, to belatedly execute him some eleven years after his arrest. Perhaps Grynszpan, too, was allowed to sit alone in a cell for years until the day when Hitler finally issued an oral order for his summary execution.

An even more telling and provocative clue is provided by the fate of Georg Elser, the man who very nearly succeeded in assassinating Hitler in 1939. Elser had attended Hitler's address in Munich during the commemoration of the Beer Hall Putsch on November 8, 1938—the day before the death of Rath and the commencement of Kristallnacht—and he resolved to use the same occasion and venue to assassinate the leader of the Third Reich. One year later, Elser returned to Munich, where he managed to make and plant a powerful bomb in the Bürgerbräukeller on November 8, 1939, but Hitler left the hall thirteen minutes before the bomb was detonated, and thus he was not among the seventy-one victims of the resulting explosion.

Like the Grynszpan affair, the Elser case was the focus of rival conspiracy theories. Elser was accused by the Nazis of acting as an agent for the British secret service, and Goebbels agitated for a show trial to prove British complicity in the bombing. Rival theorists argued that Hitler's early departure from the beer hall proved that the Bürgerbräukeller bomb, like the Reichstag fire, was a Nazi contrivance. And, like Grynszpan himself, Elser was confined among the *Prominenten* at Sachsenhausen, but no trial was ever held.

"The Gestapo did, however, see to it that opponents of the regime in their custody, either prominent ones or those whom the Gestapo considered the most dangerous, did not survive the war," explains historian Peter Longerich.[10] Elser, for example, was taken from his cell on April 9, 1945, less than a month before the final defeat of the Third Reich, and put to death by *Genickschuss*, the same method of murder that had been used to kill more than a million Jewish men, women, children, and babies. Whether the same fate befell Herschel Grynszpan as the war ended, or at any moment after his arrest in 1940, we still do not know and, barring the unlikely discovery of some missing Nazi document, we will never know.

✦ ✦ ✦

STRANGELY, THE OFFICIAL DATE of Herschel Grynszpan's death was established by a German government agency long after the end of World War II. According to a decree of the Lower Court of Hanover issued on June 1, 1960, Herschel died on May 8, 1945. The date is Victory in Europe (VE) day, the day when the surviving leadership of the Third Reich formally surrendered to the Allies, thus putting an end to the war in Europe and, at the same time, the thousand-year Reich.

The date of death is strictly a legal fiction. The same day was routinely used by the courts in Germany whenever the actual date of a Nazi murder could not be determined. The decree was issued at the request of Herschel's parents, who had applied for reparations for the death of their youngest child from the government of West Germany on September 26, 1958, and needed a death certificate to support their claim. The proceedings lasted nearly three years, but the only evidence of Herschel's death that was submitted to the court consisted of the absence of evidence.

Both Zindel and Mordecai Grynszpan submitted affidavits in which they attested to the fact that their "strenuous and far-reaching efforts to find him had failed," and the fact that "Herschel himself, moreover, had not tried to contact the family, though this could easily have been done."[11] Herschel's older brother, Mordecai, spent a year searching for some trace of his brother in Paris before joining their parents in Israel. Uncle Abraham was arrested in Paris and deported to Auschwitz, where he was murdered, but Aunt Chava managed to survive the war and was still living in the same apartment on rue des Petites Ecuries where Herschel used to take his dinners; she still ran a tailoring business, but it was now called Maison du Tailleur.*

If Herschel had been alive and well, and especially if he had returned to Paris, it seems almost certain that he would have been found. Indeed, his zealous courtship of reporters and politicians while in French custody suggests that he would have readily and

---

* Other key figures in the Grynszpan case also survived the war, including Herschel's leading attorneys, Vincent de Moro-Giafferi and Serge Weill-Goudchaux, and his Nazi prosecutors, Wolfgang Diewerge and Friedrich Grimm.

proudly revealed the fact of his survival to anyone who would listen. The court in Hanover agreed that Grynszpan was dead, but the request for reparations was denied by the government of West Germany, which was paradoxically cited as evidence of yet another conspiracy theory in the Grynszpan case: "Might the German government have proof that Herschel is alive?" asked Karl Freund in a 1959 article in the French magazine *L'Arche*, one of several European publications that reprised the story, mostly for shock and titillation, in the postwar era.[12]

The speculation that Grynszpan somehow survived the Second World War was given a certain enduring credibility as the result of an article titled "Geheime Reichssache" (Secret Reich Matter), which appeared in the April 1952 issue of a German illustrated news magazine, *Wochenend* (Weekend). The author of the article, which was a work of sensationalism rather than scholarship, was a former Gestapo officer with an aristocratic title, Count Michael Alexander Soltikow, an opportunist and provocateur who had once authored anti-Semitic tracts but now claimed to have been an enemy of the Nazi regime and a friend of the Jews.

Soltikow endorsed the story of a homosexual encounter that Grynszpan had given to the Gestapo as his motive for shooting Rath, and he insisted that he was rendering a service to the Jewish people by doing so: "It is a necessity and a pleasure for me to be able to show that world Jewry had nothing to do with this deed," boasted Soltikow.[13] He also insisted Grynszpan was alive but remained in hiding precisely because of his confessed homosexuality. If Grynszpan refused to contact his cherished family after the war, Soltikow invited his readers to conclude, it was only because he was ashamed of his confession that he was a *faygeleh*.

One family felt shamed by the allegations in Soltikow's article, but it was not the Grynszpans. Günter vom Rath, the brother of the slain diplomat, promptly filed a lawsuit for criminal libel against both Soltikow and his publisher in Munich for characterizing the slain Nazi diplomat as a homosexual. The case did not come to trial until 1960, but it provided at least one shocking moment when a witness, who claimed to be an intelligence operative, asked why Herschel Grynszan had not been called to the witness stand, since the German police files contained a report that he was alive and well and living in Hamburg. On the day after the remarkable allegation, Soltikow offered even more shocking testimony.

"Not only was Grynszpan alive, but [he] had been in the courtroom the previous day," offered Soltikow, "and was willing to testify if granted immunity."[14]

The German judge who was hearing the libel case against Soltikow may not have taken the offer seriously, but he only complicated the matter by making a threat from the bench to arrest Grynszpan if he did appear, presumably for the shooting of Rath and possibly for violating Paragraph 175. Soltikow nonetheless vowed to bring Grynszpan to court in order to testify to the accuracy of Soltikow's article and thus defeat the libel claim. Of course, he never fulfilled his promise, and the trial ended with a guilty verdict on the charge of criminal libel. Soltikow received a suspended sentence of five months in prison and five years of probation, but the verdict was appealed and overturned in 1964.

The allegation that Grynzspan had survived the war and was living in hiding was also made by an enterprising German historian while the Soltikow trial was still pending. In 1957, Helmut Heiber published "Der Fall Grünspan" (The Grynzspan Case), the first substantial work of scholarship on the Grynzspan case. Almost as an aside, and without citing any authority for his allegation, Heiber concluded his article with the startling announcement that Grynszpan had been among the prisoners liberated from the Magdeburg prison by the U.S. Army in 1945 and that he "was living under an assumed name in Paris."[15]

As an apparent authority on the Grynszpan case, Heiber was later contacted by the Hanover court that had been asked by the Grynszpan family to declare that Herschel was dead, and a court investigator asked him to "state his reasons for thinking that Grynszpan was still alive."[16] Under judicial examination, however, Heiber finally conceded that the whole story of Grynszpan's survival began with an item of mere hearsay, and further court inquiries with INTERPOL revealed that Heiber's allegation was based only on "unsubstantiated reports transmitted by an employee of the French security police in Baden-Baden in April 1954."[17]

"As I remember, I found in the dossier, a communication stating that Grynszpan was then living in Hamburg," Heiber lamely confessed in a 1959 letter to Cuénot, "but nevertheless I cannot remember where this information came from."[18]

The story of Grynszpan's survival could not stand up under historical or judicial scrutiny. Heiber himself, the apparent author of the tale, couldn't decide whether Grynszpan was supposed to be living in Paris or in Hamburg. Nevertheless, it was picked up and elaborated upon by various reporters across Europe and in the United States. So began the *bubbemeiseh* that Herschel, the boy who had loved mechanical things, was working as an automobile mechanic in Paris, where he had married and was raising children of his own.

No less an authority than Raul Hilberg, for example, assumed that the bizarre story was true. "After the trial was dropped, Grynzpan was kept 'on ice,'" Hilberg wrote in 1980. "He was discovered in 1957, living quietly in Paris." Hilberg's cited source was an article titled "Hersche Gruenspan lebt!" (Herschel Grynszpan lives!), which appeared in *Aufbau*, a German-language Jewish newspaper published in New York.[19] Hannah Arendt, too, may have relied on nothing more than magazine articles in composing her own provocative asides on the Grynszpan case in *Eichmann in Jerusalem*, although we cannot know with certainty, because she did not bother to cite her sources.

No real evidence that Grynszpan survived the war was presented to the court in Hanover, or at the Soltikow trial, or by any of the scholars and reporters who made the same allegation, but the story is now lodged in the accumulation of myth and legend that has come to encrust the Grynszpan case.

✦   ✦   ·✦

WHAT WE KNOW WITH absolute certainty is that Grynszpan was a troubled young man who sought and savored fame. At seventeen, he aspired to put himself in the headlines: "I have to protest in a way that the whole world hears my protest," he wrote to his family on the postcard that he carried into the embassy at 78 rue de Lille.[20] Once in a French prison cell, he campaigned to maintain the celebrity—or notoriety—that he had achieved by writing letters to newspaper editors, politicians, judges, and even Hitler and Roosevelt. If we are to believe the Gestapo, he even contrived to write himself into history by composing a coded confession and attempting to pass it to his fellow inmates in the hope that they would find a way to smuggle it out of the prison.

The greatest flaw in the argument that Grynszpan survived the war is found in the fact that, as far as we know, no one—not even his own mother, father, and brother—heard a word from him after he signed and mailed a Red Cross postcard in 1940. None of the researchers who studied the Grynszpan case in the decades immediately following World War II—Dr. Alain Cuénot, Gerald Schwab, Friedrich Kaul, and Helmut Heiber—were able to find a scintilla of real evidence that Grynszpan was alive, and neither was Ronald Roizen, who conducted his own investigation in the 1980s. To be sure, the case offers a long list of unlikely deeds and events, but the ability and willingness of a glory seeker like Herschel Grynszpan to go into hiding for the rest of his life would have been the most improbable of all.

By now, Herschel Grynszpan has faded from history, and his

anonymous death is indistinguishable from those of millions of less famous Jewish victims. Herschel himself was the first one to invent the wholly imagined moments and motives that endlessly decorate his life story, but he was soon joined by his own attorneys, then by the army of conspiracy theorists, Nazis and antifascists alike, and finally by inventive reporters and historians. One novelist, Lutz van Dijk, reimagined the case in fiction—and offered an explanation for Grynszpan's disappearance after the war—in the German-language novel *Der Attentäter* (The Assassin). The novel depicts a rendezvous between Grynszpan and a journalist named Julien, another former inmate of Sachsenhausen, at a café on the boulevard Saint-Denis in November 1945. Intriguingly, Van Dijk suggests Grynszpan was actually and perhaps even openly gay.

"Herschel is dead," says the character of Herschel Grynszpan, now in hiding under a phony identity. "There are too many people who wanted my death, and still do after everything has come to an end. Too many for me to live. Some of my own people, you know, that is the worst. There are some Chaverim* who still blame me today for causing the pogroms in Germany."

"How do you know?" asks Julien.

"I heard it. Reliable. From soldiers of the Red Army, who let me leave Berlin. Then from a relative in Brussels, who was told: 'When this gay pig comes here, we will finish him!' No, Julien, Herschel is dead. I will have new papers soon and a new name and I will live somewhere else. Maybe something will change some day. Right now it does not look like it."[21]

The rumor, theory, and invention that have so richly ornamented the life story of Herschel Grynszpan make it more challenging, if not impossible, to tease out fact from fancy. We can speak only of what

---

* *Chaverim* is the Hebrew word for "friends," but it also carries the meaning of "comrades" and was commonly used among the progressive Zionists with whom Herschel socialized in Paris.

is possible and what is plausible, but we cannot know with certainty whether he was already dead on VE-day, and, if not, why he never revealed himself to the family he cherished and the public whose attention he so ardently sought. Among those who know and care about the Grynszpan case, however, the speculation has never ended.

12

THE EXTERMINATING ANGEL

THE FIRST HOLOCAUST SURVIVOR TO TAKE THE STAND AS A background witness at the 1961 trial of Adolf Eichmann was Zindel Grynszpan. "An old man, wearing a traditional Jewish skullcap, small, very frail, with sparse white hair and beard, holding himself quite erect," is how Hannah Arendt describes Herschel's father in *Eichmann in Jerusalem*. "[I]n a sense, his name was already 'famous.'"[1]

Eichmann, the self-styled "Jewish specialist" of the Third Reich, survived the war and managed to find a safe refuge in Argentina, where he was seized by Israeli commandos and smuggled back to Israel in 1960. He was then charged under Israeli law with crimes against the Jewish people and crimes against humanity, all based on his crucial and commanding role in arranging for the deportation of millions of Jewish victims to the death camps. Herschel Grynszpan, of course, was not among them. Why, then, did the Israeli prosecutor call Herschel's father as a star witness? And, if the Grynszpan name was truly famous, why has the young man himself and the murder in Paris in 1938 receded from memory and history?

The trial was held in a converted theater in Jerusalem and attended by the world press, Hannah Arendt among them. Ironically, the Eichmann trial was far more impactful than the show trial that the

Nazis had planned for Grynszpan. Indeed, although the Israeli judges who presided over the trial were more concerned with juris-prudence than with theatricality, it is also true that the Eichman trial was intended by Israeli prime minister David Ben-Gurion to remind the postwar world of the facts of the Final Solution in all of their ghastly and heartbreaking detail.

Zindel Grynszpan, for example, was called to testify about the expulsion of Polish Jews from Germany in 1938, the incident that prompted Herschel to carry out his act of protest against the Third Reich. The link between Zindel's testimony and the crimes for which Eichmann was on trial is oblique: "The assassination had triggered the pogroms in Germany and Austria, the so-called *Kristallnacht* of November 9, which was indeed a prelude to the Final Solution," explains Arendt, "but with whose preparation Eichmann had noth-ing to do." Yet Arendt, who found much to criticize in the prosecu-tion's case against Eichmann, was plainly moved by Zindel's testimony: "No one either before or after," she writes, "was to equal the shining honesty of Zindel Grynszpan."[2]

The quotation marks that Arendt puts around the word "famous" when she invokes the Grynszpan family name, however, are unset-tling. Perhaps she meant to signify that Herschel Grynszpan was famous only in the sense that he was among the few victims of Nazi terror whose name is known at all. But there is something dismissive and even derogatory in Arendt's pointed use of those quotation marks, as if to suggest that Herschel and his deed were ultimately inconsequential and thus unworthy of remembrance. After all, as we have already noted, Arendt dismisses him as a "psychotic" and slan-ders him with the speculation that he "might have acted as an unwit-ting tool of Gestapo agents in Paris"[3] As a refined German-Jewish intellectual who cherished the *Kultur* of her native land, Arendt betrayed a certain disdain for *Ostjuden* in general, and she treated Grynszpan with unalloyed contempt.

Nor did the prosecutors of Eichmann pay much respect to the boy with the "famous" name. He was mentioned during the Eichmann trial only when the prosecution played a recording of the Israeli police interrogation in which the defendant recalled his questioning of Grynszpan at Gestapo headquarters in Berlin. The prosecution sought to demonstrate that Eichmann was regarded within the Nazi regime as the *Sachbearbeiter* (competent specialist) for the Jewish Question "in its totality," whether the fate of a single Jew or millions of Jews was at stake.[4] If a show trial was being planned for the Jewish boy who shot a Nazi diplomat in Paris, then Eichmann was the one to interrogate him, and if 100,000 Jews were to be rounded up in France and shipped by rail to the death camps, Eichmann was the one to manage the task. Otherwise, the exploits and the ultimate fate of Herschel Grynszpan went unnoticed in the Eichmann trial itself and in Arendt's influential account of the proceedings in the Jerusalem courtroom.

Even those who knew Grynszpan best were unwilling to lionize him. None of the three principal investigators of the case were much impressed by the young man whom they studied so intensively. "Grynszpan was no hero," concludes Dr. Alain Cuénot.[5] Gerald Schwab insists that his own interest in the case "was not predicated on the assumption that the assassination of vom Rath in itself was either an exceptionally important act—it gained importance out of all proportion only because the Nazis chose to make it so—or that it was somehow a heroic or meaningful symbolic gesture, which it was not."[6] Ron Roizen is not nearly so dismissive but he ultimately declares himself to be undecided: "Grynszpan's action cannot be condemned or justified on pragmatic grounds alone."[7]

Herschel Grynszpan, to borrow Trotsky's enduring phase, ended up in the dustbin of history. The Grynszpan case is not even mentioned in most scholarly studies of Jewish resistance to Nazi Germany. Indeed, if Grynszpan is remembered at all, it is only as a footnote to the history of Kristallnacht. Thus, for example, a black-and-white photograph of Herschel Grynszpan—looking small, lonely, and haunted—is displayed for a second or two in an audiovisual display about the events of Kristallnacht at Yad Vashem in Jerusalem, but only to acknowledge the pretext on which the Nazis relied in carrying out the first official act of collective violence against the Jews in Germany. Some accounts of Kristallnacht, in fact, mention the victim of the assassination in the Paris embassy of the Third Reich but leave out the "famous" name of his assassin.

"Neither Grynszpan nor Frankfurter—or Schwartzbard, the assassin of Petliura—entered the pantheon of Jewish heroic figures, which they were in their way," observed historian Saul Friedländer in an interview with the author.* "To bring the attention of the world to what was being done to the Jews was an act of resistance. Why Herschel Grynszpan has been overlooked, even if his act had unfortunate consequences, is strange and baffling."[8]

One answer, of course, can be found in Grynszpan's nature and conduct, which were not the stuff of which heroes are readily made. He was a tormented adolescent, surely not psychotic in a clinical sense but plainly afflicted by visions of catastrophe and delusions of grandeur. There's something of Hamlet in Herschel Grynszpan, a young man whose conflict with his uncle over a perceived wrong against his father only stoked his anxieties and fantasies. If Herschel was, in fact, a gay man, his inner life would have been torqued in even more damaging ways by the homophobia that prevailed in the

* Saul Friedländer was a young child when his family arrived in Paris as refugees from Czechoslovakia in 1940. His parents managed to hide him in a Catholic boarding school before they were arrested and deported to Auschwitz, where they were both murdered. So meticulous was German record keeping, and so dutiful were the French police, that gendarmes (rather than the Gestapo) later showed up at the apartment where the Friedländers had been staying and demanded of the neighbors, "Where is the boy?" Interview with the author, August 9, 2010.

Jewish immigrant community in the 1930s, and especially among religious Jews.

Then, too, the fact that Grynszpan lived alone in an attic room, brooding over the insults and outrages that he and his family were made to suffer, is more than faintly reminiscent of Lee Harvey Oswald and Sirhan Sirhan and various other lone gunmen who acted on their private grievances in the same way that Herschel did. Assassination may be intended and understood as a public act of protest, but the mind of every assassin teems with motives and meanings that are seldom if ever fully revealed to history. "What is a man?" muses André Malraux in *Anti-Memoirs*. "A miserable little pile of secrets."[9] The unsavory details of Herschel's secret life, whether real or invented, are hardly endearing or elevating, which may explain why he is so off-putting to so many of those who have studied his case.

Yet we should not be so distracted by what Auschwitz survivor Primo Levi dismisses as "small-change Freudianism" that we overlook the moments of courage that can also be detected in the life of Herschel Grynszpan.[10] "A story like this one is not self-contained," wrote Levi in an altogether different context in *The Drowned and the Saved*, although Levi's words may help us to understand Grynszpan, too. "It is pregnant, full of significance, asks more questions than it answers, sums up in itself the entire theme of the gray zone and leaves one dangling. It shouts and clamors to be understood, because in it one perceives a symbol, as in dreams and the signs of heaven."[11]

✦　✦　✦

DOROTHY THOMPSON IS THE only observer of the Grynszpan case to characterize the shooting of Ernst vom Rath as an early and momentous example of Jewish armed resistance to Nazi terror: "Only the second act of counter-violence by a Jew," as she wrote in 1938, obliquely crediting David Frankfurter, assassin of Wilhelm Gustloff, for the first such act.[12] Yet, aside from Thompson's passing remark, Grynszpan has been wholly excluded from the ranks of Jewish resisters. The fact that he is not honored for his "act of counterviolence" is especially troubling precisely because so much effort has been expended to single out and praise the Jewish fighters who can be found among the victims of the Holocaust.

"In Israel and many other places," explains historian Deborah E. Lipstadt in *The Eichmann Trial*, "there was a persistent leitmotif when the discourse turned to Holocaust survivors: Why didn't you resist? Why did you comply with the orders?"[13]

The question itself has been condemned as cruel and unfair by most historians of the Holocaust. After all, nothing is said about the several million Soviet prisoners of war—young men in uniform who had been issued weapons and trained to use them in battle—who were disarmed, herded into camps, and slowly starved to death by the Germans during World War II without fighting back. Yet a different standard has been applied to the Jewish victims, few of whom had ever handled a firearm, none of whom were actually armed, and all of whom were brutalized and terrorized by their Nazi captors. Even the Israeli prosecutor in the Eichmann trial, as Hannah Arendt points out in *Eichmann in Jerusalem*, felt obliged to ask the survivors on the witness stand, "Why did you not protest?" "Why did you board the train?" "Fifteen thousand people were standing there and hundreds of guards facing you—why didn't you revolt and charge and attack?"[14]

The fact is that Jewish armed resistance took place all over Nazi-occupied Europe, and some acts of resistance are remembered and celebrated. The young fighters in Warsaw, Vilna, and other ghettos rallied to the words of Abba Kovner, poet and Zionist leader: "Let's not allow ourselves to be led like sheep to the slaughter."[15] The Bielski partisans granted refuge to any Jewish man, woman, or child who managed to reach their encampment in the forests of what is now Belarus: "This is our way—we don't select," declared Tuvia

Bielski, an ironic reference to the selection of victims for the gas chambers that took place on arrival at the death camps.[16] Even inside the concentration camps, a few courageous Jewish men and women rose up against their SS guards, most famously in Treblinka, Sobibor, and Birkenau. Other acts of armed resistance in cities, forests, ghettos, and camps have been thoroughly documented even though they are rarely, if ever, pointed out.

"Is there such a thing as useful violence? Unfortunately, yes," writes Primo Levi, who praised not only the fighters in the camps and ghettos but allowed that meaning can be found in other acts of violence. "Nor in general is murder useless: Raskolnikov, in killing the old moneylender, set a purpose for himself, albeit a culpable one; and so did Princip at Sarajevo."[17]

Nor was armed resistance the only form of resistance. Historian Yehuda Bauer borrowed the Hebrew word *amidah* (standing), a reference to a Jewish prayer that is recited while standing, to describe how Jewish men, women, and children "stood up against" the Germans in ways that did not always require a firearm. *Amidah*, as the term is used by Bauer, included "smuggling food into ghettoes; mutual self-sacrifice within the family to avoid starvation or worse; cultural, educational, religious, and political activities taken to strengthen morale; the work of doctors, nurses, and educators to consciously maintain health and moral fiber to enable individual and group survival; and, of course, armed rebellion or the use of force (with bare hands or 'cold' weapons) against the Germans and their collaborators."[18]

One stirring example is the Jewish self-help movement that emerged in Poland in response to the Nazi threat. When Hitler expelled those 12,000 Polish Jews in October 1938, Jewish volunteers hastened to the camp at Zbąszyń to provide the refugees with bread, soup, clothing, medical care, and even Yiddish classes. "A committee from Warsaw has come here," wrote Esther, Herschel's sister, in her second postcard from Zbąszyń. "These people do what they can for us."[19] Later, when all of Poland was under German occupation, the same organization provided the same kind of sustenance to the hundreds of thousands of Jews who were herded into the ghettos that served as holding pens for the death camps. So it turns out that Herschel Grynszpan's parents and siblings were among the earliest beneficiaries of a Jewish resistance movement, wholly unarmed and nonviolent, that carried out its final act of *amidah* in the last days of the Warsaw ghetto.

"This major effort by an impoverished and beleaguered community was much more than a natural response to the tragedy of their persecuted brethren," explains historian Samuel D. Kassow in *Who Will Write Our History?* "It was a defiant challenge to anti-Semites and a proud assertion of national dignity and solidarity."[20]

Still, there is an undeniable difference between armed resistance and passive resistance—or, to put it more bluntly, between resistance and revenge—and something in human nature demands vengeance. Raul Hilberg, for example, disdains what he calls the "inflation of resistance," and he recognizes a distinction between "dy[ing] with dignity" and spilling the blood of one's murderer before dying. "When Jewry was threatened with destruction, the independent-minded breakaway Jews made a sharp distinction between themselves and all those others who had not joined them. 'Do not walk like sheep to the slaughter,' they said, and they meant every word."[21]

The ghetto fighters who made a last stand against the Germans in the Warsaw ghetto, for instance, demonstrated the moral and emotional power of armed resistance to the 40,000 or so Jewish victims who still remained alive in the ghetto after the deportations to the death camps—an example that has resonated through subsequent generations, both in Israel and elsewhere. The Warsaw ghetto uprising did nothing to spare the remaining Jews from death by *Genick-*

schuss or gas chamber, but it changed the narrative of German mass murder in a crucial and dramatic way. "When we threw our grenades and saw German blood on the streets of Warsaw, which had been flooded with so much Jewish blood and tears," said one ghetto fighter, "a great joy possessed us."[22]

Herschel Grynszpan, of course, never reached the ghettoes and death camps where these celebrated heroes of the Jewish resistance managed to spill the blood of their torturers and murderers before going to their own deaths. Indeed, when Herschel carried his little revolver into the German embassy in 1938 and opened fire on a Nazi diplomat in a business suit, no such places yet existed, and if Grynszpan had been able to imagine the Bosch-like horrors that were to come a few years later, he would surely have been dismissed as a psychotic. History reveals, however, that he would not have been wrong.

✦　✦　✦

THE NUMBER OF JEWISH men and women who fought back against Nazi Germany and its collaborators, whether with "hot" or "cold" weapons, was small in absolute terms, and the number of casualties they inflicted was even smaller. Apart from the half-million Jews who served with distinction in the armed forces of the Soviet Union, the number of Jewish resistance fighters who took up arms against Nazi Germany as partisans and ghetto fighters can be counted in the thousands, a tiny fraction of the six million Jews who were murdered during the Holocaust. The death toll they inflicted on the Germans and their collaborators must be counted in the hundreds. The vast majority of Jewish victims, like the survivor of Kristallnacht who tossed his Browning pistol into the Pegnitz River in Fürth, did not fight back at all.

"The reaction pattern of the Jews is characterized by almost complete lack of resistance," argues Raul Hilberg. "In marked contrast to German propaganda, the documentary evidence of Jewish resistance, overt or submerged, is very slight. On a European-wide scale the Jews had no resistance organization, no blueprint for armed action, no plan even for psychological warfare. They were completely unprepared."[23]

Indeed, the young men and women who called upon their elders to join in the armed resistance against Nazi Germany were regarded as "hotheads who would bring disaster upon the whole ghetto," according to Lucy Dawidowicz, whose words accurately describe how Herschel Grynszpan was regarded by both Jews and non-Jews when the shooting of Rath was seized upon by the Nazis as a pretext for the catastrophic events of Kristallnacht. "In some ghettos the populace responded with unvarnished fear and hatred to the would-be resisters, seeing them as foolish fanatics or even raving lunatics," explains Dawidowicz. "Observant Jews even assembled in the prayer house [of Radoszkowice, a shtetl near Vilna] to excommunicate the ten members of the resistance who intended to join partisans in the woods."[24]

The courageous few who carried out acts of armed resistance, in other words, were beset with insuperable obstacles on all sides. They had no weapons of their own, and they took dire risks to acquire them. They were shunned by the majority of their fellow Jews who rightfully feared that the Nazis would impose collective punishment on the Jewish community if a Jew took a single German life. Jews who lived in the cities and larger towns could not readily escape into the forests where the partisan bands were operating. Even if they reached the forests and managed to find a Jewish partisan band, they were at risk of being turned away if they were old or infirm or unarmed. (The Bielski partisans, as we have noted, were one exception.) If they happened upon non-Jewish partisans, they might have been killed outright.

Israeli prosecutor Gideon Hausner prompted a witness to make the same point during the Eichmann trial when he asked Moshe Beisky why the Jewish inmates of the slave labor camp at Plaszów, who vastly outnumbered their guards, did not rise up in revolt. Beisky's answer summed up the predicament of the Jewish victims: "Nearby us there was a Polish camp," explained the witness. "There were 1,000 Poles. One hundred meters beyond the camp they had a place to go to—their homes. I don't recall one instance of escape on the part of the Poles. But where could any of the Jews go? We were wearing clothes which were dyed yellow with yellow stripes. And at that moment, let us suppose that the 15,000 people within the camp even succeeded without armed strength to go beyond the boundaries of the camp—where would they go? What could they do?"[25]

Historians continue to argue among themselves over the origin, meaning, and extent of Jewish armed resistance. "There was a great deal of Jewish armed resistance, very much more than could have been expected," insists Yehuda Bauer, who squarely contradicts the assertions of Raul Hilberg.* Even Bauer, however, concedes that Jewish resistance fighters achieved little or nothing on the field of battle. "To measure Jewish armed resistance in terms of the numbers of Germans killed, or the effect it had on German policies, or even on chances of survival is futile," writes Bauer. "All such results are negligible. Instead, the measuring rod has to be the effect this type of resistance had on those who engaged in it and on postwar Jewish consciousness."[26]

When we try to apply the measuring rod to the Grynszpan case, however, we find that the boy assassin himself seems to have disappeared from the history of Jewish resistance to Nazi Germany in the

---

* Raul Hilberg and Lucy Dawidowicz, both now deceased, focused on the perpetrators and victims of German mass murder rather than on the resisters. More-recent scholarship has revealed additional details about Jewish armed resistance. Yehuda Bauer, for example, "identifies armed resistance to the Nazis and their henchmen in twenty-four ghettoes of western and central Poland," points out historian Michael Marrus, "and even more in eastern parts of the country." See Marrus, *The Holocaust in History* (New York: Meridian, 1987), 143.

same way that he seems to have vanished from the German prison in which he was last seen. Ironically, even though every act of Jewish resistance during the Holocaust, whether active or passive, "hot" or "cold," is nowadays singled out and celebrated, Grynszpan's act of counterviolence has been wholly forgotten.

✦ ✦ ✦

ONLY ONE OF THE five shots that Grynszpan fired at Rath—small-caliber bullets with a relatively low muzzle velocity—inflicted a fatal injury, and it took his victim two days to die. By contrast, the para-military death squads known as the *Einsatzgruppen* (Special-Duty Groups), the German police and army units that operated alongside them, and their collaborators in various occupied countries suc-ceeded in killing more than a million Jewish men, women, children, and babies, each one with a *Genickschuss* from a military weapon of large caliber and high velocity.[27] Indeed, they were carefully instructed by the military doctors attached to their units on how to fire a single fatal shot at an unarmed civilian in their custody.*

"Dr. Schoenfelder sketched on the ground—so that we could all see—the outline of the upper part of a human body," said one mem-ber of Police Battalion 101, "and marked on the neck the spot at which we should fire."[28]

Even so, a wounded man, woman, or child sometimes survived the first volley of gunfire, and then it was necessary to administer what the Germans called, astoundingly, a *Gnadenschuss* (mercy

* "Today Auschwitz stands for the Holocaust, and the Holocaust for the evil of the century," observes historian Timothy Snyder. Yet an even greater number of Jewish victims died "in other German death factories . . . whose names are less often recalled," Snyder points out, and "[s]till more Jews, Polish or Soviet or Baltic Jews, were shot over ditches and pits." See Snyder, *Bloodlands: Europe between Hitler and Stalin* (New York: Basic Books, 2010), viii.

shot) to finish off the victim.[29] Heinrich Himmler himself was a participant in one such incident, which took place during one of his inspection tours of the killing fields of eastern Europe and Russia. "After the first salvo Himmler came right up to me and looked personally into the ditch, remarking that there was still someone alive," testified a lieutenant of the Landeskriminalpolizeiamt (Criminal Police) after the war. "He said to me, 'Lieutenant, shoot that one!' Himmler stood beside me while I did it. . . ."[30]

One of the cruelest ironies of the Holocaust is that Nazi Germany sought to justify the mass murder of Jews by, among other things, characterizing the victims as partisans when, in fact, the vast majority of them were self-evidently defenseless civilians. "As a matter of principle any Jew [was] to be regarded as a partisan," said an SS commander named Erich vom dem Bach-Zelewski, one of the men in charge of the campaign of mass murder in Russia.[31] Every Jew, regardless of gender, age, or physical ability, was assumed to be willing and able to pick up a gun and use it against the Germans, a notion that echoes the Nazi insistence that Herschel Grynszpan was acting in service of a vast Jewish conspiracy against Germany.

"That is the greatest lie of anti-Semitism because it gives lie to the slogan that the Jews are conspiring to dominate the world," Bach-Zelewski later admitted. "If they had had some sort of organization, these people could have been saved by the millions; but instead they were taken completely by surprise. Never before has a people gone as unsuspectingly to its disaster. Nothing was prepared. Absolutely nothing."[32]

The body count of German mass murder as meticulously recorded by the Nazis themselves provides corroborating evidence for Bach-Zelewski's testimony. On February 9, 1942, for example, the commander of Einsatzkommando 3 submitted a formal report on the number of partisans, mentally ill, Communists, and Jews that his men had managed to shoot in a single operation in the Baltic. Jews and partisans were placed in different categories precisely because, as the Nazis seemed to concede when it came to official reports of the body counts, not every Jewish victim was also a partisan. The report of the commander was precise:

Partisans	56
Mentally ill	653
Communists	1,064
Jews	136,421

Of the 138,194 victims of Einsatzkommando 3 who were murdered by gunfire in a single action in the winter of 1942, according to Nazi records, exactly 55,556 were women and 34,464 were children.[33] Even if they were plainly *not* partisans, however, the mass murder of Jewish children was rationalized by the Nazis as a necessary precaution against future acts of Jewish vengeance. Not once but repeatedly, even obsessively, Himmler told his comrades in the highest circles of Nazi leadership that it would have been "cowardly" for him to spare Jewish children from mass murder precisely because they would "grow up to be the avengers who would kill our fathers and our grandchildren."[34]

Herschel Grynszpan clearly would have savored the prospect of Jewish vengeance that Himmler claimed to fear, and perhaps he even experienced a moment of joy like the one described by the ghetto fighter when he spilled German blood. After all, long before he offered his tale of homosexual seduction and betrayal in a Gestapo cell, Herschel frankly told a German diplomatic official in Paris that he shot Rath "to avenge the great wrong which had been visited on his fellow Jews in general and on his family in particular."[35] Nonetheless, Himmler's oft-stated anxiety over Jewish child avengers, even if we are willing to take it seriously, was misplaced. Precious few Jewish children grew up to be avengers in the Nazi era.

Something profound is at stake in the debate over the extent and quality of Jewish resistance during the Holocaust. "There is no doubt that this issue touches a sensitive nerve in the Jewish consciousness," writes historian Michael Marrus, "an unspoken assumption of which has been that Jewish resistance somehow validates Jewish self-worth."[36] That is why resistance has been so broadly defined by historians like Yehuda Bauer, although he also concedes that "individual acts of resistance constitute a slippery and awkward topic, because what to include and what to exclude is difficult to determine."[37] Grynszpan, as we have seen, has been mostly excluded.

"This was a purely private act of revenge for what his family went through as Polish citizens in Germany," Bauer told the author in an interview. "If his parents had been given a visa, he wouldn't have done anything."[38]

Among the various and sometimes conflicting motivations of Jewish resistance fighters—escape and survival, revenge against the murderers of their fellow Jews, participation in the larger struggle to defeat Nazi Germany on the field of battle—perhaps the most resonant one was an urgent need to write themselves into history, a yearning that Grynszpan himself also shared. "The message for the Jews sometimes included the notion that they were defending Jewish honor," explains Bauer in *Rethinking the Holocaust*, "as in the famous words of Dolek Liebeskind of the Zionist underground in Cracrow: 'For three lines in history that will be written about the youth who fought and did not go like sheep to the slaughter, it is even worth dying.'"[39]

✦   ✦   ✦

THE SEARCH TO FIND examples of Jewish resistance has failed to acknowledge the exploits of Herschel Grynszpan. A street in Israel, as we have seen, is named *Ha Nokem* (The Avenger) in memory of Sholom Schwartzbard, the assassin of Petliura. *Lohamei HaGetaot*

(The Ghetto Fighters), a kibbutz founded in 1949, honors the men and women who took up arms against the Germans in Warsaw and other ghettoes. The Bielski partisans have earned the ultimate badge of honor in Western popular culture—a T-shirt emblazoned with the image of Zul Bielski and a cautionary message: "Stand up to tyranny, oppression and discrimination . . . early."[40]

The message can be plausibly applied to the deeds of Herschel Grynszpan. Yet, remarkably, there is no street named after Grynszpan, no kibbutz, no T-shirt, as if the "famous name" carries a certain taint. Even Weill-Goudchaux, one of his own attorneys, refused to call him a hero. "Personally, I would prefer to choose my heroes from such men as Mordechai Anielewicz, commander of the Warsaw ghetto revolt, or [French resistance fighter] Colonel Gilles Epstein, who was shot by the Germans."[41] Grynszpan's deed, in fact, is still regarded in some circles as a *shanda*, a scandalous act that brings shame on the Jewish people: "Jews would prefer that talk of this embarrassing assassin not be too detailed," observes Cuénot, "if it is not to glorify him."[42]

The case against Herschel Grynszpan begins with the undeniable fact that his act of violence in Paris was seized upon by the Nazis as a pretext for Kristallnacht. Although historians agree that Kristallnacht—or some other escalation of Hitler's war against the Jews— would have taken place sooner or later even if Grynszpan had not shot Rath, the aftermath of the shooting was so catastrophic for the Jewish population of Germany and Austria that Grynszpan's act has been regarded almost universally, both at the time and thereafter, as "useless, dangerous, and a great disservice to Jews everywhere," in the words of Gerald Schwab.[43]

Yet it is also undeniable that *all* resistance, and especially armed resistance, led to collective punishment of hundreds and thousands of innocents. Moshe Beisky, for example, passed up every opportunity to escape from the labor camp at Plaszów precisely because "he

knew that the commander, Amon Göth, would apply collective punishment, probably death, to the eighty other prisoners in his barracks if he escaped," as Deborah Lipstadt explains.[44] Even the
celebrated Mordechai Anielewicz, the doomed leader of the Warsaw
ghetto fighters, understood that armed resistance would cost Jewish
lives rather than save them.

"He foresaw the destruction of the ghetto and he was sure that
neither he nor his combatants would survive the liquidation of the
ghetto," wrote Emmanuel Ringelblum, the founder of the Oyneg
Shabbes ghetto archives—yet another example of *amidah* in the
Warsaw ghetto—and, not incidentally, one of the leaders of the rescue effort at Zbąszyń in 1938. "He was sure that they would die like
stray dogs and no one would even know their last resting place."[45]

Indeed, every effort at armed resistance, Jewish or otherwise, led
to reprisals that were directed against the innocent. When a pair of
Czechoslovakian commandos assassinated SS leader Reinhard Heydrich in 1942, for example, the town of Lidice was wholly eradicated
as an act of collective punishment because the Nazis wrongly
believed that the attackers had hidden there. (Like Rath, Heydrich
was only wounded during the incident and actually died of medical
complications in the hospital.) Even though the Heydrich assassination was wholly unrelated to Jewish resistance, the incident prompted
Hitler to order a sudden acceleration of the mass murder of Jews: "It
is time now to wipe the slate clean," reported Himmler to a gathering of SS generals after taking his orders from the Führer.[46] Significantly, the death camps at Belzec, Sobibor, Treblinka, and Majdanek
were dubbed Aktion Reinhard camps in honor of Heydrich.

So the suggestion that Grynszpan is somehow culpable for provoking Nazi violence against the Jews is not merely unsupported by
the facts of history but is also morally bankrupt. At worst, Grynszpan was what used to be called a "premature antifascist" because he
seemed to perceive the existential threat that Nazi Germany posed

to the Jewish people at a time when the Western democracies—and some elements of the Jewish community in Germany itself and elsewhere around the world—were still seeking to appease Hitler and ride out the worst excesses of the Nazi regime. Indeed, the argument has been made that Kristallnacht had a salutary effect precisely because it destroyed any remaining delusions about how Nazi Germany intended to solve the Jewish Problem once and for all. Herschel's notion of his role in history may have been delusional, but, to his credit, he suffered from no comforting hallucinations about Hitler's intentions toward the Jews.

To be sure, the Einsatzgruppen and the gas chambers were not yet in operation on the day when Grynszpan assassinated Rath, and the sufferings of the expelled Polish Jews at Zbąszyń seem shockingly trivial when compared with the mass murder that would shortly be carried out at Auschwitz and Babi Yar, a genocidal campaign that would have seemed biblical in its severity if it had not been carried out with the assistance of twentieth-century industrial technology. But the nightmares that disturbed the sleep of the seventeen-year-old boy in his room at the Hôtel de Suez on the night before the assassination—"Again and again I asked myself, 'What have we done to deserve such a fate?'"—turned out to be prescient.[47] If Grynszpan had carried out the same act of armed resistance against Nazi Germany in 1942 rather than 1938, he would surely enjoy a more honorific place in the annals of the Holocaust.

It is also true that the circumstances of the shooting of Rath are rather less than chivalrous, which may explain why Weill-Goudchaux expressed greater admiration for ghetto fighters and members of the French underground than for his own client.* "What

* Ironically, the Germans made much of chivalry except when it came to the mass murder of Jews: "With regard to the non-Jewish peoples we want only to accomplish our vital interests," goes the text of an indoctrination booklet for German soldiers titled *The Jew in German History*. "We respect

most people perceive as heroic is shooting back at someone who is shooting at you," observed Alan E. Steinweis in an interview with the author. "To pull out a pistol and shoot an unarmed person by surprise is seen more as an assassination than an act of resistance."[48] The target of the assassination also makes a difference in how Grynszpan is perceived; after all, the German officers who tried but failed to assassinate Hitler in 1944 were vilified by no one but the Nazis themselves, whereas Ernst vom Rath was imagined by some commentators on the Grynszpan case, including Hannah Arendt, as a man with "openly anti-Nazi views" and "sympathy for Jews" whose death at the hands of a Jewish assassin was a cruel irony, although no real evidence suggests that Rath was other than a dutiful Nazi careerist.[49]

Then, too, Grynszpan's stature suffered from the fact that he was so closely and so publicly examined while in French and German custody. Significantly, we know much more about his frailties and failings than we do about those of the resistance fighters whose reputations are more highly varnished. Yet Herschel was not always well served by his legal team; after all, it was one of his attorneys—Weill-Goudchaux, the man who later refused to call him a hero—who stoked rather than tempered Herschel's vaunting self-regard: "Never in his life did he think there existed a young man of seventeen," wrote Herschel in his prison diary after a visit from Weill-Goudchaux, "who would have the courage to carry out an act as I had."[50]

His youth, in fact, works against his plausibility as a hero of the Jewish armed resistance to Nazi Germany. At seventeen, after all, Herschel was still only a child under both French and German law,

---

them and conduct a chivalrous argument with them. But we fight world Jewry as one has to fight a poisonous parasite; we encounter in him not only the enemy of our people, but a plague of all peoples." Quoted in Lucy S. Davidowicz, *The War Against the Jews, 1933–1945* (New York: Holt, Rinehart and Winston, 1975), 114–15.

and he appeared to be even younger because of his diminutive stature. Yet the transcripts of his interrogations make it clear that Herschel was an alert and savvy observer of the world in which he was forced to grow up; he read the newspapers, and he must have discussed what he read with his family and his friends. Indeed, he saw himself as an agent rather than a victim of history. "The world was visibly shaking under the blows of economic catastrophe, political mob hysteria, the Fascist domination of Europe, fear of another world war," writes Alfred Kazin about the zeitgeist of the 1930s, although he did not have Grynszpan in mind. "And no one was likely to feel the burden of the times so keenly as a young Jew starting life in a Yiddish-speaking immigrant family. . . ."[51]

Herschel was clearly a voluble young man, which also undermined his credibility with both detectives and historians. Even when he was still asserting that he had acted on high-minded principles in killing Rath, he couldn't keep his facts straight. According to the various versions of his testimony, Grynszpan could not decide whether he went to the embassy with a plan to shoot the German ambassador, or any available German diplomat, or himself. Sometimes he avowed his intent to kill his victim, and sometimes he insisted that he intended only to wound him. When it struck him as convenient to do so, he claimed that Rath provoked him by calling him a "dirty Jew." Herschel wanted to be regarded as an avenger of the Jewish people—Himmler's worst nightmare—but the talkative young man succeeded only in diminishing himself whenever he opened his mouth, which he did often and with real gusto.

One story, above all, tainted the standing of Herschel Grynszpan, and it, too, fell from his own lips. Perhaps young Herschel was gay, and perhaps not, but once Herschel embraced the version of his exploits that Moro-Giafferi had suggested—the sordid tale of a homosexual *crime passionelle*—he forfeited his claim to the role of heroic avenger. At the time when Herschel offered his confession of sexual adventure to a Gestapo interrogator, homophobia was nearly universal, homosexuality was clinically defined as a psychiatric aberration, and homosexuals were treated as criminals under the law, not only in the Third Reich but throughout the world. Indeed, that is why Herschel was able to use the story of an affair with Rath to derail the show trial.

Exactly here, in fact, we encounter what is arguably his greatest act of courage. Herschel understood Hitler's fear and loathing of homosexuality, and he fearlessly exploited it, not to save himself but to deny the Nazis an opportunity to justify their war on the Jews. Alone in a Gestapo cell in Berlin, wholly without the hope of escape or rescue, young Herschel must have understood that once he succeeded in destroying the propaganda value of the Nazi show trial, he was courting a *Genickschuss*. At the same time, however, he put his own reputation gravely at risk.

"I guarantee you, if everything about Grynszpan's case was the same, except that he slept with Anne Frank, or some other nice Jewish girl, instead of Ernst Vom Rath," wrote journalist Jonathan Mark in the *New York Jewish Week* in 2010, "he'd be the subject of symposiums and seminars every Kristallnacht and Yom HaShoah, too, and day school lesson-plans, and there'd be floats in his honor at the Salute to Israel Parade."[52]

We do not know whether or not Grynszpan was gay, but it seems improbable that he ever engaged in a sexual encounter, paid or otherwise, with Rath. No more evidence exists for the truth of the tale he told the Gestapo than for Arendt's surmise that Herschel was a Gestapo agent. Still, the homoerotic elements that entered the Grynszpan life story are now ineradicable. André Gide alluded to Grynszpan's supposed love affair with Rath in his diaries, and the same rumors cast a curious light on the libretto of Michael Tippett's oratorio in honor of Grynszpan: "I am caught between my desires and their frustration as between the hammer and the anvil."[53]

So we are left with a spectral figure whose real nature remains a mystery and whose historical significance is profoundly enigmatic. The musings of Dr. Cuénot—"Was Grynszpan an exterminating angel . . . or an agent of execution in the pay of obscure international powers . . . or a sort of juvenile delinquent, isolated, paranoiac, debauched, anti-social and in revolt?"—are all good and plausible questions, but the answers are still obscure seven decades after his probable if still mysterious death.[54]

Yet, at the end of the short, strange, and turbulent life of Herschel Grynszpan, we are left with two ineradicable facts of history. Only weeks after the prime ministers of England and France had trembled before Hitler in Munich, Grynszpan walked into the German embassy in Paris and shot a Nazi diplomat, an "act of counter-violence" in explicit protest against Hitler's war against the Jews. And, three years later, a time when appeasement of Nazi Germany had manifestly failed and its murderous intentions were being carried out, the same young man, alone and abandoned in a Gestapo cell in Berlin, succeeded in denying his Nazi captors the opportunity to justify the mass murder of the Jewish people in the show trial they had planned for him.

For these two acts of courage and defiance, the young man paid with his life. If Jewish armed resistance to Nazi Germany deserves more than "three lines in history," then we are obliged to remember Herschel Grynszpan and to regard him as the hero he sought to be.

CHRONOLOGY

The Early Years of Herschel Grynszpan

March 28, 1921   Herschel Feibel Grynszpan is born in Hanover.

July 1936   Grynszpan, at the age of fifteen, leaves Germany and arrives in Belgium.

September 1936   Grynszpan crosses illegally from Belgium to France and arrives in Paris.

Key Events in 1938

March 13, 1938:   *Anschluss* (Annexation), the formal union of Austria and Germany under Nazi rule.

July 6–15, 1938:   International conference on the plight of Jewish refugees from Nazi Germany held in Evian, France. German observers report that "no coun-

try, America not excepted, declared itself ready
to accept unconditionally any number of Jews."

August 11, 1938   Herschel Grynszpan is denied legal residency
in France, and an expulsion order is issued.

August 22, 1938   Issuance of German police order revoking all
residence permits for Polish Jews and other
foreigners living in Nazi Germany by March
31, 1939.

September 30, 1938   Signing of the Munich pact, which detached
the Sudetenland from Czechoslovakia and
annexed it to Nazi Germany, by the leaders of
France, England, Italy, and Germany.

October 27–29, 1938   Polish Jews living in Germany (including the
family of Herschel Grynszpan) are rounded
up, transported to the German–Polish frontier,
and interned by the Polish authorities.

THE ASSASSINATION OF ERNST VOM RATH

November 3, 1938   Herschel Grynszpan receives a postcard from
his sister describing the deportation of Polish
Jews from Germany and despairs over the fate
of his family.

November 6, 1938   Herschel Grynszpan leaves his uncle's apartment after an argument, presumably over the
plight of his family in Poland and a threat of

suicide. He spends a sleepless night alone in
the Hôtel de Suez.

November 7, 1938   Grynszpan enters the German embassy in
Paris, fires five shots at Ernst vom Rath, and is
arrested by the French police.

Kristallnacht

November 9, 1938

4:00 p.m.   Death of Rath in Paris.

7:00 p.m.   Hitler and Goebbels confer on the German
response to Rath's death at the commemora-
tion of the Beer Hall Putsch in Munich.

9:00 p.m.   Goebbels announces the pogrom later known
as Kristallnacht to Nazi party leaders.

11:55 p.m.   Secret teletype from Gestapo headquarters in
Berlin to units across Germany alerting units
to prepare for anti-Jewish demonstrations and
mass arrest of Jews and authorizing use of SS
units to assist in operations.

November 10, 1938

1:20 a.m.   Orders are issued by telephone and telex from
Munich to local Gestapo and Brownshirt
officials for posting of approved signs on

Jewish-owned buildings (e.g., "Revenge for the murder of vom Rath"), burning and bombing of synagogues, destruction of Jewish-owned shops, disarming of Jews, etc.

2:00 a.m.   First death of a Jewish victim of Kristallnacht reported to Goebbels. Burning of synagogues and Jewish-owned shops and apartments, and assaults on Jewish men, women, and children continue throughout the day.

THE FATE OF HERSCHEL GRYNSZPAN

November 17, 1938   State funeral of Ernst vom Rath.

January 7, 1939   Gustav vom Rath, father of Ernst vom Rath, appears before the French magistrate in Paris who is preparing the trial of Herschel Grynszpan on murder charges.

September 1, 1939   German invasion of Poland.

September 3, 1939   World War II begins with declaration of war by Great Britain and France.

Michael Tippett starts work on *A Child of Our Time*, an oratorio based on Herschel Grynszpan.

March/April 1940   Last direct communication from Grynszpan received by his family.

June 8, 1940	Herschel Grynszpan is formally indicted in France for the murderof Ernst vom Rath.
June 14, 1940	German troops enter Paris, and Grynszpan escapes to Toulouse, where he seeks refuge in a French prison.
July 17, 1940	After futile efforts to find Grynszpan by a Nazi task force, he is turned over to German authorities by Vichy France and flown to Berlin.
October 16, 1941	Herschel Grynszpan is formally indicted in Germany on charges of high treason.
October 29, 1941	Adolf Eichmann and other German officials meet in Berlin for the first of several meetings to plan the show trial of Grynszpan.
April 17, 1942	Memo submitted to Hitler asking for a decision on whether and when to put Grynszpan on trial.
May 11, 1942	Scheduled date of the trial of Grynszpan in Berlin.
May 13, 1942	Hitler orders the indefinite postponement of the Grynszpan trial.
September 26, 1942	Grynszpan is transferred from Sachsenhausen concentration camp to the prison at Magdeburg.

December 7, 1942   Last documentary evidence in German archives suggesting that Grynszpan was still alive.

May 8, 1945   VE day, the end of World War II in Europe, and the nominal date of Herschel Grynszpan's death, as decreed by the Lower Court of Hanover on June 1, 1960.

ACKNOWLEDGMENTS

My first grateful thought, as always, is for my beloved wife and *b'sheret*, Ann Benjamin Kirsch; my children, Adam and Jenny Kirsch; my grandson, Charlie; and the other members of our family who are mentioned with love in the dedication.

Also mentioned in the dedication is my late father, Robert Kirsch, who first told me the story of Herschel Grynszpan at a time when he was planning to write a novel based on Grynszpan's life story. Alas, my father did not live long enough to undertake the project, and I think of this book—a work of nonfiction—as a memorial to both my father and to Grynszpan.

I owe a special debt of appreciation to Judy Woo, my co-worker and cherished friend, who assisted me in the research and writing of this book from its inception.

As a reader and a book reviewer, I have known and admired Robert Weil since he first introduced me to the posthumously published fiction of Henry Roth. It has been a privilege and a pleasure to work with Bob and his colleagues at the Horace Liveright imprint of W. W. Norton, including Peter Miller, Phil Marino, Will Menaker, and Otto Sonntag, on this book.

I am grateful to the distinguished scholars who kindly agreed to be interviewed for this book: Saul Friedländer, Yehuda Bauer, Alan E. Steinweis, Deborah E. Lipstadt, Michael R. Marrus, and Ron Roizen. Any errors of fact and all of the opinions expressed in this book, of course, are mine alone.

Stefanie Gaines translated French source materials, and Esther Singer translated German source materials. Professor Janet Hadda generously assisted me with advice on Yiddish words, phrases, and names. Louise Steinman shared her firsthand knowledge of Radomsk and other points of information about the Jewish experience in Poland.

Adaire J. Klein, director of Library and Archival Services at the Simon Wiesenthal Center—Museum of Tolerance, Kyra Schuster at the U.S. Holocaust Memorial Museum, and Sandra Costich at the *American Scholar* assisted me in locating and accessing important research sources.

Ronald S. Rosen shared materials about Michael Tippett and his oratorio, *A Child of Our Time*. Chuck Hawks enlightened me on various aspects of the weapon and ammunition used by Herschel Grynszpan. Carl Weiner pulled down his copy of the *Plan de Paris* at his home in St. Paul and photocopied the page that showed the location of the Pletzel, the starting point for my own visits to the places where many of the events in this book took place.

Laurie Fox, my agent of long standing but also a dear friend and one of my favorite writers and artists, has bestowed upon me the opportunity to write my last eight books, including this one.

Rob Eshman and Susan Freudenheim at the *Jewish Journal*, where I serve as book editor, have opened their pages to expanded book coverage in an era when many newspapers have done exactly the opposite.

Finally, I want to acknowledge the friends and colleagues who have enriched my life and work in various ways:

Angie Yoon, my dear friend and valued co-worker.

Maret Orliss, Ann Binney, and their colleagues at the *Los Angeles Times* Book Festival.

Terry Nathan, Florrie Binford Kichler, and their colleagues at the Independent Book Publishers Association.

Andrea L. Chambers, Libby Jordan, Jennifer Anne Goodwin, and their colleagues at the New York University Summer Publishing Institute.

Rabbi Naomi Levy, Erika Dreifus, Elaine Margolin, Steve Weinberg, Leslie S. Klinger, Lisa Silverman, Mirjana Urosev, Jay Dougherty, Susan Pollyea, Jacob Gabay, Dora Levy Mossanen and Nader Mossanen, Maryann Rosenfeld and Shelly Kadish, and Raye Birk and Candace Barrett.

NOTES

Author's Note on Sources

To access the primary sources in the Grynszpan case, I have relied mostly upon the work of two principal researchers, Gerald Schwab and Dr. Alain Cuénot, each of whom retrieved and examined the documents that were collected during the French and German investigations of the case in the 1930s and 1940s and who also interviewed or corresponded with various surviving participants in the case.

The results of Schwab's research are embodied in *The Day the Holocaust Began: The Odyssey of Herschel Grynszpan*. Cuénot's research appears in an unpublished work titled *L'Affaire Grynszpan–vom Rath*, and I worked from an English-language abridgment titled *The Herschel Grynszpan Case*, which was translated by Joan Redmont, edited by David Rome, and deposited as a type-script by Rome in various libraries and institutions.

Whenever I have cited Schwab as my source for quotations from archival documents, I have included a description of the document in the applicable endnote unless Schwab himself does not provide a citation. The English-language abridgement of *L'Affaire Grynszpan* from which I worked does not consistently include citations to specific documents, and so I have cited the pages in Cuénot's work where such documents are quoted.

I also conducted additional research in the library and archives of Yad Vashem in Jerusalem and the Simon Wiesenthal Center in Los Angeles, interviewed various Holocaust scholars, and consulted the published works that are listed in the bibliography.

ABBREVIATIONS

Cuénot	Alain Cuénot, *The Herschel Grynszpan Case*, trans. Joan Redmont; ed. David Rome (Beverly Hills, Calif.: privately published by David Rome, 1982)
Diewerge	Wolfgang Diewerge, *Anschlag gegen den Frieden* (Munich: Franz Eher Nachf., 1939)
Friedländer	Saul Friedländer, *Nazi Germany and the Jews*, vol. 1, *The Years of Persecution, 1933–1939* (New York: Harper-Perennial, 1997)
Grimm, 1940	Friedrich Grimm, *Denkschrift über die in Paris im Juni-Juli 1940 von der Deutschen Feldpolizei in der Grünspan-Sache beschlagnahmten Akten* (n.p., n.d.)
Grimm, 1942	Friedrich Grimm, *Der Grünspan Prozess* (Nuremberg: F. Willmy, 1942)
MoP files	Documents from the files of the Reichs Ministry for Public Enlightenment and Propaganda, Central State Archives, Potsdam, Germany
Read and Fisher	Anthony Read and David Fisher, *Kristallnacht: The Unleashing of the Holocaust* (New York: Peter Bedrick Books, 1989)
Schwab	Gerald Schwab, *The Day the Holocaust Began: The Odyssey of Herschel Grynszpan* (New York: Praeger, 1990)
Steinweis	Alan E. Steinweis, *Kristallnacht 1938* (Cambridge, Mass.: Belknap Press of Harvard University Press, 2009)

Prologue: The Boy Avenger

1. Cuénot, 159.

2. Schwab, 40.

3. Quoted in Cuénot, 101.

4. Hannah Arendt, *Eichmann in Jerusalem: A Report on the Banality of Evil*, rev. and enl. ed. (New York: Penguin Books, 1965), 227.

5. Don DeLillo, *Libra* (New York: Penguin Books, 1988), 248.

Chapter 1: The Day Hitler Dined Alone

1. Friedrich Percyval Reck-Malleczewen, *Diary of a Man in Despair*, trans. Paul Rubens (New York: Macmillan, 1970), 27.

2. Ibid., 20 ("our Minister of Lies") and 52 ("obviously mentally deranged").

3. Ibid., 27, 28.

4. Ibid., 195 (ellipses omittted).

5. *Julius Caesar*, act 4, scene 3, in G. B. Harrison, ed., *Shakespeare: The Complete Works* (New York: Harcourt, Brace and World, 1952), 836.

6. Quoted in Felix and Miyoko Imonti, *Violent Justice: How Three Assassins Fought to Free Europe's Jews* (Amherst, N.Y.: Prometheus Books, 1994), 82.

7. Quoted ibid.

8. Quoted ibid., 82, 92.

9. Quoted ibid, 88.

10. Quoted ibid., 86.

11. Quoted ibid., 103.

12. Quoted ibid.

13. Quoted in Schwab, 100–101.

14. Cuénot, 10–11.

15. Giles MacDonogh, *1938: Hitler's Gamble* (New York: Basic Books, 2009), 43.

16. Quoted in Friedländer, 182.

17. Cuénot, 8.

18. Quoted ibid., 47, 113, 114.

19. Leon Trotsky, "For Grynszpan: Against Fascist Pogrom Gangs and Stalinist Scoundrels," *Socialist Appeal* (New York), February 14, 1939, available at http://www.marxists.org/archive/trotsky/1939/xx/grnszpan.htm.

20. Quoted in Kenneth Gloag, *Tippett: A Child of Our Time* (Cambridge: Cambridge University Press, 1999), 5 (ellipses omitted; I have standardized the spelling of Grynszpan's name, which Tippett gives as "Grynspan").

Chapter 2: The Prodigal Son

1. Quoted in Saul Friedländer, *The Years of Extermination: Nazi Germany and the Jews, 1939–1945* (New York: HarperPerennial, 2007), 368 (ellipses omitted).

2. "In August 1941 Hitler was attuning the regime to the idea of fighting the war in future under the banner of a 'war against the Jews.'" Peter Longerich, *Heinrich Himmler: A Life*, trans. Jeremy Noakes and Lesley Sharpe (Oxford: Oxford University Press, 2012), 529.

3. Quoted in William L. Shirer, *The Rise and Fall of the Third Reich: A History of Nazi Germany* (New York: Simon and Schuster, 1960), 194.

4. Quoted in Friedländer, 282.

5. Saul Friedländer, for example, refers to "the Jewish question" in *Nazi Ger-*

many and the Jews, 72, whereas Daniel Jonah Goldhagen translates *Judenfrage* as the "Jewish Problem" in *Hitler's Willing Executioners: Ordinary Germans and the Holocaust* (New York: Vintage Books, 1997), 63.

6. Peter Longerich, *Holocaust: The Nazi Persecution and Murder of the Jews* (Oxford: Oxford University Press, 2010), 113.

7. Quoted in Goldhagen, *Hitler's Willing Executioners*, 93.

8. Quoted in Friedländer, 21 (ellipses omitted).

9. Quoted ibid., 111.

10. Quoted in Lucy S. Dawidowicz, *The War Against the Jews, 1933–1945* (New York: Holt, Rinehart and Winston, 1975), 162.

11. Quoted in Friedländer, 171.

12. Quoted ibid., 245.

13. Quoted in Deborah E. Lipstadt, *The Eichmann Trial* (New York: Nextbook Schocken, 2011), 70.

14. Quoted in Friedlander, 201 (ellipses omitted).

15. Dawidowicz, *War Against the Jew*, 106.

16. Tom Segev, *The Seventh Million: The Israelis and the Holocaust*, trans. Haim Watzman (New York: Hill and Wang, 1993), 22.

17. Friedländer, 299.

18. Joseph Roth, *Report from a Parisian Paradise: Essays from France, 1925–1939*, trans. Michael Hofmann (New York: W. W. Norton, 2004), 145.

19. Herbert von Bismarck, state secretary, Prussian Ministry of the Interior, quoted in Friedländer, 35.

20. Quoted in Dawidowicz, *War Against the Jews*, 190.

21. Schwab, 45 (letter from Arnold Edber to Schwab, February 5, 1951).

22. Quoted ibid.

23. Cuénot, 10–11.

24. Schwab, 45 (ellipses omitted; report of February 21, 1939, in MoP files).

25. " 'The human material coming from Germany is getting worse and worse,' the [German Immigrants'] Association charged after almost a year of Nazi rule. 'They are not able and not willing to work, and they need social assistance.'" Segev, *Seventh Million*, 43.

26. Quoted ibid., 100.

27. Quoted in Read and Fisher, 43.

28. *The Collected Stories of Isaac Bashevis Singer* (New York: Farrar, Straus and Giroux, 1982), 372–73.

29. "Mizrachi," *Encyclopaedia Judaica* (Jerusalem: Keter Publishing House, n.d.), 12:175.

30. "Ha-Tikvah," ibid., 7:1471.

31. Quoted in Cuénot, 10.

32. Quoted ibid., 12.

33. Quoted in Schwab, 46–47 (MoP files).

34. Quoted ibid.

35. Quoted in Cuénot, 164.

36. Quoted ibid.

37. Quoted in Friedländer, 182.

38. Quoted in Cuénot, 61.

39. Quoted in Schwab, 161 (from Grimm, 1942).

40. Quoted in Cuénot, 165.

41. Quoted in Friedländer, 181, 180.

42. Quoted ibid., 236.

43. Quoted ibid., 182. The journal entry was dated November 6, 1936, and was prompted by a pamphlet about the Gustloff case by Emil Ludwig, a prolific and well-known Jewish writer who had managed to leave Germany in 1932 and was then living in Switzerland.

44. Ibid., 195.

45. Grynszpan, quoted in Schwab, 47.

46. Quoted in Cuénot, 112, 111.

47. Quoted ibid., 112, 113.

48. Quoted ibid., 113.

49. Ibid., 14.

50. Quoted ibid.

Chapter 3: Tout Va Bien

1. Letter to Benno Reifenberg, May 16, 1925, in Michael Hofmann, trans. and ed., *Joseph Roth: A Life in Letters* (New York: W. W. Norton, 2012), 38.

2. *Pepe le Moko*, Paris Film, 1937.

3. Alan Riding, *And the Show Went On: Cultural Life in Nazi-Occupied Paris* (New York: Alfred A. Knopf, 2010), 26.

4. Quoted in William Wiser, *The Twilight Years: Paris in the 1930s* (New York: Carroll and Graf, 2000), 195.

5. Quoted in Riding, *And the Show Went On*, 7–8.

6. Quoted in Wiser, *Twilight Years*, 198.

7. Ibid., 6.

8. Ibid., 57.

9. Quoted in Riding, *And the Show Went On*, 50–51.

10. Quoted in Wiser, *Twilight Years*, 112.

11. Quoted in Riding, *And the Show Went On*, 21.

12. Joseph Roth, *Report from a Parisian Paradise: Essays from France, 1925–1939*, trans. Michael Hofmann (New York: W. W. Norton, 2004), 13.

13. Ibid., 147–48.

14. "In the Bistro after Midnight," ibid., 246–47. The piece appeared in *Die Zukunft*, a German-language newspaper in Paris, on November 11, 1938, in the days following Kristallnacht.

15. Schwab, 51 (ellipses omitted).

16. Ibid., 57–58.

17. Wiser, *Twilight Years*, 202.

18. Schwab, 53.

19. Quoted in Cuénot, 159.

20. Quoted in Schwab, 53 (Grynszpan to French medical experts during the pretrial investigation).

21. Ibid., 58.

22. Cuénot, 51, quoting an account published in *L'Intransigeant* on November 8, 1938.

23. Quoted in Schwab, 16–17 (from French judicial files, as quoted by Grimm, 1942).

24. Quoted ibid.

25. Giles MacDonogh, *1938: Hitler's Gamble* (New York: Basic Books, 2009), xi.

26. Victor Brombert, *Trains of Thought: From Paris to Ohama Beach, Memories of a Wartime Youth* (New York: Anchor Books, 2004), 144 (ellipses omitted).

27. Quoted in MacDonogh, *1938*, 46.

28. Quoted ibid., 6.

29. Quoted in Friedländer, 248.

30. Ibid., 249.

31. Quoted ibid. (ellipses omitted).

32. Quoted in William L. Shirer, *The Rise and Fall of the Third Reich: A History of Nazi Germany* (New York: Simon and Schuster, 1960), 420.

33. Quoted in Schwab, 56 (as quoted by Grimm, 1942; ellipses omitted).

34. Ibid., 55.

35. Quoted in Friedländer, 220.

36. Quoted in MacDonogh, *1938*, 145.

37. Quoted in Friedländer, 224.

38. Quoted ibid., 283.

39. Quoted in Schwab, 60 (*Dziennek Ustaw* [the Law Journal], no. 22, item 91, April 1, 1938).

40. Quoted ibid., 61 (MoP files).

41. Quoted ibid. (German police order, August 22, 1938)

***Chapter 4*: Special Handling**

1. Paraphrased in Schwab, 17 (statement of Herr Auer, private secretary to the German ambassador in Paris, from French judicial files).

2. Quoted ibid. (statement of Herr Auer, from French judicial files).

3. Quoted ibid., 16 (statement of Mlle Taulin, from French judicial files).

4. Cuénot, 67 (an erroneous spelling of Rath's name in the quoted material has been corrected).

5. Quoted ibid.

6. Ibid., 52.

7. Friedländer, 195.

8. Quoted in Schwab, 64 (from testimony of Zindel Grynszpan at Eichmann trial, 1961).

9. Raul Hilberg, "The Nature of the Process," in *Survivors, Victims, and Perpetrators: Essays on the Nazi Holocaust*, ed. Joel E. Dimsdale (Washington, D.C.: Hemisphere Publishing, 1980), 18.

10. Andrew Morris-Friedman and Ulrich Schädler, "'Juden Raus!' (Jews Out!)—History's Most Infamous Board Game," *Board Game Studies* 6 (2003): 48.

11. Quoted ibid., 238 (ellipses omitted).

12. Quoted ibid., 144.

13. Quoted in Lucy S. Dawidowicz, *The War Against the Jews, 1933–1945* (New York: Holt, Rinehart and Winston, 1975), 106.

14. Quoted in Schwab, 64–65 (from testimony of Zindel Grynszpan at Eichmann trial, 1961).

15. Quoted ibid., 4 (MoP files; some punctuation marks and ellipses have been omitted).

16. Quoted ibid. (MoP files; Schwab notes that a sentence in the postcard is crossed out but appears to read, "Could you send us something to Lodz.")

17. Quoted ibid., 65 (from testimony of Zindel Grynszpan at Eichmann trial, 1961).

18. Quoted ibid.

19. Quoted in Read and Fisher, 47.

20. Quoted in Schwab, 65 (from testimony of Zindel Grynszpan at Eichmann trial, 1961).

21. Quoted in Cuénot, 38 (ellipses omitted).

22. Quoted in Schwab, 66–67 (from Diewerge).

23. Quoted ibid., 66 (from Diewerge).

24. Quoted ibid., 64 (from *Times* of London; ellipses omitted).

25. Quoted in Read and Fisher, 40.

26. Quoted in Schwab, 64 (from Grimm, 1942).

27. Quoted in Cuénot, 31 (ellipses omitted).

28. Quoted in Schwab, 72 (from Grimm, 1942; Kaufmann's account is paraphrased by Schwab, and I have rendered some of it here in dialogue form).

29. Quoted ibid., 73 (from Grimm, 1942).

30. Victor Brombert, *Trains of Thought: From Paris to Omaha Beach, Memories of a Wartime Youth* (New York: Anchor Books, 2004), 49.

31. Schwab, 58.

Chapter 5: "So That the World Would Not Ignore It"

1. Cuénot gives the name of the hotel as "Hotel Ideal-Suez"; see, e.g., Cuénot, 46. Schwab (and other sources) refer to the hotel as the "Hotel de Suez"; see, e.g., 148 and 153.

2. Alice Kaplan, *French Lessons: A Memoir* (Chicago: University of Chicago Press, 1993), 119.

3. Schwab, 74 (from Diewerge; Schwab paraphrases the testimony of Mlle Laurent, which I have rendered here as dialogue).

4. Quoted in Cuénot, 46.

5. Quoted ibid.

6. Quoted ibid., 47

7. Schwab, 75 (paraphrase of the testimony of M. Carpe, which I have rendered here as dialogue).

8. Read and Fisher, 3–4.

9. Schwab, 58.

10. Quoted in Read and Fisher, 6.

11. Schwab, 1 (paraphrase of the testimony of Autret, which I have rendered here as dialogue).

12. Cuénot, 51 (paraphrase of the testimony of Mme Mathis, which I have rendered here as dialogue; the phrase rendered by him as "a gentleman from the embassy" is given by Schwab, 2, as "an embassy official").

13. Quoted in Schwab, 6, 2 (from Grimm, 1942, and MoP files).

14. Cuénot, 51, quoting an account published in *L'Intransigeant* on November 8, 1938.

15. Schwab, 2, and Cuénot, 51 (paraphrases of the testimony of Nagorka, which I have rendered here as dialogue).

16. Quoted in Schwab, 2.

17. Quoted ibid.

18. Quoted ibid., 3.

19. Quoted in Cuénot, 47.

20. Quoted in Read and Fisher, 55.

21. Schwab, 1990, 3 (paraphrase of Herschel Grynszpan's response, which I have rendered here as dialogue).

22. Quoted in Mitchell G. Bard, *48 Hours of Kristallnacht: Night of Destruction/Dawn of the Holocaust: An Oral History* (Guilford, Conn.: Lyons Press, 2008), 7. ("Jewish Murder Attempt in Paris" etc. appeared on November 8, the day after the shooting of Rath. "The Shots in Paris . . ." appeared on November 9.)

23. Quoted in Cuénot, 52, 55.

24. Quoted ibid., 53.

25. Schwab, 7 (cites Cuénot and identifies Diewerge as Cuénot's source).

26. Quoted in Cuénot, 58.

27. Quoted ibid.

28. Ibid., 59.

Chapter 6: **The Blood Flag**

1. Quoted in William L. Shirer, *The Rise and Fall of the Third Reich: A History of Nazi Germany* (New York: Simon and Schuster, 1960), 68.

2. Read and Fisher, 58.

3. Steinweis, 41.

4. Quoted in Friedländer, 271 ("intense conversation"), and Read and Fisher, 62 ("allowed to have its fling").

5. Quoted in Steinweis, 43.

6. Quoted ibid., 42.

7. Louis P. Lochner, ed. and trans., *The Goebbels Diaries* (Garden City, N.Y.: Doubleday, 1948), 41.

8. Quoted in Steinweis, 43. (The quotation is from the November 10, 1938, entry in Goebbels's diary: "If we could now just once unleash the wrath of the people!" Goebbels does not say, however, that he uttered these words to Hitler.)

9. Quoted in Read and Fisher, 62.

10. Quoted ibid.

11. Quoted ibid.

12. Quoted in Friedländer, 271 (ellipses omitted).

13. Quoted in Martin Gilbert, *Kristallnacht: Prelude to Destruction* (New York: HarperCollins, 2006), 27–28.

14. Steinweis, 20, quoting a directive issued by the Deutsches Nachrichten-büro (DNB).

15. Quoted in Gilbert, *Kristallnacht*, 29.

16. Quoted in Schwab, 22 (from testimony of the chief of staff of the SA Group Nordsee before the Nazi Party High Court).

17. Quoted ibid., 23.

18. "Kristallnacht Memories of Edgard Rosenberg," *Haiti Holocaust Survivors*, available at http://haitiholocaustsurvivors.wordpress.com/anti-semitism/kristallnacht/kristallnacht-memories-of-edgar-rosenberg/.

19. Ibid.

20. Gilbert, *Kristallnacht*, 30.

21. Quoted in Read and Fisher, 65.

22. Quoted in Friedländer, 270.

23. Schwab, 25 (from letter of Harry Naujoks to Schwab of February 18, 1951).

24. Read and Fisher, 112.

25. Ibid., 69.

26. Steinweis, 2.

27. Quoted in Bard, *48 Hours*, xiii.

28. Steinweis, 2.

29. Ibid., 25–26.

30. Ibid., 7.

31. Quoted ibid., 84.

32. "Kristallnacht Memories of Edgard Rosenberg."

33. Steinweis, 31.

34. Friedrich Percyval Reck-Malleczewen, *Diary of a Man in Despair*, trans. Paul Rubens (New York: Macmillan, 1970), 27.

35. Quoted in Steinweis, 100 (ellipses omitted).

36. Quoted in Schwab, 20–21 (from proceedings of the Nazi Party High Court).

37. Quoted in Steinweis, 118.

38. Quoted ibid.

39. Ibid.

40. Gilbert, *Kristallnacht*, 26; Steinweis, 55.

41. Steinweis, 9.

42. Quoted ibid., 49.

43. Daniel Jonah Goldhagen, *Hitler's Willing Executioners: Ordinary Germans and the Holocaust* (New York: Vintage Books, 1997), 140–41.

44. Quoted in Friedländer, 201.

45. Quoted in Read and Fisher, 131 (ellipses omitted).

46. Quoted in Shirer, *Rise and Fall*, 432 ("I wish you had killed"), and in Read and Fisher, 138 ("in the future").

47. Quoted in Peter Longerich, *Holocaust: The Nazi Persecution and Murder of the Jews* (Oxford: Oxford University Press, 2010), 117.

48. Quoted in Gilbert, *Kristallnacht*, 29.

49. Victor Klemperer, *I Will Bear Witness: A Diary of the Nazi Years, 1933–1941*, trans. Martin Chalmers (New York: Modern Library, 1998), 281.

50. Ibid., 294.

51. "Kristallnacht Memories of Edgard Rosenberg."

52. Quoted in Schwab, 10.

53. Quoted in Read and Fisher, 175.

54. Quoted ibid., 170.

55. Lucy S. Dawidowicz, *The War Against the Jews, 1933–1945* (New York: Holt, Rinehart and Winston, 1975), 343, 345 (ellipses are omitted and some punctuation is altered).

56. Quoted in Cuénot, 76.

57. Quoted in David H. Weinberg, *A Community on Trial: The Jews of Paris in the 1930s* (Chicago: University of Chicago Press, 1977), 183.

58. Leon Trotsky, "For Grynszpan: Against Fascist Pogrom Gangs and Stalinist Scoundrels," *Socialist Appeal* (New York), February 14, 1939, available at http://www.marxists.org/archive/trotsky/1939/xx/grnszpan.htm.

59. Quoted in Schwab, 4, 88 (from MoP files and Grimm, 1940).

Chapter 7: Higher Powers

1. Susan Hertog, *Dangerous Ambition: Rebecca West and Dorothy Thompson, New Women in Search of Love and Power* (New York: Ballantine Books, 2011), 214.

2. *Time*, June 12, 1939.

3. Quoted in Read and Fisher, 234.

4. Louis P. Lochner, ed. and trans., *The Goebbels Diaries, 1942–1943* (Garden City, N.Y.: Doubleday, 1948), 114 (entry of April 5, 1942).

5. Dorothy Thompson, *Let the Record Speak* (Boston: Houghton Mifflin, 1939), 256.

6. Ibid., 256, 259, 260 (ellipses omitted).

7. Ibid., 260.

8. Dorothy Thompson, "Give a Man a Chance," *New York Herald Tribune*, November 16, 1938.

9. Quoted ibid.

10. Lochner, *Goebbels Diaries*, 41 (entry of February 10, 1942).

11. Schwab, 78.

12. *Le Temps*, November 10, 1938, quoted ibid.

13. Quoted ibid., 78.

14. Quoted in Cuénot, 91 (ellipses omitted).

15. Quoted in Schwab, 88 (from Grimm, 1940).

16. Quoted in Cuénot, 91.

17. Quoted in Cuénot, 113 (ellipses omitted).

18. Quoted in Read and Fisher, 234–35.

19. Quoted in Schwab, 81, 83 (from MoP files).

20. Quoted ibid., 82–83 (from Friedrich Grimm, *40 Jahre Dienst am Recht* [1953]).

21. Quoted ibid., 68 (from MoP 1939 pamphlet).

22. Ibid.

23. Quoted in Steinweis, 138.

24. Schwab, 45 (from MoP files).

25. Ibid., 84, 85 (from Diewerge).

26. Quoted ibid., 90 (from MoP files).

27. Quoted ibid., 89–90.

28. Quoted in Cuénot, 55.

29. Ibid., 17.

30. Quoted in Schwab, 157–58 (from Friedrich Grimm, "Testimony in the Grysnszpan Trial [Final Draft]," July 1942; ellipses omitted).

31. Schwab, 158.

32. Quoted ibid., 159 (from Grimm, "Testimony").

33. Cuénot, 163.

34. Ibid., 163, 164.

35. Quoted in Friedländer, 182.

36. Quoted in Schwab, 159 (from Grimm, "Testimony"; ellipses omitted and some punctuation altered).

37. Quoted ibid., 100–101 (from MoP files).

38. Quoted ibid.

39. Cuénot, 94–95 ("tepid Nazi"); Read and Fisher, 54 ("Jewish girlfriend").

40. Cuénot, 75.

41. Hannah Arendt, *Eichmann in Jerusalem: A Report on the Banality of Evil*, rev. and enl. ed. (New York: Penguin Books, 1965), 227 (ellipses omitted).

42. The bibliography of *Eichmann in Jerusalem* includes Helmut Heiber's "Der Fall Grünspan," a 1957 study of the Grynszpan case that Heiber himself later partly recanted. See a discussion of Heiber's work starting on p. 258.

43. Cuénot, 55 ("kill a member," "protest and vengeance," and "The person himself"); Schwab, 106 ("I did not wish").

44. Friedländer, 220.

45. Quoted ibid., 213–14.

46. Lucy S. Dawidowicz, *The War Against the Jews, 1933–1945* (New York: Holt, Rinehart and Winston, 1975), 161 (ellipses omitted).

47. Quoted in Schwab, 94, 101 (from Grimm, "Testimony").

48. Cuénot, 98.

49. Ibid.

50. Quoted ibid., 101.

51. Ibid., 98.

52. Letter from Erich Wollenberg to Günter vom Rath, May 3, 1964, quoted ibid., 101 (ellipses omitted).

53. Ibid. (ellipses omitted and variant spellings of "Grynszpan" in the original letter standardized; "Did Grynszpan really have relations with vom Rath?" is a paraphrase rather than a direct quotation from the letter).

54. Quoted ibid., 107 (ellipses omitted).

Chapter 8: Phony War

1. Quoted in William Wiser, *The Twilight Years: Paris in the 1930s* (New York: Carroll and Graf, 2000), 224.

2. William L. Shirer, *Berlin Diary: The Journal of a Foreign Correspondent, 1934–1941* (New York: Alfred A. Knopf, 1941), 150 (entry of October 8, 1938; ellipses omitted).

3. Quoted in Schwab, 112.

4. Cuénot, 119–20.

5. *New York Times*, December 28, 1938. The article quotes Grynszpan as referring to "1,200" Jews in need of aid, which is almost certainly a typo. I have inserted the commonly used number of deported Polish Jews, which is the same number that Grynszpan invoked when he shot Rath.

6. Quoted in Cuénot, 116.

7. Ibid.

8. Quoted ibid., 118.

9. Quoted in Schwab, 90 (from Grimm, 1940; ellipses omitted).

10. Ibid., 94 ("hand-holding"); Read and Fisher, 238 (*le Grand Patron*).

11. *The Merchant of Venice*, act 3, scene 1, in G. B. Harrison, ed., *Shakespeare: The Complete Works* (New York: Harcourt, Brace and World, 1952), 597.

12. Quoted in Schwab, 94 (from Grimm, 1940; ellipses omitted).

13. Quoted in Cuénot, 113–14. The letter that Berenbaum brought back from Zbąszyń was dated November 27, 1938.

14. Ibid.

15. Quoted ibid., 108 (ellipses omitted).

16. Ibid., 94–95.

17. Schwab, 82–83.

18. Quoted ibid., 111 (from MoP files).

19. Quoted ibid., 16 (from *Völkischer Beobachter*, January 8, 1939).

20. Ron Roizen, "Herschel Grynszpan: The Fate of a Forgotten Assassin," *Holocaust and Genocide Studies* 1, no. 2 (1986): 227, n. 23.

21. Schwab, 17.

22. Quoted in William L. Shirer, *The Rise and Fall of the Third Reich: A History of Nazi Germany* (New York: Simon and Schuster, 1960), 519.

23. Quoted in Cuénot, 108.

24. Quoted ibid., 107.

25. Quoted in Schwab, 120 (from Grimm, 1940; ellipses omitted).

26. Quoted in Pierre Dumoulin [Friedrich Grimm], *L'Affaire Grynspan: Un Attentat contre la France!* (Paris: Éditions Jean-Renard, 1942), 33 (translation of the original French text by Stefanie Gaines).

27. Adam Kirsch, "The Jewish Question: Martin Heidegger," *New York Times*, May 7, 2010, available at http://www.nytimes.com/2010/05/09/books/review/Kirsch-t.html?pagewanted=all.

28. Quoted in William L. Shirer, *The Nightmare Years, 1930–1940*, vol. 2 of *20th Century Journey: A Memoir of a Life and the Times* (Boston: Little, Brown, 1984), 503.

29. Ibid., 528.

30. Victor Brombert, *Trains of Thought: From Paris to Omaha Beach, Memories of a Wartime Youth* (New York: Anchor Books, 2004), 163.

31. Alan Riding, *And the Show Went On: Cultural Life in Nazi-Occupied Paris* (New York: Alfred A. Knopf, 2010), 42, 43.

32. Quoted in Shirer, *Nightmare Years*, 522.

33. Quoted in Riding, *And the Show Went On*, 44.

34. Quoted in Shirer, *Nightmare Years*, 524.

35. Quoted in Riding, *And the Show Went On*, 45.

36. Shirer, *Rise and Fall*, 742 (ellipses omitted).

37. Ibid., 782 (ellipses omitted).

38. The following is based on Cuénot, 129.

39. Quoted in Schwab, 125 (from Friedrich Karl Kaul, *Der Fall des Herschel Gryszpan* [Berlin: Akademie-Verlag, 1965]).

40. *New York Times*, September 7, 1940.

41. Varian Fry, *Surrender on Demand* (New York: Random House, 1945), 52.

Chapter 9: In the Belly of the Beast

1. Schwab, 126.

2. Quoted in Alan Riding, *And the Show Went On: Cultural Life in Nazi-Occupied Paris* (New York: Alfred A. Knopf, 2010), 48.

3. Cuénot, 130 (the phrase "new order" has been capitalized).

4. Quoted in Schwab, 127 (from article 19 of Franco-German armistice, June 22, 1940).

5. Ibid., 129 (ellipses omitted).

6. Paraphrased ibid., 128 (from MoP files).

7. Quoted in Cuénot, 107.

8. Quoted in Pierre Dumoulin [Friedrich Grimm], *L'Affaire Grynspan: Un Attentat contre la France!* (Paris: Éditions Jean-Renard, 1942), 33.

9. Quoted in Jochen von Lang, ed., in collaboration with Claus Sibyll, *Eichmann Interrogated: Transcripts from the Archives of the Israeli Police*, trans. Ralph Manheim (New York: Da Capo Press, 1999), xxii.

10. Nizkor Project, "The Trial of Adolf Eichmann," sess. 11, available at http://www.nizkor.org/hweb/people/e/eichmann-adolf/transcripts/Sessions/Session-011-03.html. Eichmann places his interrogation of Grynszpan in late 1943 or 1944 but he is probably wrong about the timing, for the reasons discussed in chapter 10.

11. Ibid.

12. Ibid.

13. Ibid.

14. Quoted in Schwab, 161 (from Friedrich Grimm, "Testimony in the Grynszpan Trial [Final Draft]," July 10, 1942).

15. Quoted ibid., 146, 147 (from Goebbels diary entry of September 2, 1942).

16. Quoted in William L. Shirer, *The Rise and Fall of the Third Reich: A History of Nazi Germany* (New York: Simon and Schuster, 1960), 192.

17. Ibid.

18. Quoted ibid., 193.

19. Fritz Tobias, *The Reichstag Fire* (New York: G. P. Putnam's Sons, 1964), 284.

20. A. J. P. Taylor, introd. to Tobias, *Reichstag Fire*, 9.

21. Roland Freisler, quoted in H. W. Koch, *In the Name of the Volk: Political Justice in Hitler's Germany* (New York: Barnes & Noble Books, 1989), 6.

22. Schwab, 141 ("circus atmosphere"); quoted ibid., 137 ("solemn and effective manner")—from a memorandum by Friedrich Grimm, December 10, 1941).

23. Ibid., 164–65 (from Grimm, "Testimony").

24. Ibid., 53.

25. Cuénot, 7, 18.

26. Schwab, 44, 45.

Chapter 10: **Paragraph One Hundred Seventy-Five**

1. Read and Fisher, 251.

2. Ibid., 252.

3. Quoted in Cuénot, 150.

4. Quoted ibid.

5. Quoted in Richard Plant, *The Pink Triangle: The Nazi War Against Homo-sexuals* (New York: New Republic Book/Henry Holt, 1986), 49.

6. Ibid., 56.

7. Quoted ibid., 52.

8. Quoted ibid., 57.

9. Ibid., 113.

10. Quoted ibid., 30 (ellipses omitted).

11. Louis P. Lochner, ed. and trans., *The Goebbels Diaries, 1942–1943* (Garden City, N.Y.: Doubleday, 1948), 63.

12. Quoted in Peter Longerich, *Heinrich Himmler: A Life*, trans. Jeremy Noakes and Lesley Sharpe (Oxford: Oxford University Press, 2012), 231 ("plagues" and "abominations"); see also 237, 239.

13. Quoted in Jacob Robinson, *And the Crooked Shall Be Made Straight: The Eichmann Trial, the Jewish Catastrophe, and Hannah Arendt's Narrative* (Philadelphia: Jewish Publication Society of America, 1965), 317, n. 74.

14. Lochner, *Goebbels Diaries*, 114 (entry of April 5, 1942).

15. Notation by Minister Krümmer of the Foreign Ministry, quoted in Schwab, 155.

16. Ibid., 164 (from Friedrich Grimm, "Testimony in the Grynszpan Trial [Final Draft]," July 10, 1942).

17. Pierre Dumoulin [Friedrich Grimm], *L'Affaire Grynspan: Un Attentat contre la France!* (Paris: Éditions Jean-Renard, 1942), 12.

18. Ibid., 13, 14.

19. Cuénot, 51, 50. The phrase rendered by Cuénot as "a gentleman from the embassy" is given by Schwab, 2, as "an embassy official."

20. Quoted in Schwab, 2 (from Grimm, 1942).

21. Cuénot, 77.

22. Quoted ibid. The author of the note spelled Grynszpan's name "Grynspan."

23. Lochner, *Goebbels Diaries*, 144 (entry of April 5, 1942).

24. Cuénot, 150, citing Helmut Heiber ("and would thus furnish proof").

25. Hannah Arendt, *Eichmann in Jerusalem: A Report on the Banality of Evil*, rev. and enl. ed. (New York: Penguin Books, 1965), 227–28.

26. Schwab, 129, citing Friedrich Karl Kaul, *Der Fall des Herschel Grynszpan* (Berlin: Akademie Verlag, 1965).

27. Quoted ibid., 183 (from "Führer Information," July 3, 1942; spelling and punctuation have been altered).

28. Quoted in Read and Fisher, 253.

29. Quoted in Schwab, 186.

30. Quoted ibid., 181–82 (from a teletype from Guenther to Ambassador Abetz, May 8, 1942).

31. Dumoulin [Grimm], *L'Affaire Grynspan*, 15.

32. Quoted in Schwab, 181–82 (from a teletype from Guenther to Abetz, May 8, 1942).

33. Quoted ibid.

34. Quoted ibid., 175 (from a communication between Bormann and Ribbentrop, April 17, 1942).

35. Quoted ibid., 175, 176 (from "Führer Information," April 17, 1742, and telegram from Krümmer to Ambassader Abetz, April 18, 1942).

36. Quoted ibid., 182 (from "Führer Information," July 3, 1942; some punctuation and capitalization have been altered).

37. Ibid., 182.

38. Lochner, *Goebbels Diaries*, 159. (Goebbels cited the questionable availability of former French foreign minister Georges Bonnet as a trial witness as another reason for postponement of the trial.)

Chapter 11: Grynszpan's Ghost

1. The text is quoted from a postcard provided by the International Red Cross to Allied prisoners of war who were interned by the Japanese Imperial Army. See http://commons.wikimedia.org/wiki/File:Dad-pow-postcard-wwII.jpg. The postcard used by Grynszpan was similar but not identical.

2. Quoted in Schwab, 183.

3. Quoted ibid., 200 (from Krümmer memorandum of December 7, 1942).

4. Raul Hilberg, *The Destruction of the European Jews*, student ed. (New York: Holmes & Meier, 1985), 285.

5. Lucy S. Dawidowicz, *The War Against the Jews, 1933–1945* (New York: Holt, Rinehart and Winston, 1975), 136.

6. Quoted ibid., 106.

7. Quoted in Schwab, 199 (attributed to Harry Naujoks).

8. Quoted in Ron Roizen, "Herschel Grynszpan: The Fate of a Forgotten Assassin," *Holocaust and Genocide Studies* 1, no. 2 (1986): 223.

9. Schwab, 200 (attributed to Fritz Dahms).

10. Peter Longerich, *Heinrich Himmler: A Life*, trans. Jeremy Noakes and Lesley Sharpe (Oxford: Oxford University Press, 2012), 698.

11. Roizen, "Herschel Grynszpan," 222.

12. Quoted ibid., 221.

13. Quoted ibid., 220 (ellipses omitted).

14. Schwab, 1990, 198 (paraphrase of statement attributed to Soltikow).

15. Ibid. (attributed to Soltikow).

16. Quoted in Roizen, "Herschel Grynszpan," 222.

17. Ibid., 223.

18. Letter from Heiber to Cuénot, March 24, 1959, quoted in Cuénot, 155.

19. Raul Hilberg, "The Nature of the Process," in *Survivors, Victims, and Perpetrators: Essays on the Nazi Holocaust*, ed. Joel E. Dimsdale (Washington, D.C.: Hemisphere Publishing, 1980), 51, n. 80, citing Kurt R. Grossman, "Hersche Gruenspan lebt!," *Aufbau* (New York), May 10, 1957, pp. 1, 5–6.

20. Quoted in Cuénot, 47.

21. Lutz van Dijk, *Der Attentäter: Herschel Grynszpan und die Vorgänge um die "Kristallnacht"* (Hamburg: Rowolt, 1995), 11 (ellipses omitted; translation from the original German text by Esther Singer).

Chapter 12: The Exterminating Angel

1. Hannah Arendt, *Eichmann in Jerusalem: A Report on the Banality of Evil*, rev. and enl. ed. (New York: Penguin Books, 1965), 227.

2. Ibid., 227, 229–30.

3. Ibid., 227–28.

4. Jacob Robinson, *And the Crooked Shall Be Made Straight: The Eichmann Trial, the Jewish Catastrophe, and Hannah Arendt's Narrative* (Philadelphia: Jewish Publication Society of America, 1965), 22.

5. Quoted by David Rome in his introduction to Cuénot, ii.

6. Schwab, xii–xiii.

7. Quoted in Ron Roizen, "Herschel Grynszpan: The Fate of a Forgotten Assassin," *Holocaust and Genocide Studies* 1, no. 2 (1986): 225 (ellipses omitted).

8. Saul Friedländer, interview with the author, August 9, 2010.

9. André Malraux, *Anti-Memoirs*, trans. Terence Kilmartin (New York: Henry Holt, 1967), 5.

10. Primo Levi, *The Drowned and the Saved*, trans. Raymond Rosenthal (New York: Vintage International, 1989), 25.

11. Ibid., 66–67. The quoted remarks concern Chaim Rumkowski, the Nazi-appointed "elder" of the Lódź Ghetto whose collaboration with German authorities has been much criticized.

12. Quoted in Read and Fisher, 232–33.

13. Deborah E. Lipstadt, *The Eichmann Trial* (New York: Nextbook Schocken, 2011), 79.

14. Quoted in Arendt, *Eichmann in Jerusalem*, 11.

15. Quoted in Lucy S. Dawidowicz, *The War Against the Jews, 1933–1945* (New York: Holt, Rinehart and Winston, 1975), 314.

16. Quoted in Nahama Tec, *Defiance: The Bielski Partisans* (Oxford: Oxford University Press, 1993), 3.

17. Levi, *The Drowned and the Saved*, 105 (ellipses omitted).

18. Yehuda Bauer, *Rethinking the Holocaust* (New Haven: Yale University Press, 2002), 120.

19. Quoted in Cuénot, 31.

20. Samuel D. Kassow, *Who Will Write Our History? Emanuel Ringelbaum, the Warsaw Ghetto, and the Oyneg Shabes Archive* (Bloomington: Indiana University Press, 2007), 101.

21. Raul Hilberg, *The Destruction of the European Jews*, student ed. (New York: Holmes & Meier, 1985), 136. Hilberg quotes Martin Gilbert: "To die with dignity was also a form of resistance."

22. Quoted in Dawidowicz, *War Against the Jews*, 337.

23. Hilberg, *Destruction of the European Jews*, 293.

24. Dawidowicz, *War Against the Jews*, 325.

25. Quoted in Lipstadt, *Eichmann Trial*, 80–81 (ellipses omitted).

26. Bauer, *Rethinking the Holocaust*, 142, 140.

27. Dawidowicz, *War Against the Jews*, 114. "'Special-duty groups' perhaps best renders the meaning [of *Einsatzgruppen*]: 'striking force' too conveys some flavor of the German."

28. Quoted in Daniel Jonah Goldhagen, *Hitler's Willing Executioners: Ordinary Germans and the Holocaust* (New York: Vintage Books, 1997), 217.

29. Ibid., 228.

30. Quoted in Peter Longerich, *Heinrich Himmler: A Life*, trans. Jeremy Noakes and Lesley Sharpe (Oxford: Oxford University Press, 2012), 534.

31. Quoted ibid., 525.

32. Quoted in Hilberg, *Destruction of the European Jews*, 294–95. Hilberg refers to the informant as "vom dem Bach"; Longerich, *Heinrich Himmler*, 525, gives the name as "von dem Bach-Zelewski."

33. Saul Friedländer, *The Years of Extermination: Nazi Germany and the Jews, 1939–1945* (New York: HarperPerennial, 2007), 362.

34. Quoted in Longerich, *Heinrich Himmler*, 539.

35. Schwab, 3.

36. Michael R. Marrus, *The Holocaust in History* (New York: Meridian, 1987), 136.

37. Bauer, *Rethinking the Holocaust*, 119.

38. Yehuda Bauer, interview with the author, October 12, 2010.

39. Bauer, *Rethinking the Holocaust*, 140–41.

40. Jewish Partisan Educational Foundation, at www.jewishpartisans. blogspot.com.

41. Quoted in Cuénot, 2. The quotation, as given by Cuénot, begins, "Personally if I were Jewish . . ." Schwab, however, states that Weill-Goudchaux was Jewish. The explanation may be that Weill-Goudchaux was of Jewish descent but did not regard himself as a Jew.

42. Cuénot, 2.

43. Schwab, 40.

44. Lipstadt, *Eichmann Trial*, 80.

45. Quoted in Friedländer, *Years of Extermination*, 523–24.

46. Quoted ibid., 350.

47. Quoted in Cuénot, 46.

48. Alan E. Steinweis, interview with the author, October 13, 2011.

49. Arendt, *Eichmann in Jerusalem*, 227.

50. Quoted in Schwab, 106 (from Grimm, 1940).

51. Kazin, introduction to *Call It Sleep*, by Henry Roth (New York: Farrar, Straus and Giroux, 1991), x. Kazin is referring specifically to Roth in the 1930s writing about his experience growing up on the Lower East Side of New York City.

52. Jonathan Mark, "Sex and Kristallnacht: The Boy Toy (and Boy Assassin) Who Started It All," *New York Jewish Week*, November 5, 2010.

53. Quoted in Kenneth Gloag, *Tippett: A Child of Our Time* (Cambridge: Cambridge University Press, 1999), 21.

54. Cuénot, 3.

BIBLIOGRAPHY

BOOKS, PERIODICALS, FILMS, AND ONLINE SOURCES

Arendt, Hannah. *Eichmann in Jerusalem: A Report on the Banality of Evil*. Revised and enlarged edition. New York: Penguin Books, 1965.

Bard, Mitchell G. *48 Hours of Kristallnacht: Night of Destruction/Dawn of the Holocaust: An Oral History*. Guilford, Conn.: Lyons Press, 2008.

Bauer, Yehuda. *Jewish Reactions to the Holocaust*. Translated by John Glucker. Tel Aviv: MOD Books, 1989.

_____. *Rethinking the Holocaust*. New Haven: Yale University Press, 2002.

Brombert, Victor. *Trains of Thought: From Paris to Omaha Beach, Memories of a Wartime Youth*. New York: Anchor Books, 2004.

Caspary, Gerard. "From the Edge of the Holocaust: Letters from My Mother and Grandmother." Unpublished manuscript, 2000. (Quoted with permission of Paula Fass, executor of the estate of Gerard Caspary.)

Cuénot, Alain. *The Herschel Grynszpan Case*. Translation by Joan Redmont of unpublished manuscript "L'Affaire Grynszpan–vom Rath." Edited by David Rome, Beverly Hills, Calif.: privately published by David Rome 1982.

Dawidowicz, Lucy S. *The War Against the Jews, 1933–1945*. New York: Holt, Rinehart and Winston, 1975.

DeLillo, Don. *Libra*. New York: Penguin Books, 1988.

Dimsdale, Joel E., ed. *Survivors, Victims, and Perpetrators: Essays on the Nazi Holocaust*. Washington, D.C.: Hemisphere Publishing, 1980.

Dumoulin, Pierre [Friedrich Grimm]. *L'Affaire Grynspan: Un Attentat contre la France!* Paris: Éditions Jean-Renard, 1942.

Duvivier, Julien, writer and director. *Pépé le Moko*. Paris Film, 1937.

Friedländer, Saul. *When Memory Comes*. Translated by Helen R. Lane. New York: Farrar, Straus and Giroux, 1979.

――――. *Nazi Germany and the Jews*. Vol. 1, *The Years of Persecution, 1933–1939*. New York: HarperPerennial, 1997.

――――. *The Years of Extermination: Nazi Germany and the Jews, 1939–1945*. New York: HarperPerennial, 2007.

Fry, Varian. *Surrender on Demand*. New York: Random House, 1945.

Gilbert, Martin. *Kristallnacht: Prelude to Destruction*. New York: HarperCollins, 2006.

Gloag, Kenneth. *Tippett: A Child of Our Time*. Cambridge: Cambridge University Press, 1999.

Goldhagen, Daniel Jonah. *Hitler's Willing Executioners: Ordinary Germans and the Holocaust*. New York: Vintage Books, 1997.

Goralski, Robert. *World War II Almanac, 1931–1945: A Political and Military Record*. New York: Perigee Books, 1981.

Harrison, G. B., ed. *Shakespeare: The Complete Works*. New York: Harcourt, Brace and World, 1952.

Hertog, Susan. *Dangerous Ambition: Rebecca West and Dorothy Thompson, New Women in Search of Love and Power*. New York: Ballantine Books, 2011.

Hilberg, Raul. *The Destruction of the European Jews*. Student edition. New York: Holmes & Meier, 1985. Originally published in 1961.

――――. *The Politics of Memory: The Journey of a Holocaust Historian*. Chicago: Ivan R. Dee, 1996.

Hofmann, Michael, trans. and ed. *Joseph Roth: A Life in Letters*. New York: W. W. Norton, 2012.

Howe, Irving. *World of Our Fathers*. New York: Harcourt Brace Jovanovich, 1976.

Imonti, Felix and Miyoko. *Violent Justice: How Three Assassins Fought to Free Europe's Jews*. Amherst, N.Y.: Prometheus Books, 1994.

Isaacson, Walter. *Einstein: His Life and Universe*. New York: Simon and Schuster, 2007.

Kaplan, Alice. *French Lessons: A Memoir*. Chicago: University of Chicago Press, 1993.

Kassow, Samuel D. *Who Will Write Our History? Emanuel Ringelbaum, the Warsaw Ghetto, and the Oyneg Shabes Archive*. Bloomington: Indiana University Press, 2007.

Kazin, Alfred. Introduction to *Call It Sleep*, by Henry Roth. New York: Farrar, Straus and Giroux, 1991.

Keegan, John. *The Second World War*. New York: Penguin Books, 1989.

Kirsch, Adam. "The Jewish Question: Martin Heidegger." *New York Times*, May 7, 2010.

Klemperer, Victor. *I Will Bear Witness: A Diary of the Nazi Years, 1933–1941*. Translated by Martin Chalmers. New York: Modern Library, 1998.

Koch, H. W. *In the Name of the Volk: Political Justice in Hitler's Germany*. New York: Barnes & Noble Books, 1989.

Lang, Jochen von, ed., in collaboration with Claus Sibyll. *Eichmann Interrogated: Transcripts from the Archives of the Israeli Police*. Translated by Ralph Manheim. Introduction by Avner W. Less. New York: Da Capo Press, 1999.

Levi, Primo. *The Drowned and the Saved*. Translated by Raymond Rosenthal. New York: Vintage International, 1989.

_____. *Survival in Auschwitz*. New York: Classic House Books, 2008.

Lipstadt, Deborah E. *The Eichmann Trial*. New York: Nextbook Schocken, 2011.

Lochner, Louis P., ed. and trans. *The Goebbels Diaries, 1942–1943*. Garden City, N.Y.: Doubleday, 1948.

Longerich, Peter. *Holocaust: The Nazi Persecution and Murder of the Jews*. Oxford: Oxford University Press, 2010.

_____. *Heinrich Himmler: A Life*. Translated by Jeremy Noakes and Lesley Sharpe. Oxford: Oxford University Press, 2012.

Lubitsch, Ernst, producer and director. Charles Brackett, Billy Wilder, and Walter Reisch, writers. *Ninotchka*. Metro-Goldwyn Mayer, 1939.

MacDonogh, Giles. *1938: Hitler's Gamble*. New York: Basic Books, 2009.

Malraux, André. Translated by Terence Kilmartin. *Anti-Memoirs*. New York: Henry Holt, 1967.

Marcus, Greil. Foreword in Alexander Trocchi. *Cain's Book*. New York: Grove Press, 1992.

Mark, Jonathan. "Sex and Kristallnacht: The Boy Toy (and Boy Assassin) Who Started It All." *New York Jewish Week*, November 5, 2010.

Marrus, Michael R. "Vichy before Vichy: Antisemitic Currents in France during the 1930's." *Wiener Library Bulletin* 33 (1980).

_____. *The Holocaust in History*. New York: Meridian, 1987.

_____. "The Strange Story of Herschel Grynszpan." *American Scholar* 57, no. 1 (Winter 1988): 69–79.

Morris-Friedman, Andrew, and Ulrich Schädler. "'Juden Raus!' (Jews Out!)—History's Most Infamous Board Game." *Board Game Studies* 6 (2003): 47–58.

Nizkor Project. "The Trial of Adolf Eichmann." Session 11. Available at http://www.nizkor.org/hweb/people/e/eichmann-adolf/transcripts/Sessions/Session-011-03.html.

Plant, Richard. *The Pink Triangle: The Nazi War Against Homosexuals*. New York: New Republic Book/Henry Holt, 1986.

Read, Anthony, and David Fisher. *Kristallnacht: The Unleashing of the Holocaust*. New York: Peter Bedrick Books, 1989.

Reck-Malleczewen, Friedrich Percyval. *Diary of a Man in Despair*. Translated by Paul Rubens. New York: Macmillan, 1970.

Riding, Alan. *And the Show Went On: Cultural Life in Nazi-Occupied Paris*. New York: Alfred A. Knopf, 2010.

Robinson, Jacob. *And the Crooked Shall Be Made Straight: The Eichmann Trial, the Jewish Catastrophe, and Hannah Arendt's Narrative*. Philadelphia: Jewish Publication Society of America, 1965.

Roizen, Ron. "Herschel Grynszpan: The Fate of a Forgotten Assassin." *Holocaust and Genocide Studies* 1, no. 2 (1986): 217–28.

Rosenberg, Edgar. "Kristallnacht Memories of Edgard Rosenberg." *Haiti Holocaust Survivors*. Available at http://haitiholocaustsurvivors.word press.com/anti-semitism/kristallnacht/kristallnacht-memories-of-edgar-rosenberg/.

Roth, Joseph. *Report from a Parisian Paradise: Essays from France, 1925–1939*. Translated with an introduction by Michael Hofmann. New York: W. W. Norton, 2004.

Schwab, Gerald. *The Day the Holocaust Began: The Odyssey of Herschel Grynszpan*. New York: Praeger, 1990.

Segev, Tom. *The Seventh Million: The Israelis and the Holocaust*. Translated by Haim Watzman. New York: Hill and Wang, 1993.

Shirer, William L. *Berlin Diary: The Journal of a Foreign Correspondent, 1934–1941*. New York: Alfred A. Knopf, 1941.

_____. *The Rise and Fall of the Third Reich: A History of Nazi Germany*. New York: Simon and Schuster, 1960.

_____. *The Nightmare Years, 1930–1940*. Vol. 2 of *20th Century Journey: A Memoir of a Life and the Times*. Boston: Little, Brown, 1984.

Singer, Isaac Bashevis. *The Collected Stories of Isaac Bashevis Singer*. New York: Farrar, Straus and Giroux, 1982.

Smith, Howard K. *Last Train from Berlin*. New York: Alfred A. Knopf, 1943.

Snyder, Timothy. *Bloodlands: Europe between Hitler and Stalin*. New York: Basic Books, 2010.

Steinweis, Alan E. *Kristallnacht 1938*. Cambridge, Mass.: Belknap Press of Harvard University Press, 2009.

Tec, Nahama. *Defiance: The Bielski Partisans*. Oxford: Oxford University Press, 1993.

Thalmann, Rita, and Emmanuel Feinermann. *Crystal Night: 9–10 November 1938*. Translated by Gilles Cremonesi. New York: Coward, McCann & Geoghegan, 1974.

Thompson, Dorothy. *Let the Record Speak*. Boston: Houghton Mifflin, 1939.

Thirwell, Adam. "Genocide and the Fine Arts." *New Republic*, May 10, 2012, pp. 25–31.

Tobias, Fritz. *The Reichstag Fire.* Introduction by A. J. P. Taylor. New York: G. P. Putnam's Sons, 1964.

Trotsky, Leon. "For Grynszpan: Against Fascist Pogrom Gangs and Stalinist Scoundrels." *Socialist Appeal* (New York), February 14, 1939. Available at Leon Trotsky Internet Archive 2005.

van Dijk, Lutz. *Der Attentäter: Herschel Grynszpan und die Vorgänge um die "Kristallnacht."* Hamburg: Rowolt, 1995.

Weinberg, David H. *A Community on Trial: The Jews of Paris in the 1930s.* Chicago: University of Chicago Press, 1977.

Wiser, William. *The Twilight Years: Paris in the 1930s.* New York: Carroll and Graf, 2000.

INTERVIEWS

Yehuda Bauer. Yad Vashem, Jerusalem, Israel. October 12, 2010.

Saul Friedländer. Los Angeles, California. August 9, 2010.

Deborah E. Lipstadt. By telephone. February 15, 2011.

Michael Marrus. By telephone. February 17, 2011.

Ron Roizen. By telephone. December 20, 2010.

Alan E. Steinweis. By telephone. October 13, 2011.

INDEX

Page numbers beginning with 295 refer to endnotes.